⤳ ❦ ⤲

A Toast to Magic!

In magic, the cup is a symbol of the fruitful Goddess, from whom wisdom and blessings flow. *A Witch's Brew* is unique in its focus on the symbolic heritage of beverages, offering options for creating a wide variety of fermented and non-fermented drinks that have magical associations in folklore and myth.

This creative handbook explains everything you need to know to brew beverages to give you an emotional lift, ease a minor illness, deepen the meaning of your rituals and celebrations, or magically aid goals such as increasing psychic awareness, fertility, productivity, or luck. The luscious ingredients and magical associations described in these recipes enable you to choose the perfect beverage for that special occasion, whether you're custom-brewing a juice-based love potion for you and your mate or brewing a tasty apple mead for a harvest celebration. *A Witch's Brew* also describes how to call on the appropriate deity to bless the components and metaphysical aims of your brew, so that creating your beverage is in itself a form of worship.

Magical brewing will enrich any spiritual path or seasonal celebration, and here you'll find a bewitching array of elixirs, teas, punches, ciders, wines, beers, tonics, coffees, and coolers sure to tantalize your tongue and work their special magic on you!

⤳ ❦ ⤲

About the Author

Patricia Telesco is a trustee for the Universal Federation of Pagans and a professional member of the Wiccan-Pagan Press Alliance. Her hobbies include Celtic illumination, antique restoration, historical costuming, writing and singing folk music, sufi dancing, historical herbalism studies, carving wood and soapstone, writing poetry, and participating in the Society for Creative Anachronism. Many of these activities have extended themselves into her small mail-order business called Hourglass Creations. Her articles and poems have appeared in journals such as *Circle*, *The Unicorn*, *Moonstone* (England), *Demeter's Emerald*, *Silver Chalice*, and *Llewellyn's New Worlds of Mind and Spirit*. She welcomes the opportunity to do workshops and lectures. Patricia lives in Buffalo, New York, with her husband, son, daughter, dog, and four cats.

To Write to the Author

If you wish to contact the author or would like more information about this book, please write to the author in care of Llewellyn Worldwide and we will forward your request. Both the author and publisher appreciate hearing from you and learning of your enjoyment of this book and how it has helped you. Llewellyn Worldwide cannot guarantee that every letter written to the author can be answered, but all will be forwarded. Please write to:

Patricia Telesco
c/o Llewellyn Worldwide
P.O. Box 64383-K708, St. Paul, MN 55164-0383, U.S.A.
Please enclose a self-addressed, stamped envelope for reply, or $1.00 to cover costs.
If outside U.S.A., enclose international postal reply coupon.

Free Catalog From Llewellyn Worldwide

For more than 90 years Llewellyn has brought its readers knowledge in the fields of metaphysics and human potential. Learn about the newest books in spiritual guidance, natural healing, astrology, occult philosophy, and more. Enjoy book reviews, new age articles, a calendar of events, plus current advertised products and services. To get your free copy of *Llewellyn's New Worlds of Mind and Spirit*, send your name and address to:

Llewellyn's New Worlds of Mind and Spirit
P.O. Box 64383-K708, St. Paul, MN 55164-0383, U.S.A.

A Witch's Brew

The Art of Making Magical Beverages

Patricia Telesco

1995
Llewellyn Publications
St. Paul, Minnesota 55164-0383 U.S.A.

FIRST EDITION
First Printing, 1995

Cover painting by William Giese
Cover design by Linda Norton
Technical consultation on brewing methods and procedures by Jeffrey Donaghue
Interior design by Jessica Thoreson and Connie Hill
Edited by Connie Hill

Library of Congress Cataloging-in-Publication Data
Telesco, Patricia, 1960–
    A witch's brew : the art of making magical beverages / Patricia Telesco —
1st ed.
      p.   cm.
    Includes bibliographical references and index.
    ISBN 1-56718-708-0 (alk. paper)
      1. Witchcraft. 2. Recipes. 3. Beverages—Folklore—Miscellanea.
4. Beverages—History. 5. Brewing—Miscellanea. I. Title.
BF1572.R4.T45 1995   95-3215
641.2—dc20   CIP

Printed in the United States of America

Llewellyn Publications
A Division of Llewellyn Worldwide, Ltd.
P.O. Box 64383, St. Paul, MN 55164-0383

Dedication

To the spirit of hospitality
which makes any dwelling
a welcome sanctuary
for kindred spirits to share.

Other Books by the Author

A Victorian Grimoire
The Urban Pagan
Llewellyn's 1994 Magical Almanac
The Victorian Flower Oracle
A Kitchen Witch's Cookbook

Forthcoming

Folkways

ᷓ Table of Contents ᷔ

Part Three
The Magical Brew Pot—Recipes for Non-Alcoholic Beverages

Part Four
Appendices, Glossary, Bibliography, and Index

Acknowledgements

To my extended family, who not only now know why the letters X and Y are different, but who are rallying to have at least one of them stricken from the alphabet, my thanks for keeping my wit keen and my *pun*sils sharp.

To Tiger, I hereby donate one set of keys firmly attached by ball and chain. For the great bard Luke, a special fire log all his own so he will actually sleep in his tent at night.

To Paul and Karl, no, I don't know where it is, and yes I will look for it when I get home, along with a hug or two.

For Kevin, I'm keeping safe one return bus ticket, from Anywhere USA, just in case.

To David, whose gift for finding things rivals that a Kender, looking down on yourself causes stiff necks. Remember your heart is as big as you are (and that's a lot in a 6' 6" package).

To Karen J., my confidante and level-minded friend. Thank you for giving me good advice repeatedly, and always with kindness.

To the three wives' men, thanks for being such good sports when the three associated ladies want to "cut loose."

Finally, and most appropriately to this book, to the God/dess for the miracle of wine provided in Summer of 1992, and the wonders of "magic fountains" built by dwarves and fairy folk every August.

Foreword

Our ancestors must have experienced intoxication from naturally fermented fruits and berries. Perhaps they observed birds falling drunk from the trees. Cedar waxwings present us with the same sight today after feasting on over-ripe berries. Whatever may have happened in the distant past, our ancestors soon sought to duplicate this intoxication. They became brewers. They must have been profoundly moved, and as they sought to understand their experiences, they imbued both the process of brewing and the beverages brewed with mystic qualities. How else to explain the altered feelings and change of consciousness? Fermented beverages have become an important part of the religious and social life of every human culture.

As humans have sought to harness and control the process which we now know of as fermentation, brewing has grown from a simple household activity to a cottage industry, then to a major part of the world's economy. Today's bio-technology industries began with the attempt to understand and control fermentation.

We have seen the explosion of "boutique" wineries in the 1970s and 1980s, and the growth of micro-breweries and brewpubs in the 1980s and 1990s. *A Witch's Brew* is a recognition of the ever-increasing popularity and importance of home brewing which is part of the above trend, but with a twist. Here the New Brewer meets the New Age.

Experienced brewers and wine makers may wish to alter the recipes to suit their own preferences. The metaphysical and magical aspects of the ingredients will apply wherever they are being used. This book offers the practicing brewer a chance to incorporate new meaning and significance into his or her art. The practicing metaphysican is likewise shown a simple means to begin learning the brewer's craft.

An appendix with more detailed information about the general process of home fermentation has been added to help novices succeed in their first brewing endeavors.

—Jeffrey Donaghue
Founder and President,
Minnesota Home Brewers' Association
Edina, Minnesota

Introduction

I rejoice with the land, when it rains, and all that dwells
drinks from one common cup of sky.

—Marian LoreSinger

In magic, the cup is a symbol of the Goddess, that ever-fruitful fountain from which the nectars of originality, wisdom, and blessings flow. Like the Horn of Plenty or Cauldron of Cerridwen, there is always enough of these vibrant liquids to quench the thirst. This well-spring metes out to each of us exactly what we need; one person gets a chalice of compassion, another a goblet of gladness, another a tumbler of tolerance.

Upon altars across the world, cups adorn holy places. Sometimes they hold water, sometimes wine. Whether it be a Shaman's bowl or a Catholic's communion chalice, the cup's presence is a strong reminder that beverages are a significant part of many religious traditions.

This book comes to you with that heritage in mind, offering options for an assortment of enchanted drinks. Some are presented for health, some to help celebrate the Wheel of the Year, some to encourage specific positive attributes, and others for simple pleasure. All have potential, from a magical perspective, to enrich your life.

In addition to the recipes presented here, I have included information on the history of refreshments, specifically those used for worship, medicine, and magic. Drinks and potions played a key role in these areas, one application frequently overlapping another. For example, a Medieval monk may have prepared angelica tea to help a sickly patient. His reason for doing so probably survives in the folklore that says angels gave humanity the angelica herb specifically for treating illness.

History and folklore help us appreciate the many possible metaphysical applications for beverages. Angelica wine or tea can be used in rituals for overall well-being. When wishing for better understanding of, or communion with, guardian spirits, either choice would be an excellent addition to your altar. In both cases, history provided a foundation from which to build your magical construct.

I find brewing to be a tremendously satisfying activity. It has become a household tradition to share samples of homemade wines with our guests. We also make special mixtures for holiday gift-giving, much as other people bake cookies! This activity developed into a family hobby where everyone participates by adding an ingredient, taste-testing, and weaving in their own magic.

Similarly, brewing can give your imagination and creativity another outlet, and an alternative means to express your Path. Each new creation provides an opportunity to stir in a spell to meet your needs. By adding elements of ceremony to your preparation process, these beverages become part of the same Divine source that permeates "New Age" ideals.

Let's take the example of apple mead, a beverage dating back to ancient Rome, where it was used in everything from celebrations to treating wounded soldiers. Magically speaking, mead symbolizes joy and health. To these ends, you would stir clockwise around the brew pot while chanting, "health to me, joy be free!" Apples also are tokens of beauty and wisdom, giving you an alternative focus. In addition, apples are traditionally a part of harvest festivals like Halloween, making mead a perfect addition to any fall table.

The greatest beauty of beverage creation is that its magic doesn't have to be complicated. Even the simplest drinks have spiritual implications hidden in their folklore, myths, and correspondences. Water is a perfect example. Magically, water is symbolic of purification, healing, insight, and the lunar nature. Because of its importance to humankind, there are a wealth of Divine figures dedicated to spring and fresh water. Included in this list are Ahurani, the Persian water Goddess, and Baldur, the Norse God of wells. Either of these deities could be called upon to bless your water or any other drink (see Appendix B).

Putting this information together takes only a little resourcefulness. For example, to create a drink that will improve spiritual perception, invoke Llud (from Arthurian traditions) to sanctify the water. Visualize bright, inspirational light filling the cup. Finally, sip the water to internalize the magic.

Another good illustration is fruit juice. Nearly all fruits have positive correlations with love, joy, or health (if not all three). The next time you need an emotional lift, visualize bright blue light (the color of peace or happiness) filling your juice before you drink it; for romance, create a love potion for yourself and your mate with specially chosen fruit juices as a base. Strawberry and passion fruit are good choices here (see Appendix A).

Alcoholic beverages, especially wine, present a different set of variables to consider. In magic for awareness, consuming too much alcohol would induce the opposite of the desired result. On the other hand, wine is important to religious ceremonies, especially those involving transsubstantiation (Catholicism) and libation (Pagan/Wiccan). Positive "kitchen witchery" provides the balance necessary to make these factors work together harmoniously.

Wine has been an appropriate presentation to Gods and Goddesses, and a seemly drink for them (see Chapter 2). This casts the art of brewing in a slightly different, and Divinely inspired, light. Various orders of monks, including those at Notre Dame and St. Gall, produced widely acclaimed liquors, beers, and wines. It was as if the preparation of sacred drinks could not be left to commoners. Instead, the trust lay with holy people, whose skills improved their orders' finances.

Part of New Age ideology is the belief that everyone, not just selected individuals, has a Divine vocation. We can discover this vocation through many of mediums, techniques, and paths. Thus, I offer these recipes as a sensitive and enjoyable exploration of beverages as a potential medium for magic.

Some members of the metaphysical and New Age community do not approve of any use of alcohol. Nonetheless, the history of beverages indicates that spirituous drinks can contine to assume an honored place in our rituals, should we desire. To truly honor something means that it is not abused, but used whenever appropriate to the occasion.

Just as with magical cooking (see *The Kitchen Witch's Cookbook*), preparing metaphysically enhanced beverages for yourself or a group should be considered carefully. Ask yourself simple questions: Are your guests driving? Are any members of your circle allergic to alcohol or pregnant? Are any recovering alcoholics going to be present? If the answer to any of these questions is yes, then having alternatives to alcoholic libations is a thoughtful courtesy.

This book offers options and variations to personalize each recipe, reflecting your needs, or those of family and guests. History is one part of this picture, providing cultural richness and a variety of traditions to accentuate your Path and spiritual goals. The remainder of the portrait comes from your own capable hands and creative spirit.

The Appendices list suggestions for brewing Gods and Goddesses, include an inventory of additives and ingredients with their magical correspondences, a list of mail order suppliers, folklore examples that can furnish ideas or themes for your brewing efforts, and the basics of modern brewing methods. In addition, there is a glossary of terms and a bibliography.

By making your own ritual brews, you can share in an honored heritage. Whether for an offering, libation, or pure enjoyment, begin reclaiming this legacy. Blend your talent with innovation, vision, love, and discretion to make tasty, magical blessings for yourself, friends, family, and visitors. Stir up your witch's brew today!

Part One

Customs, Beliefs, and Practices

*The thirsty earth soaks up the rain
and drinks, and gapes for drink again
the plants suck in the earth and are
with constant drinking lush and fair...
Fill all the glasses then, for why
should every creature drink, but I?*

—Abraham Cowley

Chapter One

The History of Brewing

As he brews, so shall he drink.
—Ben Johnson

To understand better how brewing has evolved, first roll back the pages of time; past the advent of pasteurization, before chlorinated water, before even indoor plumbing! In those days, fermented drinks could be found in almost any home.

Throughout ancient civilization, fermented or boiled beverages were a means of thwarting the plague, consumption, and other communicable diseases (see Chapter 3). People believed in the healthful nature of these drinks, crediting some with life-prolonging attributes. During earlier centuries, when many children did not live to see their first birthday, any protective remedy was worth trying. European children are still permitted wine with their meals, a legacy from their ancestors. In Germany, for instance, children can even purchase beer because it is classified as food.

We do not have to look far today to observe remnants of these and similar practices. We still call beverages with alcoholic content, "spirits."[1] There is the traditional toast at weddings or recognition gatherings. When people come to

---

1. This phrase originates with the ancient idea that an actual spirit abides in all living things (Animism). In this case, the spirit of the wine fruit is literally given free access to the individual through drinking, making one act crazy when fully "possessed by the spirit."

our homes, we offer coffee, tea, or wine by way of hospitality. We christen ships with champagne bottles, and in some rural settings folks still brew by the waxing to full moon to insure the success of their endeavors, on the premise that the energy of a "growing" moon gives the mead or wine a fuller flavor. Truth be known, you can find such a person in these pages!

Some brewers keep their recipes guarded with great secrecy, passing them on to only carefully chosen successors. Collectors of rare wines invest hundreds to thousands of dollars in their prized bottles, many of which will never be opened. There is some type of magical mystique to fermented beverages that is powerful and effective, so let's take a little closer look at the background of these bewitching beverages.

Beer

The hoary sage replied, "come my lad and drink some beer."
—Samuel Johnson

Somewhere in the Euphrates valley, a Sumerian farmer, peasant, or perhaps a cook, stumbled on the notion of soaking barley in water, and grinding those grains into flour for bread. Eventually this led to using bread as an agent for brewing. When floated in a liquid, bread provided yeast for fermentation.

Exactly how this application came about is a mystery. One possibility is that dry journey cakes softened in water were neglected for some reason. When their owner discovered the error, there were small bubbles in the liquid and an intriguing aroma. Once the concoction was tasted, the world would never be the same.

History records brewing techniques as far back as 6000 B.C. Even at this early date, farmers in Babylon and Egypt dedicated 30 to 40 percent of their grain crops to brewing efforts, which leads us to speculate that beer is far older. Beer-like beverages appeared in China around the twenty-third century B.C.

Egyptians attributed the success of beer to Osiris, and offered Him libations at many festivals (see also Chapter 2). By 2300 B.C., cuniform writings and Theban tomb inscriptions show both light and dark beers being available in Southern Egypt. There were also special beers set aside for ritual use.

Unlike a modern brewery, which uses exacting instruments and measures to achieve perfect results, ancient brewers tried everything at least once. By so doing, they hoped to stumble on a formula that would bring fame and fortune. Religious communities credited many of their experimental flavorings (especially herbs) with mystical symbolism appropriate to the region and culture (see also Mead in this chapter).

Personalized rituals and customs developed and were handed down through the centuries, with individual brewers protecting their best creations as carefully as they did family treasures. Basic recipes, however, were not kept secret. These formulas traveled first to Greece, then Rome, and then slowly spread throughout the European continent. Each brewer tried to develop unique versions of his or her recipes. The joy of discovery was contagious.

During this period, beer tended to be thicker than today's, usually had remnants of the brewing process at the bottom of the cup, and a questionable flavor.

Hops was but one among many sources of flavoring until about 8 A.D. (except in the region of Bavaria, where it was the preferred choice). In general, however, hops did not catch on until around 1400.

An English book of lists from the 1100s shows at least 40 breweries. Not surprisingly, this was also the period when King Henry II taxed ale for the first time.

In Medieval times in Europe, an interesting transformation was evident. Brewing and malting became an art, frequently practiced by at least one member of every good-sized household, usually a woman, who was known by the semi-official title of "Malster" or "Brewster." Ales also appeared on the European continent during these years.

In the late 1400s, when Europeans became restless and sailed toward the horizon, they did not leave their beers behind them. Once settled in Plymouth in the early 1600s, one of the first priorities for the Pilgrims, other than basic survival, was discovering grains for brewing. They regarded beer as a Divine, wholesome blessing that held a place of honor alongside bread. Even religious folk extolled beer's benefits, perhaps because it kept the settlers from the temptation of drinking the stronger spirits available as trade routes developed.

The scientific aspects that made brewing work (or fail) were completely unknown to these people. To them, it seemed almost a whim of the Gods if one batch was tasty and another unfit for even the dogs. This mystery remained until at least 1870, when Pasteur came on the scene.

In the late 1800s, thousands of small brewing companies were established in the United States. This number slowly dwindled as the public decided what it liked best. By 1930, regional brewers began exploring the possibility of national distribution. Low-calorie beers appeared during World War II, and resurfaced around 1960 when the growing awareness of health and physical fitness created renewed demand.

While commercial production grew, home brewers, like their ancestors before them, worked quietly in a cellar, barn, or spare room, refining techniques and recipes. During prohibition, distilling proved a most profitable skill for those who were wise or reckless enough to avert the authorities.[2]

MODERN BREWER'S NOTE: The Federal Bureau of Alcohol, Tobacco and Firearms (BATF) regulates the production of alcohol in all its forms and enforces the laws pertaining to alcohol production. Title 26 of the Internal Revenue Code makes private distillation of any amount of alcohol for any reason a Federal crime. It is a crime to intend to distill witout a license. It is a crime to own or make distillation devices. It is not a crime to know how to do these things. Penalties for breaking these laws include prison and confiscation of personal property, such as your home where the illegal activity took place. Don't do it. — J.D.

In modern society, brewing has gained renewed interest, although mostly as a hobby. Then too, there are the die-hard enthusiasts who enjoy keeping an old, venerable art alive.

Wine

While wine and friendship crown the board,
we'll sing the joys they both afford.

—John Dryer

Grapes were discovered around 3000 B.C. in the region now known as Russia. The Bible, Edda, and memorial tablets from Ramses IV (1166 B.C.) and Euripides, among other notable texts, all speak of various uses for wine. Wine has probably been made for nearly as long as beer.

In its earliest stages, only the wealthy enjoyed wine. Its preparation was long, arduous, and costly. First, the grapes were pressed carefully, the juice poured into jugs, and the jugs then "stopped up" with leaves and mud. The pulp

---

2. While private distillation is illegal, wine and beer making is not. One may produce, for personal consumption, up to 100 gallons a year as head of household, or 200 gallons per family legally. This cannot be sold without a license.

remaining was repressed, creating poorer wine for the commoners. Because of this, one contemporary symbol for wine in magic could be prosperity.

Egyptians had a special panache for wine making, equal only to their veneration of the drink. Their favorite wines were made with dates, pomegranates, and palm sap. If tasty, the resulting drink was given to kings with pride, or placed before altars to implore the Gods'[3] blessings. For those whose patron Goddess is Isis, wine is a perfect offering, and brewing is an art venerating Her.

In Greece, wine making became a major source of income and eventual wealth. Like the Egyptians, Greek brewers had a Divine inspiration, in their God, Dionysus. As the story goes, when being held captive on a ship (with true flamboyance), Dionysus tossed his prized goblet into the sea, turning the water into wine. Later Biblical writers may have drawn on this story in their portrait of Christ at the marriage at Cana.

The Greeks also enjoyed playing games with wine. One such game was called Kottabos. Here, a vessel known as a *kylix* (a double-handled, flat, saucer-shaped cup) was filled with wine, held in one hand, and tossed from one player to another. If the cup was not caught, the players pragmatically used the wine spatters for divination! This particular technique is messy, but functional with blessed wine, sprinkled lightly on a surface. The result is similar to interpreting the symbolism in an ink blot or cloud formation.

Of all cultures and peoples, however, France made the greatest impact on the history of wine making. The Rhine valley proved a rich harvesting ground for grapes of fine quality. The wines of France quickly gained acclaim throughout the Roman empire. Thousands of casks moved down rivers on barges to merchants, who in turn delivered the wine to eager consumers.

The Celts had a passion for beer and wine, and for bawdy festivals. Of all the drinkers in history, they are known for their appetite for the "vine," and consumption to a state of drunkenness. In Scotland, more than one robust party has erupted into battle, the alcohol acting on the warrior clans like fire in a pot-bellied stove.

There was another, less violent, side to Celtic drinking traditions, though. Clan ties, and the larger ties to the entire Celtic community, were a serious matter. Here, wine was reserved mostly for nobility, who drank from a communal cup to show mutual trust and kinship. The Celts also left us the beautiful symbol of the Grail[4] to enhance our magic.

---

3. When I use the term "Gods," I am referring to all of the ancient pantheons including both masculine and feminine aspects.

4. In the Celtic tradition, the Grail symbolizes humankind's inescapable link to the natural world. In the Arthurian legends, it was sought as the implement to reclaim the sanctity of the land from war, and secure Kingship alongside Excalibur. Even today, the sword/dagger and cup remain very important icons of magical traditions; together being an emblem of perfected balance.

It seems that people once had greater alcohol tolerance than we do today. It was not unusual for a wealthy householder in Rome to make seven gallons of good drink available to valued handmaidens, on a weekly basis. In this context, "good drink" was the equivalent of any wine or beer that did not have to be drunk with clenched teeth to strain out sediment. Certain householders also mixed the drinking wine with water in proportions of two *kraters*[5] of wine to three of water. This might explains such seemingly exorbitant generosity and consumption.

Apples and grapes were the main ingredients for most early wines, but as people refined their techniques, other fruits were used. Of these, berries were most popular, being plentiful. Citrus was not widely used in Europe because of prohibitive import costs. Instead, brewers added small portions of rind for light flavoring. As we now know, citric acid also aids the fermenting process. Fresh herbs such as ginger root seasoned the wine, introducing tannin which yielded smoother, well-balanced, aromatic beverages.

Mead, Melomel, and Metheglin

I, in these flowery meads would be; these crystal springs should solace me.
—Thomas Carew

With the Saxons, we see only little change in brewing customs and a minor broadening of varieties. The major addition in home life was a "mead hall," where celebrations took place. Should one be banished from the hall, it was a great disgrace, being likened to a betrayal of trust.

Mead was a honey wine popular in Europe, Africa, Central America, and Australia.[6] In the Middle Ages, it warranted a special drinking vessel known as the Mather cup. This vessel, which had several handles and a squared-off top, exclusively held this fermented honey nectar.

Wines or beers flavored with honey owe at least part of their beginnings to Rome, where a fermented honey water called "mulsum" was used as a dessert. Two alternatives to this were concoctions flavored with myrtle berry (myritis) or

---

5. A *krater* is an ancient Roman drinking vessel which was also sometimes used for measurement.

6. It is difficult, when reading older texts, to differentiate one type of beverage from another because of overlapping ingredients. From what I can gather, anything prepared with a grain was considered a "beer," while fermented fruit juice was wine. Yet, in certain medieval settings, fruited beer such as strawberry stout could be found, seemingly combining the ingredients of beer and wine. For consistency, I will use the term beer in the remainder of this book for those drinks whose major alcohol content is formed by grain; wines by fruits and sugar; and meads by honey. Melomel is mead with fruit flavoring and metheglin is a mead with herb flavoring to which "spirits" may be added.

fruit juices (melomeli). Romans used honey as a base for medicinal liquors and just about anything else they could imagine.

The great Greek healer, Hippocrates, also employed honey in his prescriptions, especially those pertaining to colds and wounds. This lead to broader acceptance of honey drinks in Greece, the closest to mead being called hydromel. Like the Romans, Greeks varied this base by adding rose petals (omphacomel) and even wine and cheese (kykeon). The latter was a ritual beverage exclusively used during harvest festivals.

About the only difference between a mead and melomel is the addition of fruit (or fruit juice) to the base. From here, the next logical step for early brewers was adding other flavorings from their own pantry. This practice developed into the beverage known as metheglin, praised by Sir Kenelm Digby[7] as one of the best all-purpose tonics. Metheglin is from two Welsh words, meddy gllyn, meaning medicinal liquor. It is a heavily spiced mead that was favored by the Welsh and other Celtic people. A similar drink, made with sugar rather than honey, was called hippocras, or more simply, spiced wine.

I am in awe of what the old-time brewers managed to create. With innovation and common sense they overcame difficult conditions and poor equipment. The successful early beverages were a tribute to the power of the inquisitive human spirit.

Distilled Drinks

Brandy must be a decoction of hearts and tongues,
because after drinking it I fear nothing and I talk wonderfully.
—James G. Frazer, *The Golden Bough*

Individuals in many countriess try to credit themselves with inventing distillation. An essay by an Egyptian philosopher, Zozimos, living in the third century, describes certain apparatus, including a tripod-like configuration, which, according to him, priests used for distillation. These individuals also zealously guarded the secret for making a magic potion called the "spirit of wine." Unfortunately, historians question the translations of this information.

We know that Aristotle discussed distillation of water to make it drinkable, and that Pliny the Elder wrote of flammable[8] wine, but even this is inconclusive.

---

7. Digby was an acclaimed fourteenth century writer on cookery, brewing, and other subjects. One of his most famous books is *The Closet Opened*, in which he shares many recipes from contemporaries.

8. It is very difficult to get ordinary wine to ignite; this statement appears to refer to a distilled beverage.

Then too, we could look to China, where brewers used a slightly different method: freezing instead of boiling. This led to the development of certain rice liquors, as observed by Marco Polo. In A.D. 800, a mixture similar to those he described was transported through Japan (*sake*) to the Mediterranean, where Arab alchemists employed their traditional approaches to the whole idea.

Arabs already distilled herbs and flowers for perfume and cosmetics. One powder used in makeup was called al-kohl. This was actually a byproduct of distillation, to which we owe the modern word "alcohol." An Arabian writer, living in Spain, described the distillation of wine around the tenth century, but the technique itself did not make a strong appearance on the European continent until around A.D. 1100, in Italy.

Generally speaking, European alchemists of Medieval times were nobility or clergy. During this time distilled liquids earned the title "Aqua Vitae," or water of life. Here, and in China, Greece, and Rome, drinking such "beneficent spirits" was a perfectly acceptable means of encouraging longevity and health. Unfortunately, such acclaim led to more than one household accident involving candles and liberal amounts of distilled liquor, with tragic ends.

Whiskey, gin, vodka, and rum were available in the sixteenth century. They quickly became the base for other drinks, vodka being most popular because of its neutral taste. By the eighteenth century, merchants throughout Europe were distributing a wide assortment of flavored liqueurs.

In reviewing the restaurant menus of France from that period, I gleaned the following selections from an astonishingly intricate list: a grand chartreuse, a "fine" orange, absinthe, a ginger-flavored drink, cacao with vanilla, brandy, armagnac, and rosé. Among them, the recipe for chartreuse, which incorporates 130 plants and herbs, is still a secret to all but three friars at a time!

Small amounts of distilled beverages are flammable (if used with care). Thus, they can act as a symbol of the fire element on our altars, and can be offered to the Gods or consumed according to their associations. For example, Vulcan

(the Roman God of fire and metalworking) might appreciate a libation of "Fire Water," a modern cinnamon-flavored liqueur. In this example, both the beverage and the spice have strong associations with Vulcan's predominant element.

Drinking Vessels

Sparkling and bright in liquid light, does the wine our goblets gleam in!
—Charles Fenno Hoffman

Just as eating from fine china makes a meal more sumptuous, people of early civilizations appreciated the vessels and containers that held wines, meads, and beers. Egyptian tomb paintings from 1600 B.C. depict silver and gold drinking bowls. In Genesis 44:2, we even find Joseph requesting that his servant pack a special drinking bowl for a journey.

Besides the human hand, a sea shell, or gourds, one of the first drinking vessels was an animal horn. Some with traces of silver etchings surfaced in Greece, dated around 2000 B.C. (pre-Minoan). At first, the horns were cleaned, soaked in water several times, then soaked again in alcohol. Later, craftspeople decorated them with precious metals or emblematic carvings. Until a clever artisan came up with a stand, the drinking horn had to be emptied before setting it down.

In Asia and Africa, drinking bowls made of wood or metal, and later ones encrusted with gems or precious metals have been found. These bowls were called "mazers" in some areas, which in Old English refers to maple wood, the wood most frequently used in bowl construction on the European continent.

Bowls were sometimes placed on small stands, giving yet another astute artisan something to think about in the development of the goblet or chalice. Goblets made from crude glass have been found in the Mediterranean region. The word "chalice" comes from the Latin *calix*, meaning cup, which later became associated with the Grail.

Every culture had unique ways of forming a goblet to personal tastes. Normans preferred round-bottomed cups, and the Gothic style had feet and toes below conical cups, rather like gargoyles. In Tudor England, sculpted, flowing bases were balanced with hemispheric bowls. Of the lot, the Scandinavians were probably the most stubborn crew, preferring silver tankards to goblets, right up until the 1700s.

Before the advent of rapid transportation, people took traveling drinking sets with them. Small carved wooden boxes held decanters and glasses to accompany the drinking that helped pass the time of long voyages. During the Victorian era, this idea moved into the woods with huntsmen, who carried special flasks filled with cherry brandy.

No matter the design, however, the use of cups in religious ceremonies remains customary (see also Chapter 2). The raising of a cup came to symbolize an invocation for blessing. It also implored the Gods to witness a promise.

When two people drank from one cup, it made them one in the eyes of the Divine. This particular symbol was used in early Pagan marriage rites. Gypsies felt that if two people drank from a common glass, it symbolized kinship. Then why is this glass sometimes broken, as in the Jewish marriage ritual? So that the oath can never be reversed.

We have many choices for magical drinking vessels. For someone who follows a huntsman God, for example, the drinking horn might adorn the altar, while in rituals for animal health and well-being, a simple bowl is more appropriate.

The Future

Years mature into fruit so that some small seeds of moments may outlive them.
—Rabindranath Tagor

Our ancestors' lives were laden with superstition. Beverages too were subject to magics, medicines, and folklore. Records of early recipes and approaches are available for adaptation by the home brewer today.

Mingling this heritage with our own creative contemporary sensibilities, accomplishes two important ends. First, the richness of the past becomes a sharing experience. This continues the legacy of oral traditions, encouraging others toward research and eventual production.

Second, this process may serve to inspire new family customs. Here, rather than a trip to the nearby convenience store, old-fashioned experimentation and personal vision rule. Home beverage making can take its place again among crafts being handed down from generation to generation.

You will discover that making juices, wines, and ales can be relaxing and fun to do. Then too, there is the lovely magic of this art, just beneath the surface.

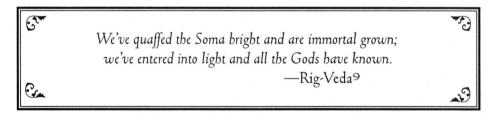

We've quaffed the Soma bright and are immortal grown;
we've entered into light and all the Gods have known.
—Rig-Veda[9]

---

9   The Rig-Veda is the oldest Vedic text, celebrating the nature religion of the Hindus. Here Soma is the father of the gods, a liquid which affords immortality.

Chapter Two

Religious Use of Beverages

There is naught, no doubt, so much the spirit calms as rum and true religion.
—Lord Byron

Alongside scholarly, political or personal pursuits, people have always enjoyed bountiful quantities of inebriating substances privately, or offered them to the Gods publicly as the perfect gift of nature. Anything admired by commoners and kings alike will eventually find its way into religious lore, observances, and ritual. The question remains, why? What inspired such reverence?

In Native American tradition, when a person fashions something, a little part of his or her spirit (essence) enters that creation.[1] So, if one makes wine and drinks it, are we then drinking of our own inherent Divine power? It is worth considering, especially in a ritualized setting (see also Legends, pages 18-20).

Even this analogy leaves the modern curiosity seeker pondering. Since not all cultures have the same religious foundation, the Native American belief presented above is only one part of a vast picture. It alone cannot explain the broad-ranging use of inebriants throughout the ancient world's greatest cultures. To discover the roots of our own religious drinking traditions, we first have to explore the archaic uses and their meanings in diverse settings.

---

1. This mirrors the belief that there is something of the Great Spirit in each soul. Many religions, including Christianity, talk about God breathing life into humankind. By imparting that breath, a vital essence, a sacred, special connection to the Creator is implied.

Early Civilization

Remove not the ancient landmark.
—Proverbs 22:28

The drawings made by cave dwellers depict nature as fearsome, wondrous, and often unforgiving. Every incident held importance to these growing minds; the sun was an ally, the storms an angry spirit. Wind was the breath of life, and creatures provided food or were an enemy of which to be wary. Slowly, these observations translated into beliefs about "spirits" in animals, plants, and every breeze.[2]

Little by little, reverence for the life force patterned itself into small, simple rituals. In tribal cultures of South America, Africa, and other regions, these rituals combined song, dance, and drink around a natural object or fire. During the rite, worshippers offered food and drink to the spirits, especially those of deceased tribal members. This gift provided the individual some of the pleasures he or she had experienced in life. There was always a special spot set aside for this, usually where the spirit could eat undisturbed by inquisitive stares.

Egyptian tombs reveal that this idea did not subside with evolutions in thinking—it simply changed form. In Egypt, hearty portions of food, drink, money, and even beloved pets were placed in tombs to help the spirit exist happily in his or her new reality. Beyond the idea of the Creator being part of all things was the firm conviction that whatever makes us alive cannot really die. If the spirit is not actually dead, then the living should supply it with the things of enjoyment—among them, of course, wine![3]

Goodheartedness was not the only motivation for these gifts. People also believed that offerings kept an angry or restless spirit from wandering about. Just when you think contemporary society has progressed beyond such views, observe a contemporary wake. Today, you will still notice people slipping a small airline bottle of alcohol, a coin, or other "charm" into the casket of a loved one, unwittingly following this age-old practice.

---

2. Even contemporary Pagans hold a little of these ancient ideas as valid, feeling that the Divine best expresses itself in the most perfect creation of nature.

3. Wine here is a generic term. Each social group valued specific beverages. Those most precious became offerings to the Gods or gifts to the dead. If the deceased was someone of rank, the gifts were of higher quality to provide the spirit in a manner to which it was "accustomed." In this way, the family knew the spirit would rest well and not haunt them.

Offerings

In the days of festivals of the Gods, who gave men wine for their banquets.
—Plato[4]

We have already seen that the ancients started a long tradition of leaving offerings before the Gods. To understand this better, we need to remind ourselves that these people regarded spirits with both wonder and honest apprehension. In German, the word *ehrfurcht*, for "offerings," says it all: "to honor in fear."

The earliest offerings were very simple ones. Water, a life-giving force, and milk, the juice of motherhood, accompanied first fruits, grains, and sometimes livestock. Sacrificial practices developed, in part, because of the joyful feeling engendered when people drank. Any liquid so full of life must be a gift from the spirits. At least part of this gift should be returned to the netherworld with a grateful heart.

Whether in thankfulness, to plead for aid, or as a remembrance, wine filled special vessels upon many ancient altars to specific Gods; among them Gestin of Sumeria, Pagat in Ugarit, Ishtar in Mesopotamia, Horus in Egypt, Poseidon in Greece, and Liber in Rome. In Greece, for example, a deep-stemmed cup for libations was the *kantharus*. A shallower bowl/plate for wine offerings was the *philae*. Here, people considered it unseemly to drink oneself to drunkenness, except during holy festivals. Throughout Greek observances, alcoholic beverages were a potent symbolic force, bringing bliss to the worshipper and delight to the Gods.

---

4.   As translated in 1854 from the *Sixth Book of the Laws*, by C. D. Young.

One example of this is the Choes Festival. From 800-300 B.C. this celebration marked the transition of boys into adulthood in Greece. As part of an observance honoring Dionysus, boys assembled in front of the Acropolis to get their first draught of wine. Henceforth they were adults, with all the duties of an adult citizen.

The Hebrews had two offerings that included liquid libation.[5] The first was a monthly donation to God that included bread, a ram, seven lambs, and two bullocks, along with a beverage. The other was strictly an offering of drink, usually meaning wine.

Germans called those who brewed beer for Pagan offerings *dasture*, until Christianity became more prevalent. The Dasture's office was sacred, and always chosen on New Year's Day. The holder of this office received a few assistants to cut firewood and tend to other chores so the Dasture could be fully mindful of his or her duties. One brew of the Dasture, created solely for offerings, was a mead called *sinnreger*. This roughly translates as "kettle stirrer" because of its invigorating effect. Priests offered sinnreger to the Gods of the Sacred Grove, then shared it among celebrants during festivals such as the Winter Solstice.

Central Asian and Sanskrit writings mention *soma*, a mountain plant that devout Hindus gathered by moonlight in a sacred area. Priests or faithful followers of Indra crushed soma with stones to extract the juice, then left the juice to ferment for future offerings.

Soma was usually placed on rustic altars made from turf, stones, and kindling. Aryans threw it into their fires by the ladle-full and distributed it among their priests. So powerful was the acclaim of this beverage that the Rig-Veda calls it a "master of a thousand songs," and "leader of sages." It even gives power to the Gods. In later years, soma shared with others at any gathering became the symbol of devoted friendship.

Another intoxicant mentioned in Sanskrit writings is *sura*. This is millet, water, curds, butter, and barley fermented together. Sura was as popular as soma (see footnote, page 12), but gained some negative implications because of its potency. From this, it is but one short step to the Persian sacred drink known as *haomas*.[6] White haomas was the drink of immortality, given to the Persians by the god, Ormuzd. Accordingly, priests presented haomas to Ormuzd alongside meat and holy water.

---

5. According to Thomas Hartwell Horne, in his 1856 treatise on Jewish offerings. This seems well confirmed by Biblical evidence.

6. The similarity between the word *soma* and *haomas* should not be overlooked. Persians and central Asians had the same racial origin, which created interesting similarities in their verbiage and religious rites.

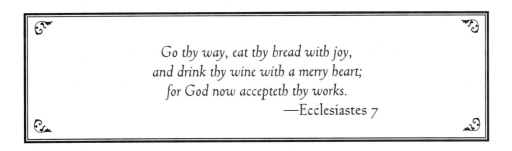

Go thy way, eat thy bread with joy,
and drink thy wine with a merry heart;
for God now accepteth thy works.
—Ecclesiastes 7

The meting out of this beverage for Persian Gods is especially significant since people regarded it as a panacea. Haomas symbolized the bounty of earth and morality. No more precious substance could be returned to the gods to implore their favor.

Chinese sacred writings from 3000 to 4000 years ago, known as the Shoo King and the Shi King, describe the spirituous offerings of these people. The priests of the region made sacred beverages only when heaven bid them to, and then these drinks were only consumed on sacrificial days. Stern warnings about the dangers of abusing Divine gifts accompanied the creation and enjoyment of such drinks (see also, Legends, pages 18-20).

Tablets from the time of Ramses III in Egypt indicate that similar practices occurred there. "Proper" offerings were so abundant that wine flowed throughout the valley of the Nile. Other suitable gifts included mead, oxen, and heady-smelling incense.

At one point, the populace acclaimed the House of Ramses for its generous contributions to the temples. By the end of his reign these gifts totaled over 500 oxen, 5 million sacks of corn, 6 million loaves of bread, 250,000 jugs of wine, and 460,000 gallons of beer.

Leftover offerings from religious rites were distributed first to the priests and servants of a temple, then to supplicants. To waste any portion insulted the Divine. Worshippers of Amun, for example, claimed the only appropriate offering to this God had to include 40 jars of fine mead along with other items, all of which they then ate. Since the Gods accepted the offerings as pleasing, the foods and beverages were full of blessings, and considered healthy to consume.

Finally, in Alexandria, there was the curious custom, devoted to the Goddess (probably Isis), of placing a glass of honeyed wine on the table on the last day of the month. This is a lovely and subtle offering, which I see no reason not to "borrow." It reminds me a bit of the Old Testament custom of leaving one seat at the table for the prophet. Small gestures like these let the Divine powers know that we remember them and welcome them in our sacred space, our home.

Legends, Lore, Customs, and Tales

If ancient tales say true, nor wrong these holy men.
—Lord Byron

It is difficult to separate the legends of beverages from actual applications in a reli-gious or cultural setting—the stories themselves were often the basis for analo-gous liturgical or domestic actions. Allegorical tales help us understand early civilization's indigenous and ritual employment of drinks with greater clarity, pro-viding marvelous symbols and ideas to adapt in contemporary magical settings.

Not all of these customs or legends directly relate to religion *per se.* Nonetheless, early people did not separate mundane life from spiritual. The events of day-to-day existence always had a basis in "other realms," so if folk tra-ditions do not specifically speak of faith, they usually have connections some-where along the way. Time's passage has simply obscured the relationship.

We begin with the Norse, who claim that before entering Valhalla one must first consume all the beer, wine, or other alcohol spilled in this life. This belief acts as gentle encouragement to take care with such precious liquids, and a reminder to offer all spilled beverages to the gods. A feasting hall is prepared for those who pass this vigorous test, and a special drinking horn is passed at the welcoming banquet, filled with mead from the base of the Yggdrasil tree.[7] This insures the horn will never run dry, and the mead heals any wound sustained in life. Happy Norsemen share divine liquids here (specifically ale), while keeping company with Odin and Frigg in the netherworld.

Another Norse legend holds that all red-fruited plants are sacred to Thor, the god of thunder. The first goblet of red wine at a wedding should be offered to him, in return for his promise to join the festivities and bestow good weather.

The Norse legend of Bragi, the son of Odin, and a god of muse, relates that in his keeping was the mead of poets, captured from the giants. This mead granted ardor to any who could steal a sip. As such a guardian, Bragi becomes

---

7.   In function and symbolism this tree is very similar to the Jewish Tree of Life.

a good choice to call on for Divine aid in brewing efforts.[8] Legend also tells of Oegir, whose sacred duty was to tend beer production in Asgard. At every harvest festival (most likely Lammas), it was the duty of the gods to drink with Oegir in memory of his service, so a small offering to Oegir from your first batch of wine should encourage continued success.

Another story comes from Euripides. In *Bacchae*, Euripides writes of Dionysus, saying, "he, born a God, is poured out in libations to the Gods." In other words, the god and the substance were one in the same. Each time the Greeks poured wine, Dionysus was there sharing Divine energy. Thus, when the Gods drank of this beverage, they reclaimed part of their own power! Therefore, if you follow a Grecian-style magical path, use wine as a libation for your gods.

The above reading, coupled with the writings of Aristotle (circa 300 B.C.) in the *Book of Drunkenness*, makes it apparent that Greeks preferred wine over beer. Wine could bring a bright flush to the face and ease sadness. Conversely, beer "tends to stupefy" and cause men to fall on their "hinder parts."[9]

Romans of high birth shared the Greek distaste for beer, probably considering it a drink for barbarians and peasants. However, the Latin term for beer *(Cerevisia)* may owe its origins to the Roman goddess of agriculture, Ceres. Literally translated in this context, the word "cerevisia" could mean "strength (or life) of Ceres." While some Roman philosopher would groan at the connection, this definition makes beer a marvelous beverage to choose for any altar honoring Ceres.

Less wealthy Roman citizens had ideas of their own about beer. In the Illyrian province on the Adriatic coast, people enjoyed a beer called *Sabaia*, and adopted a humorous custom along with its consumption. Athenaeus, in *Deipnos x.60*, wrote that when quaffing large commodities, the Illyrians first tightened their belts, as one places a barrel hoop on a keg to keep it from bursting.

As a group, the Celts often ate their meals at a circular table, with the leader taking a central seat, along with any entertainers. Servants brought wine in one cup, always passing it in a clockwise fashion, following the movements of their worship. Individuals of lower rank received *corma* (beer) in the same manner, so that even when separated by status, a communal purpose was implied. This symbolism could be adapted in a modern magical circle for much the same goals.

In China, ancestor worship played a key role in the way people used alcoholic beverages. Legends of this culture teach that when one leaves fermented beverages for the deceased, the ancestors partake of it, and are made happy by the drink. For the Chinese, this was a way of blessing their family, even in the hereafter.

---

8. This story can be found in the Edda, two ancient books of Norse-Icelandic mythology. The earliest written versions of the Edda date to A.D. 1000, having far older origins in oral tradition.

9. *Athenaeus*, book 10, chapter 67; book 1, chapter 68.

In the Hindu culture, an Indus legend claims that Indra drank the magic soma from three mighty bowls to absorb life-giving essence (considered lunar and feminine in nature). Most powerful in this state, Indra continues to receive soma at any celebration honoring Him. In this instance, the production of soma became a ritual, taking place in stages at morning, noon, and night. This procedure magically improved potency for both the worshipper and the gods.

The Persians honored their version of soma (see Offerings, pages 15-17) in a very special way. The spirit of anger (aeshma) and other malignant spirits were associated with most fermented beverages in this region. Haomas, however, was protected by and filled with the Goddess Ashi, who presides over fortune and wealth. Thus, this drink provided victory in battle, and the golden version of haomas nurtured the soul.

Persians regarded another drink called banga as saturated with aeshma, until Zoroaster arrived on the scene. As the leader of many wise people (and eventually a religious sect named for him), Zoroaster elevated banga to a divine level, claiming it transported the drinker to a heavenly plain. This may very well have been true, since the primary ingredient of banga was hemp seed, which produced hallucinations. The resulting astral visions inspired Zoroaster, and he taught the value of banga to his priests.

Egyptian myths recount that Ra, when he wearied of the human race, called upon Hathor to destroy them. He later reconsidered his hasty judgment, but Hathor was not easily dissuaded. To soften her heart, he poured 7,000 jugs of beer on the fields. When Hathor reached the region, she found her reflection glimmering off the brew, instead of the people she had come to destroy. Hathor drank of the beverage, was satisfied, and was calmed; Ra's quick thinking saved humankind. The modern magician might use beer to asperge a circle in a ritual for protection. Beer also makes a good spell component for astute decisions, safety, and calming anger. It would be suitable in a cup to venerate Ra and Hawthor upon the altar.

While the Hebrews learned the art of brewing from the Egyptians, it never caught on in the same manner. The Jews used some wines in offerings, and others in special festivals, but it seems that wines and ciders were usually used in more domestic situations here. The most popular flavors were pomegranate and fig.

No matter the land or legend, however, one truth comes through. Most early cultures considered intoxicants a wonderful boon from heaven; this gift allowed humankind to see or experience the Divine being more clearly. As such, they became part of religious mysteries, remnants of which we still see today.[10]

---

10. This is most plainly evidenced in the Catholic church. While Protestant sects use communion symbolically, Catholicism still holds to the idea of transubstantiation during the communion service—that the wine and bread actually become the body and blood of Christ.

Other Applications

There is at the surface, infinite variety of things;
at the center there is simplicity of unity, of cause.
—R. W. Emerson

Experience and inspiration, though a material boost, was not unknown to religious people. The ancients believed that the body and mind, in communion with Divine power, could act as a beautiful expression of that power. To help them achieve this state, they looked toward substances that already contained part of that Great Spirit, or a demi-spirit all their own.

Experience proved the merit of these beverages in changing one's mental state. Therefore, by drinking an intoxicant, people symbolically took a godly aspect into themselves. In other words, they allowed it to possess them.

One illustration is from ancient Greece and Rome, where sibyls often prophesied in a state of frenzy, sometimes aided by alcohol. Of these, the prophetesses in Cumae (lower Italy) and Erythrea (Ionia) were most celebrated. The idea was to achieve an altered awareness, in which possession by Apollo could occur. It is interesting to note that our modern word "enthusiasm," meaning intense, rapturous feelings, takes its origins from Greece. *Entheos* literally means united with God.

Another group of women from ancient Peru used a drink called *chica*, mixed with herbs, to help them obtain a suitable state of mind to answer questions. While I doubt the contemporary magician would desire intoxication for divinatory attempts, the symbolism still has its uses. For example, you could have a glass of wine nearby to anoint divination tools, or trace protective symbols with wine on your finger tips, in place of an athame or wand.

Beyond their use for religious inspiration, certain beverages of notable reputation also improved trade, marketing, and even motivated some explorations. We know this partially due to linguistic links between cultures, shown by a word such as wine: *Gwin* = Welsh, *Fin* = Irish, *Foinos* = Greek, *Vinum* = Latin, *Vin* = French.

Another confirmation comes from the Chinese philosophers and priests. These men sent out ships searching for the elixir of immortality known as *Tze Mai*. While sailors investigated age-old stories recounted by sacred texts (and made maps), the alchemists at home tried to discover the elusive formula. In the process, the Chinese enjoyed advancement in the areas of medicine, science, geography ... and brewing, too!

From Babylon, caravans transported plum and date wines to neighboring countries. These items fetched a handsome price in cash, barter, or trade. Cities under the control of Alexander were favorite spots to stop and sell, increasing the coffers of Babylon and the city's clever merchants.

In the Middle Ages, in the castle of a king or lord, beverages pleased both guests and nobles. At any gathering, the king had the best libations available, as he gained his position through "Divine right." Nobles and lords also received better wines than the remaining company. In this setting, the ruling authority accepted "offerings" on behalf of the gods.

From this point forward, wine and beer became more available or affordable. Their popularity and a growing understanding of brewing processes displaced much of the mystery surrounding alcohol. The country villager might periodically offer wine to the land, the well, or the Gods in thankfulness. The Church maintained communion. Even so, most people lost sight of brewing as a religious expression, and of its origins and importance throughout their history.

Today

And the vine said unto them, should I leave my vine
which cheereth both God and man?

—Judges 9:12

Science has given us so much that old mysteries are no longer mysteries, but commonplace knowledge. How can we reclaim wonder and appreciation for things that we can buy readily?

People cherish their traditions. In Japan, for example, tea and sake are still venerable drinks, accompanied by ceremonies and customs that defy understanding by Western minds. Voodoo sects use rum in certain rituals, and followers of Hawaiian Huna employ gin for some spells.

In China, rice wine continues to appear at harvest festivals, where everyone raises pledge cups in thankfulness to the ancestors, symbolizing unity. Similar actions, by way of a toast, can be seen in modern marriage ceremonies. Communion is still taken by Christians. But what of the remainder; what of the Gods?

Pagans and Wiccans have an opportunity to revitalize ancient reverence for beverages as a Divine gift. While we serve cakes and wines at our rituals, are we truly aware of their significance to us? History, heritage, and related symbolism can serve as a foundation for instructing others in this abundance. Then, in religious magical realms, beverages will be available for future generations.[11]

---

11. The main reference given for wine and bread as part of magical rites comes from *Aradia, the Gospel of Witches* (C. G. Leland), purportedly shared by an Italian Familial Witch with the author.

Chapter Three

Medicinal Mixtures

*H*ere stands mead, for Baldur brewed, over the bright potion, a shield is laid.
—The Younger Edda

Folk remedies included beverages as their base for thousands of years. For proof, we need look no further than the Roman battlefield, Polish soldiers,[1] and the Celts. In all three cases physicians used liqueurs laced with herbs to ease the pain of wounds and begin the healing process.

On the home front, teas and tonics, "physicks," and tinctures took care of family maladies. Women were both housewives and physicians to a household, usually trained in folk remedies by their mothers. While they might not read or write, many of them could put the contemporary herbal hobbyist to shame with their field knowledge of plants, preparations, and applications. Except for the occasional traveling priest, monk, physician, or sage, this familial knowledge was the backbone of health care well into the 1900s.

An integral part of these home medicines was alcohol. Liquor effectively covered up the taste of a disagreeable herbal mixture. It also provided a practical way to get a stubborn person to rest. The amount prescribed was not large, only what was necessary for efficacy. Indeed, healers used great restraint with these

---

1. Horilka, recipes for which will be included in Section Two of this book, was a Polish and Russian honey mead mixed with spirits of vodka. This was one of the most popular healing elixirs for soldiers in this area.

because of their cost. Elixirs could command exorbitant prices due to rare spices or gold and silver leaf added for effectiveness.[2]

From a magical perspective, it is important to recognize that many of these concoctions also had symbolic value. Red wine,[3] for example, became a healing drink for someone with blood problems. Then too, people believed many alcoholic beverages were inherently healthy. With Persian haomas, for example, the sacred text of *Zend Avesta* says, "of all the healing virtues, Haomas, whereby thou art a healer, grant me some." It should be noted that these medicinal liqueurs are only one part of the ancient folk medicine cabinet, as it regularly included non-alcoholic substances as well.

Beer

Oh, many a peer of England brews,
livelier liquor than the muse,
and malt does more than Milton can,
to justify God's ways to man.
—Alfred E. Houseman

The idea that alcoholic beverages are healthy is accepted in many cultures. In German society, for example, people viewed drinking large commodities of beer as a sign of strength. The Celtic peoples incorporated it into every social, civic, and religious activity. Each activity had its own special beer, as evidenced by titles such as "bride ale," "tithe ale," "inheritance beer" (*erbbier*), and "soul beer" (*seelenbier*).

Before the advent of Christianity, rulers or family priests might decree that the populace should drink until supplies were exhausted, to honor the Gods. As early as A.D. 800, brewing developed into an honorable occupation. In this atmosphere, beer drinking was considered psychologically healthy, thanks to cultural conditions.

With this in mind, we can then look to more common applications for beer, mixed liberally with ancient herbalism and customary folk medicine. Plinius, in *Natural History* (XXI, 50), noted that hops was a good nutrient. Herbalists

---

2. Folklore has granted innate magical qualities to precious metals. Gold conveyed the power of the sun, strength, and vitality. Silver comprised the lunar sphere, associated with healing, insight, fertility, etc. Thus it is that you find many medieval recipes for Aqua Vitae including gold or silver leaf as vital components.

3. This is an excellent example of what Cunning Folk called "sympathy." The color or visual impact of a plant or drink indicated its use—like a code that God left for humankind to interpret. Examples include red for blood problems, yellow for jaundice, onions to cure baldness, etc.

recommended hops to relieve
sleeplessness, dizziness, nausea,
headaches, and twitching mus-
cles. Similarly, oats appear as
a beneficial addition to tonics,
easing nervous exhaustion and
improving concentration. Therefore, any beverage made from
either of these substances was
also assumed to be beneficial.

Another ancient illustra-
tion emerged from Egypt
around 1500 B.C. In this country, to dream of drinking beer
made from barley meant a long
life; from wheat, it indicated
joy. Two recipes discovered in
the Ebers Papyrus, dating
from the same period, call for
stagnant water and beer dregs
for ischury, and an olive (or
perhaps olive oil, depending on your translation) mixed
with beer for colic.

Moving forward in history, one story of St. Brigit (A.D. 450) reveals positive religious connotations for beer. According to legend, while nursing a group
of lepers, St. Brigit changed water to beer by sheer faith. This story, combined
with the fact that medieval churches allotted as much as three sections of land
for cultivating beer ingredients, indicates that the church respected this substance. Its popularity commonly, religiously, magically, and medicinally continued to grow.

During the Middle Ages, herbalists and healers recommended small
amounts of beer to aid digestion. Since the medieval apothecary was subject to
whim, this was rarely a plain beer. Instead it often included healthful herbs and/or
honey. Medicinal beers regularly contained yarrow (a stimulant frequently applied
to wounds), rosemary, anise, caraway, ginger, and juniper berries.

The best-written example of medicinal beer comes to us through *Physica
Sacra* by St. Hildegard, an abbess of a Benedictine nunnery on the Rhine. In A.D.
1100, she wrote of the preservative qualities of hops that could decrease the

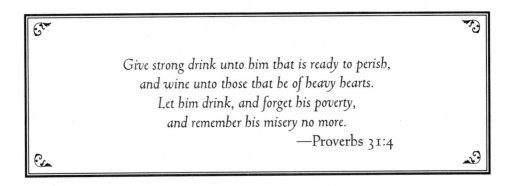

Give strong drink unto him that is ready to perish,
and wine unto those that be of heavy hearts.
Let him drink, and forget his poverty,
and remember his misery no more.
—Proverbs 31:4

occurances of many sicknesses. In one sample recipe, she claims that beer prepared with seven ash leaves[4] (a magical number) and special herbs will "purge the stomach and ease the chest."[5] St. Hildegard also tells us that certain dishes prepared with beer instead of wine are more healthful, because of the boiling process that beer incorporates.

This particular illustration also illuminates an important point about Paganism and the church. Certain purported effects of herbs and their uses by the clergy were "technically" magical. Since Christianity began in a Pagan world, many tried-and-true symbolic methods adapted to the new face of God very slowly. Typically, the approach remained unchanged, except for the attending invocation or prayer. Here, a holy person altered the prayer so that it venerated Jesus or Mary (a type of the God and Goddess). The result was a pattern familiar to the ailing individual, thereby giving them comfort. Additionally, the church saved face and gained converts by hiding Pagan techniques behind Christian words.

Time did little to transform the original notions of beer as healthful. It remained in popular use for folk medicine until the U.S. Constitutional amendment established prohibition January 16, 1920 (repealed in 1934). Those who loved beer came away from this period with a bad taste in their mouth, since many home brews were terrible. Additionally, the ill effects of alcohol began to attract public notice. As a medicinal beverage, it all but disappeared from use, except in rural settings.

---

4. The seven ash leaves recommended in this recipe probably derived from an old folk custom. Ash was a sacred tree in Europe, comparable to the fabled Yggdrasil. It shows up in hundreds of remedials. The number seven is also magical, signifying moon magic and healing. There are seven wonders in the world, seven-year cycles, seven days in the Biblical account of creation, and seven colors in the rainbow.

5. *Physica Sacra*, Lib. III, Cap. XXVII.

Cyder

With all the Gallick wines are not so boone,
as hearty Sider, y'strong drink of wood.
—Vicar of Dilwyn, 1651

Depending on the period reviewed, cyder was either a wine (ancient Greece and Rome), a long drink (Middle Ages), or a fruit juice (modern). It became popularly accepted in sixteenth century England, where healers started using it almost immediately. On one hand, certain precautions had to be maintained, as cyder-making equipment could cause lead poisoning. On the other hand, this marvelous beverage eliminated scurvy on sea voyages. In the sailing adventures of these years, sailors took cyder on board, often in diluted form. It kept far better than fruit, and could replace any drinking water that became tainted on long journeys.

In English tradition, harvest was the best time to drink cyder for health. Since cyder was alchemically a "cold" drink, it was an excellent remedy for those with fevers. Even in the 1700s, fall was cold and flu season. Cyder also helped cool farmhands who found themselves overheated from autumn's painstaking work. Today's cider (its spelling also modernized) still makes a marvelous choice for ritual cups in any harvest festival.

Distilled Beverages

Aqua Vitae is the mistress of all medicines.
—H. Braunschweig

Hieronymus Braunschweig was a notable figure in medicine and pharmacology in fifteenth-century Germany. He lauded the qualities of Aqua Vitae, and recommended it to cure headaches, renew color, stop baldness, and kill fleas! With acclaim such as this, it is easy to see why people of the Middle Ages revered distilled beverages for medicinal applications.

Over time, the capable hands of apothecaries and monks added herbs to liqueurs during preparation. Spices already played an important role in the medieval kitchen. Thus, many curative herbs were also those found readily in the pantry. Prevalent superstition and knowledge helped decide which herbs to use for each sickness. For example, sage with brandy was a remarkable panacea, or so its creators claimed. Sage takes its name from the term *alvia*, meaning "I save."

Popular belief claimed that if medicine was costly, it worked better. Around 1730, one recipe included 14 liters of brandy with bay leaves, zedoary roots, cardamom, gentian root, wild rhubarb, angelica, chamomile, sweet flag, lemon rind, fennel seed, carrot seed, licorice, anise seed, ginger, nutmeg, cinnamon, mace, cloves, sage, rue, and juniper berries. To any common household, even minute quantities of this mixture would have cost an exorbitant amount, yet to assure health to a loved one, they paid the price.

The base of medicinal liqueurs changed according to what was popular at the time. A book from the early 1700s called *Secrets of Wines* (author unknown) discusses curative waters based in brandy. These included stomach water, plague water, maternity anise, and heart cordials. In the first two cases, we see the explicit medicinal application, but the latter two definitely have roots in folklore and magic. These ideas may encourage the contemporary magician to consider brandy in spells or rituals for love and fertility.

Metheglin and Mead

This meathe is singularly good for consumption, stone,
gravel, weak-sight and many more things.
—Sir Kenelm Digby

Finnish lore says heaven is a storehouse for sacred honey that has the power to heal all wounds. Hippocrates (circa 400 B.C.) agreed with this philosophy, recommending honey in his medicinal writings for everything from coughs to skin wounds. From this vantage point, it is but a short jump to perceiving mead and mead-related drinks as similarly health-promoting.

Ancient civilizations recognized honey for its healthful qualities, and regarded mead as revitalizing. The Germans and Scots equated the strength-imparting ability of mead to that of eating meat. They also considered mead an aphrodisiac, which aided reproduction. These beliefs combined into the Northern tradition of celebrating marriage with a month of mead drinking, assuring the couple joy and fertility. Our modern term "honeymoon" comes from this practice.

As early as the first century, the Greek philosopher Dioscorides praised the healing properties of mead. The best medicinal mead was a "small" brew, prepared and aged for about five days. This amount of fermentation yielded only sufficient amounts of alcohol to relax the patient, thus the term "small" refers to alcohol content. In some lands, people added the milk of animals or nuts to the mead. The Celts, for example, treated toothaches and other maladies with hazelnut juice, which already bore magical qualities.

A review of several historical figures improves our understanding of the popular use of mead and metheglin. Julius Caesar preserved his personal vigor and keenness of mind with metheglin. St. Findian fasted six days of the week, eating only bread and water to keep his soul pure. He then partook of salmon and one cup of mead on the seventh day. Another story of St. Brigit tells how she created mead for the King of Heinster in an empty vessel. The popularity of meads grew with these "celebrity endorsements."

Another important person who wrote of the advantages of mead and metheglin was Sir Kenelm Digby, a great courtier mentioned previously. From his observations come tidbits of information that enlighten us about contemporary thought during the late 1600s. At one point, he refers to metheglin as "excellent for colds and consumption."[6]

In a report from 1695, we read, "they have likewise metheglin compounded of milk and honey, and it is very wholesome,"[7] speaking of the Welsh people.

Based on such chronicles, mead-related drinks can serve as a magical drink, even in a twentieth century setting; symbolic of vigor, miracles, alertness, health, and romance.

Physicks

Physick, for the most part, is nothing else
but the substitute of exercise or temperance.
—Joseph Addison

The physick garden of the Middle Ages included a special section for "simples,"[8] medicinal plants and herbs having a purgative effect when added to food or drink. These gardens were often found in conjunction with a monastery or an apothecary shop ... reflecting Mother Nature's abundant medicine chest.

As "simpling" became more widespread, books of the day gave directions for the preparations. These volumes, rare and almost unobtainable today, included information not only on hygienic needs, but also luxurious scent creations, so desirable in furnishing a proper home with charm and beauty.

It was very difficult in my research to sort specific "physicks" out from other "remedials." Writers used the two terms interchangeably. Even so, I dis-

---

6. From 1669, *The Closet Opened*, "Mr. Pierce's Excellent White Metheglin."

7. From *History of the Principality of Wales* by Nathaniel Church, London, England, 1695.

8. I discussed simples briefly in *A Victorian Grimoire*. I believe that the term "simples" developed due to the pragmatic and easy approach these remedials took to health. For the most part, these were herbal compounds, fromt herbs grown in the kitchen garden of old.

covered that beer spiced with dandelion, sassafras, ginger root, and lemon was recommended as a blood purifier as late as 1908 (United States). Therefore, I would suggest that any beverage using pepper, garlic, ginger, citrus, and other typical "cleansing" fruits or spices could be considered part of this category.[9]

Teas

I am glad I was not born before tea.

—Sidney Smith

Known as *Teba* in China, *Teb* in Malaysia, and *Tey* in Middle English, tea is an infusion or decoction of plants or herbs in water. I believe humankind has probably tried every plant and spice on this planet as part of a curative tea at least once.

While ancient history cites applications for teas, the best available source comes from our Victorian ancestors, who were enamored of the beverage. Besides being a social accessory, curative teas surfaced in almost all cookery books of the day. These recipe collections recommended beef tea as a food for the sick room, sage and honey tea for throat infections, mint for stomach complaints, catnip for children's maladies, pennyroyal for colds, and strawberry leaf tea to "disburse" chancre sores, just to name a few.

Some teas were blended with alcoholic beverages to enhance the physical effects; an example is whiskey, honey, and lemon tea for a cough. For the most part, though, plain tea dominated social and medicinal settings. People revered it for its cordial, diversified personality. Fortunately, information on curative teas remains available today, thanks to the efforts of many excellent, dependable authors.[10]

Physicians did not exclude coffee from the realm of health-improving beverages, though it was introduced much later than tea (probably around the fifteenth century). In a section from Bentley and Trimen's *Medical Botany*, the authors recommend coffee to stimulate the stomach and nervous system without producing a narcotic effect on the brain. Later editions advocated coffee to ease migraines, too. Magically speaking, coffee continues to carry the symbolic essence of energy and empowerment.

---

9. Most good magical and medicinal herb books can help you define what spices to use for cleansing. Just be cautious, realizing that not all purifying magical herbs can safely be taken internally. Do not eat or drink any substance whose consumable qualities are in question. Never play Russian roulette with your health.

10. Suggested readings include books by Rev. Paul Beyerl, Jude Williams, Louise Riotte, Jean Palaiseul, etc. If you are searching for sources at the library, look up herbalism, health food, natural medicine and simples first. If these don't produce results, check older cookbooks or historic reviews of alchemy and the spice trade.

Tinctures

Sweet herbs from all antiquity.
—Sidney Lanier

A tincture is an alcohol, flavored lightly with spices or vegetable matter in solution. Generally the mixture consists of 4 ounces herb to 8 ounces alcohol. This blend is warmed or allowed to soak for two weeks in sunlight, then strained. Tinctures acquire their name from the "tinge" in color afforded by the steeping process.

As late as 1919, books like *Home Made Beverages* by Albert A. Hopkins appeared, recommending tinctures like the combinations shown below. Some of these recipes added other dangerous herbs including lobelia, skullcap, hemlock, and turpentine. Not all healers used these mixtures internally; sometimes they were applied by cotton or cloth to treat external conditions.

- Raspberry vinegar, clove, and honey for asthma.
- Cohosh, myrrh, skunk cabbage, and cayenne for spasms.
- Cayenne, myrrh, and brandy for fits.
- Angelica root, catnip, motherwort, sweet flag, aniseed, dill seed, fennel seed, and lady slipper for colic, restlessness, and flatulence.
- Lavender for cough or cold.
- Bloodroot and garlic for whooping cough.

To apply any of these ideas in a magical construct takes a bit of inventive searching for symbolism. For example, the recipe that pertains to asthma might be used to enhance magical efforts that work with the "air" element. Since this condition relates directly to vital breath, the symbols are analogous. In this particular illustration, I suggest tossing raspberry leaves and cloves into the wind to empower your spell.

A recipe to alleviate swelling, by comparison, provides some components to also consider for an incense prepared to deflate a touchy situation. Tinctures have the additional advantage of a long shelf life if kept sealed and stored in a cool area. They are simple to prepare, and can be easily applied in small quantities to accent magical cooking and brewing efforts.

Tonics

*Genius, in truth, means little more than the faculty
of perceiving in an unhabitual way.*
—William James

A tonic is anything mixed with water to invigorate, revitalize, stimulate, strengthen, or give nourishment. These mixtures return the body and spirit to a normal tonal quality, thus the name "tone-ic." A modern example of a tonic is warm milk for an upset stomach or sleepless night.

Traditional herbs used in tonics include agrimony, bay, bayberry, blackberry, boneset, catnip, cayenne, century, chamomile, dandelion, golden seal, nettle, peppermint, sage, tansy, wormwood, and yarrow. The most popular modern tonics are really nothing "newfangled." Ginseng, used to reduce stress, improve recuperative powers, and enhance mental awareness, is a famous medicinal plant from China. Ginseng had its beginnings in this region at least 4000 years ago. Ginseng aids anemia, headache, forgetfulness, impotence, sores, swelling, and vertigo. Some members of the ginseng family may even prolong life.

Another herb categorized as a tonic is angelica. Students of natural medicine, including Mary SummerRain and Michael Murray, tell us that angelica is good for easing symptoms of PMS, allergies, menopause, and muscle spasms. In Europe, angelica was just as popular for remedial use as ginseng was in the Orient. It gained its name because of its "angelic" qualities, as a gift from heaven. This connotation may afford angelica-based beverages an additional magical characteristic of aiding contact and communion with guiding spirits.

I happened upon one curative that left me with a smile. An ancient English translator of Greek verse recounted a wonderful ditty from Athenaeus, revealing that the ancients knew more than their fair share about hangovers and appropriate tonics to cure them.

*Last evening you were drinking deep,
so now your head hurts, go to sleep;
take some boiled cabbage when you wake,
and there's an end of your headache.*[11]

I can't say that I've tried this, but apparently it was revered, much like contemporary society views a Bloody Mary! Some things never change.

---

11. Translated from Athenaeus, *Deipnos I*, 62.

Wine

It's a wine of virtuous powers, my mother made it of wild flowers.
—S. T. Coleridge

In 1500 B.C., priests evoked the Snake Goddess of Egypt before making wine. This seems to have nothing to do with medicinal wines, until you realize that the snake itself is an ancient symbol for health, longevity, and resurrection. The Staff of Hermes is the most potent example we have of this concept.

An interesting ancient tradition focused on health is that of Wassailing at Yule celebrations in northern Europe. Either spiced apple ale, apple cider, or apple wine was used to toast the "Great Apple" tree. Wassail comes from an Anglo-Saxon term which means "whole." All those who drink from the Wassail cup ensure themselves of good health and happiness. I cannot help but wonder if the old saying about "an apple a day" might have its origins in this bit of history. Either way, the apple continues to be a powerful symbol for good health.

In the *Household Companion* (1710), we see items like borage wine recommended for hypochondria, because it comforts the heart and relieves fainting spirits. Likewise, herbalists suggested balm wine for improving digestion and expelling melancholy. In other texts, cowslip wine appears as a curative for jaundice, elderberry for colds, raspberry for throat infections, and barley wine for kidney trouble.

As with tinctures, these country curatives can find a new home and refreshed symbolism in modern magic. Raspberry wine for throat infections might translate to drinking raspberry tea or wine in spells to improve communication skills. Alternately, burning dried raspberry leaves can help open the lines of discourse between two people who are arguing. For this example, douse the flames with cold raspberry tea or wine to chill anger.

Continuing on to the turn of the century, Edward Spenser, in *The Flowering Bowl* (1903), praised wine as effective against the "stones." In his account, he recommends cutting the end of a birch branch in March and suspending it in bottles with one gallon of water, one pound of sugar, yeast, mace and cinnamon; in truth, a kind of birch-beer wine! This attitude toward wine so late in history is not startling. As wine became more popular, many of the healthy attributes of mead were simply transferred to it, since the two were so closely related.

Summary

Too many folks aren't thankful for what they've got till they've lost it!
—Marian LoreSinger

In their search for health, our ancestors tried anything that could potentially give them and their family a better chance at survival. We are fortunate today not to have to face such a harsh world. Even so, we are no less desirous of keeping ourselves and our loved ones in good physical condition. While many historical remedies need a few revisions to reflect modern awareness of toxicity and so forth, even science agrees that some contained sound advice.

We can take these basic ideas and build on them with the knowledge available to us, and add our own magical symbolism. This should improve effectiveness, both physically and metaphysically. We, like our ancestors, need to return to an ideology that doesn't separate body and mind from the spiritual. Instead, it is a "kitchen witch's" passion to integrate this awareness into everything we do. From rising in the morning to our cup of coffee, or a glass of wine or tea come nightfall ... we are magical!

Sister, sea of welling souls
cleanse the grail
complete this bowl
caress your shores with golden dawn
till magic flows upon the lawn.
—Marian LoreSinger

Chapter Four

Brewing and Magic

There is nothing so powerful as truth, and often nothing so strange.
—D. Webster

We have seen beverages at the altar, at the sick-bed, and upon our own table. Besides necessity, myths and legends fostered some of this popularity. One Norse tale recounts how Odin visited the patroness of history, Saga, and drank a bit of mead from her golden cup. This story gave mead an immediate association with wisdom, knowledge of the past, and inspiration—all marvelous qualities for those of the Old Ways to pursue.

Some of these stories attempt to explain common occurrences, such as tides. The God Thor competed with Loki in a drinking contest. Loki chose a drinking horn, which appeared to be none too large, for the competition. Try as he might, Thor could not empty it. Finally, Thor admitted his failure and felt ashamed. It was not until the next morning that Loki explained that he had placed the end of the horn carefully in the sea, away from Thor's sight. Now the ebb tide would forever be a reminder of Thor's boastful attempt at one-up-manship!

Bill Moyers, in *The Power of Myth*, discusses the importance of cultural stories to the way people think, behave, and respond. He says, "myths are stories of our search through the ages for truth, for meaning, for significance." Thus, as Cunning Folk discerned the deeper connotations of their myths, they also realized some of their greatest needs. This recognition lead to the most wondrous and popular "potion" ever developed in the witch's cauldron—the one that insured love.

First recorded in the Near East, almost every ingredient imaginable was mixed into the love potion brewpot to improve romance, passion, or both. For a perfect example, look to the famous story of Tristan and Isolt. These star-crossed young lovers accidentally drank a magic love potion so powerful that it lasted beyond death. A tragedy, yes, but also a reminder of just how much responsibility goes with mystical efforts, especially those treading on the territory of the fragile human heart.

Another dark blot on the history of love potions occurred in the era of Louis XVI of France. The king's sorceress, Catherine LaVoisin, was an expert on herb preparations, including poison. Usually, however, her knowledge of magical arts was employed for love potions, even by the king's mistress. Herbs favored by the court for amorous ends included dill, cinnamon, caraway, coriander, nutmeg, rose petals, fennel, and celery. All of these are perfectly safe to use today.

In similar potions of that era, wine mixed with moonwort, daffodil blossoms, ginseng, myrrh, parsley, yarrow, myrtle, leek, or jasmine brought about the same results. Magicians based compounds on mythical and magical associations, the herb's inferred alchemical alignments, and governing Deities. This is exactly what we hope to do later in the recipe section of this book.

Besides the mystical attributes of herbs and fruits, there is a pragmatic element. If an item aided a certain physical ailment, that herb or fruit became part of the curative potion. Some symbolism was often combined with this sensibility. For example, to shrink an abcess, tumor, or other swelling, one healer might mix the ingredients by a waning moon[1] (see also Chapter 3).

A good example was the notion of placing toads in the witch's stew-pot to make a heart elixir.[2] Today, we know that the skin of a toad contains a chemical very similar to digitalis, so it is possible that this magical potion did, indeed, help the patient.

A third illustration comes from ancient China, where children with convulsions were given ground "dragon bone" (dinosaur bones). Contemporary physicians now administer calcium, the main substance of which bones are made, in similar situations. While some early recipes for "witch's brews" were

---

1. Waning moon, similar to the waxing, symbolically meant lessening. Specifically, the emblem appeared in healing magic to treat goiter, swellings, tumors, or any other illness which could benefit from the "shrinking."

2. Dropsy is a disease in which watery (lymphatic) fluid collects in the body, sometimes to the point of suffocation if in the lungs, or to loss of limbs through impaired circulation.

anything but appetizing, these writers unwittingly gave the Cunning Folk due recognition in history as contributors to pharmacological studies and medical breakthroughs.

It was not without knowledge of their responsibility to the community that Cunning Folk served with sensibility in one hand and magic in the other. In Germany, for example, the job of dasture was preparing ritual beer, healing the sick and banishing evil spirits. This last task was accomplished by sprinkling the beverage in the same manner as Wiccans scatter blessed salt and water around the magic circle today. (See page 20, Chapter 2, for other duties of the dasture.)

On the less pleasant side of this overview, many of the items used for magical ends were not safe or terribly savory, let alone actually helpful. In some cases, the best guess was all a country "wise person" could offer, based on all the knowledge and lore he or she had personally amassed. We see this in texts such as *The Magick of Kirani, King of Persia*,[3] where the author recommends satyrion seed, honey, and the liqueur of a roe's gall to aid conception. Such a mixture hardly ranks on my top ten list of things I always wanted to try!

This point is very important to keep in mind. While there are many wonderful ideas for magical aids presented here, not all of them are feasible in our modern reality. We must take the time to check everything first from a health standpoint. Once we have determined that all the ingredients are safe to use, we can then consider the needs of nature and our personal beliefs.

No one living a positive magical lifestyle is going to kill a deer just to drain the gall. However, if you feel the symbolism is important to results, alter the approach a bit and have a picture of a deer nearby while preparing the magically enhanced potion. This is where personal insight, creativity, and resourcefulness come in; three of the greatest talents for any kitchen wizard.

3. Cyranus, London, 1685.

Protection

Beneath the shadow of great protection, the soul sits, hushed and calm.
—James F. Clarke

A Norse legend recounted in *Nibelung Lay* tells of the warrior Sigurd, rescued by a Valkyria who had been disowned by Odin. Sigurd implores the Valkyria to teach him wisdom, and she replies by giving him a horn of beer with runes carved into it. The runes were those for health, victory, protection, and winning favor. She also instructs him on how to inscribe and bless the runes for his sword hilt (Tyr) and cup (Naud-need). Then, if he felt there was treachery or poison afoot, he could cast garlic (also known as the magic leek) into his cup, along with any liqueur. If there was danger, his cup would shatter or the drink turn a hideous color.

This story may have some basis in the idea that Odin created runes specifically for magic. Protective runes on beverage cups became a potent spell, powerful enough to cause a person's voice to change if he or she held the cup and spoke falsely. Such an action insulted Odin himself, because his runes adorned the vessel. This is also why you can see runes carved into corner stones on farmer's land in Celtic regions. Only the foolish dared to desecrate such monuments.

If no such a tankard was immediately available, a method used in Peru was claiming a beverage before the Gods. In the Yasha liturgy, there is a psalm to the sacred haomas where the celebrant raises the cup to the sky, saying, "I claim to thee, O yellow one, for inspiration, for strength, for vigor."[4] The hope was that by blessing the drink, there would be no ill effects, even as we pray before meals today.

Apollonius wrote of the Argonauts pouring mead on the waters before a ship sailed. This action may have been a means to invoke and placate the Gods of the sea, and thus insure a safe voyage. It is likely that our contemporary custom of launching ships with champagne or good wine has roots in this ancient custom. This affords honey-wine some symbolism and application in modern magics pertaining to the sea or the water element.

Mead, wine, and beer were not the only substances used in rites for protection. On New Year's Eve in the West Country of England, people ritually burn the piece of hawthorn that hung in the kitchen during the previous year, accompanying this rite with "Auld Cider," a song praising cider. The words are repeated in a mantra-like manner over a deep note. With each syllable, participants make a bow, (nine bows over three repetitions). While cider does not play an active role in this rite, its name is an important pivotal point. The phrase "Auld Cider" is repeated

---

4. *Zend Avesta*, Yasha liturgy, verse 17.

three times, the number of body, mind, and spirit in symmetry. Bowing nine times equates to the number of inspiration and universal law. In this manner, people used the magical symbolism of numbers, combined with an age-old tradition, to empower their observance and guard their lands.[5]

Water and religion have worked hand in hand for such a long time that we often don't recognize the connection, or we take it for granted. Christianity has maintained strong beliefs about water's ability to cleanse and heal; Catholicism's use of holy water is an example of that connection. Among the sacred sites of Europe are hundreds of holy founts, wells, and rivers.

If all these defensive approaches fail, there are still more suggestions. Jet powdered in water will help keep snakes at bay, boneset tea repels evil spirits, and myrrh, white frankincense, and flaked jet stone in wine will cure you of elf magic. For the latter to work effectively, fast one night and partake of the substance for three, nine, or twelve mornings to break the spell.[6] Finally, angelica steeped in vinegar and drunk quickly turns away any negative magic.

Since I doubt anyone wants to consume jet powder or myrrh, these kinds of recipes can be updated. In this example, instead quaff a crystal tincture—water in which a stone has rested by the light of sun or moon for a period of three hours—or apply the substance externally.

Health and Curatives

May what I see increase and what I suffer decrease.[7]
—Jacob Grimm, 1883

Some magical curatives had time-proven results corroborated by modern science. Many of the magical beverages used for cures were symbolic or sympathetic in nature. Before creation, the magician carefully considered everything about the potion, including when it should be made, the malady being treated, and the potency of the herbs.

In this process, many items including colors, numbers, astrology, and moon phases influenced results. A woman seeking aid for fertility received treatment during the waxing to full moon. In this example, the growing lunar sphere

---

5. Circuits around land as a means of protection and blessing were common in the ancient world. One example is the festival of Termenalia in Rome, where farmers walk the boundaries of their land and leave offerings for the boundary God Terminus.

6. *Anglo Saxon Charms* by Felix Gordon, New York, 1909. Here again, we see extensive use of numerological symbolism. Three and nine appear repeatedly in folk remedials. Twelve is the number of fullness, a completed cycle, thus bringing an end or a beginning, depending on your desire.

7. This was spoken while looking at a waxing moon.

resembles the Mother Goddess with a full womb. She might also receive yellow potions for creativity and productivity, and the number of ingredients could total seven, the traditional number of lunar influence. Refer to Appendix A for color and number correspondences.

Truly astute wise people also chose components according to their astrological significance, or picked them at special times to enhance potency.[8] For example, herbs harvested when the moon is in Pisces or Virgo will improve fertile energy. Such efforts also can amplify magical beverages today.

Beverages to Enhance Food

Magical beverages offer more than thirst-quenching attributes. With a little creativity they become another valuable resource for the sacred kitchen. Varying amounts may be added to food recipes to accentuate magical goals and for improved culinary diversity. Some ideas to spark your imagination include:

- Additional or alternative flavoring for soups, stews, and casseroles. Match the beverage to your cooking intentions, like plum wine added to lemon chicken for an abundance of pure romantic energy.

- Basting and marinating accents when blended with natural juices, such as a hint of mulled mead added to a ham baste to encourage joy and health.

- A base for glazes, with the addition of butter, sugar and/or herbs, for ham, poultry, and even breads.

- Options for desserts and dessert toppings in place of extracts and/or spices. For example, making a thin sugar syrup out of rose wine and introducing it into an angel cake via toothpick holes, to return innocence to love.

- A base for syrups, sauces, and gravy. Syrups usually require boiling with sugar to create a thick enough texture, while the addition of flour or cornstarch to sauces and gravy works marvelously for meat and poultry. Sauces offer the additional benefit of sometimes being able to "reclaim" slightly burned dishes by hiding the scent and flavor of the overdone portion.

- A component in conserves, jellies, and jams. In this case the liquid is substituted for any water content in your recipe. For best results, however, you may need to reduce the sugar content when using a sweeter beverage.

---

8. Each day of the week and each hour of the day is dedicated to different spheres of influence by the heavens. For accurate information on this, order *Llewellyn's Sun Sign* and *Moon Sign* books or *Astrological Calendar* for the year to use as a guide.

Restorative Potions

Below are some historical restorative potions. If you wish to try any, be careful to update them with modern knowledge and personal insight.

- **Lust**—gather vervain by the first day of new moon before sunrise, and drink the juice. This will hinder the tendency to "stray" for seven years (Europe).

- **Fertility**—carrot or sunflower seeds in wine (England); dock tea three times a day for one full cycle of the moon (U.S.). Mare's milk drunk by a woman unaware (Asia).

- **Foolish thoughts and fear**—chrysolite powdered in wine (Greece).

- **Youth**—elder picked on Midsummer Day and dried. Add this to borage water, and drink two times a day for a month (England).

- **Memory**—eyebright juice, rosemary, and water (early American).

- **Longevity**—pine resin in water or wine (China).

- **Jaundice**—saffron potion. The sun traditionally ruled saffron. Interestingly enough, doctors today place babies with jaundice under sun lamps to relieve the problem (Asia).

- **Ague**—take water in equal quantities from three different ponds. Mix and taste it frequently (rural European). Why the author recommends pond water here I can't even guess. Instead, I think gathering it from three separate sources is the important part of this magical cure. The number three brings harmony to the body, mind, and spirit.

- **Hiccough**—dill wine sipped as needed (Mediterranean).

- **Dysentery**—egg mixed with whiskey and taken in the morning (Ireland).

- **Healing** (general)—alum bark, hornbeam, beach, wild will, blackberry, hemlock, and red spruce gathered in the fall. Get the bark sections just before noon, from a place where the sun shines on the wood to purify it. Gather all roots from the sunny side to assure healthful qualities. Make into a potion. This recipe appeared in the 1896 *Journal of American Folklore*, compiled by Stansbury Hagas. Notice the use of seven ingredients, the number of completion.

- **Aphrodisiac**—asparagus wine (rural U.S.) or ambergris in coffee (Europe).

- **Birth Pains**—potion of bindweed. Here we see an instance of a name given to an herb according to its suggested use, "to bind" (Germany).

• **Wounds**—in 1658, Sir Kenelm Digby wrote about the powder of sympathy which was placed on a cloth with blood from a wound, to effect magical healing. This is a variant on a medieval weapon salve, where people treated the instrument of injury with ointment as a way of forgiving its harm.

Blessing, Fertility, and Weather Magic

Good health and good sense are two of life's greatest blessings.
—Publilius Syrus

In reviewing magical techniques, one appears again and again for a multitude of applications; that of sprinkling a beverage on an item or around an area. In the West Country of England, there is the Twelfth Night custom of taking cyder to an apple tree, encircling it, and pouring the cyder out on the roots while chanting a poem for bounty. Up until the eighteenth century, cyder was consumed at Maypole dances in Britain in much the same manner. We can bring this tradition back to life by serving apple juice during these holidays, or placing a glass of apple wine upon our altars.

On St. Swithin's Day (July 15, Anglo Saxon), each tree is blessed, then anointed with cyder over the trunk, and tapped three times. If it rains on this day, it portends fertility and a long rainy season (continuing for 40 days). Rain or shine, the trees are graced with cyder to insure their health and fruitfulness.

Wine and water also both figure in rituals to help bring rain. Ceremonial sprinkling water from a sacred well was one way of coaxing the Gods to open heaven's vaults to save a dying crop. Rural people applied wine similarly when a well ran dry. Today, you might pour out wine to the land and the Powers during times of drought, or when you personally need refreshing.

In all cases, the meting out of the beverage becomes an offering imploring the favor of Nature or the Gods. In the process, a type of cleansing is also implied, such as during the dedication of a child. Even in non-Christian traditions, a priest/ess introduces the young one to water by a drop on the lips, or a misting (Wiccan Blessing-Ways). This action insures health and protection and bestows Divine favor.

This imagery finds a slightly different expression in modern magical traditions. Here, an asperger (using a heather branch dipped in water, for instance) sprinkles the members of a Circle to remove negative energy and invoke blessings.

Divination

The course of nature is the art of god.
—Edward Young

Roman sibyls used wine to encourage an altered state of awareness for the purpose of becoming a Divine Oracle (see Chapter 2). Euripides, writing about Dionysus, says that while enticing people to drink, Dionysus also provided inspiration, specifically foresight. The Divine being then may use the sacred vessel of a human worshiper as a channel for prophecy and wisdom.

In Norse legends, consider the case of Bragi, the god of eloquence and wisdom. Bragi enjoyed ale meads, specifically the mead of muse, before singing or recounting a rhyme. What is interesting here is that alliteration and other poetic structures in Germany were often runic in nature—the main form of soothsaying for this culture. Additionally, myths claim that the mead had been mingled with runes scraped off wooden rods used for divining. In this respect, Bragi[9] might be considered the patron God for early diviners and prophets. He relied not only on vision, but also on verbal skills to create rapport.

There is undeniable evidence that Christianity did not succeed in completely eradicating such stories or related magical practices. In some regions, as late as the Middle Ages, the local Pagans seemed determined not to be forced totally underground. One bit of history confirming this originates in the Slavic regions of Central Europe.

During the Middle Ages, the worship of a Sun God named Svantovit still occurred. Most popular on the island of Rugen, Svantovit's images show him carrying a drinking horn. Each harvest, the faithful placed a cup of sacred mead in the hands of a figure honoring this Being. Later, the priest would take the cup and read the quantity left as a forecast for the coming year. Then half the mead was poured out, the other half consumed by the priest, and the cup carefully refilled.

In some instances, the ingredients for brewing played a part in divination. One Egyptian technique used steeped wheat and *spelt* (a favored brewing barley) mixed together in the urine of a pregnant woman. If the wheat sprouted in the water first, superstition claimed the child would be a boy. This approach appeared again in Europe, except that the seeds were planted in the ground instead. In both cases, I believe the use of grain implied fertility, as does the watering. Additionally, water and grain together form the basic components of inspiring brews.

---

9. An interesting note in linguistic history is that the word "brag" originally pertained to poetry, instead of an exaggeration, as it is currently used. Braggi was known for his ability to sway even the Gods with his fluency, which may have led to the slow change in this word's meaning.

Finally, one of the most common ways of using beverages in divination is through spattering or scrying the surface. After being appropriately offered and accepted by the Gods, the Seer spatters the liquid onto the earth, interpreting the images much like reading tea leaves. In scrying, the Seer gazes on the surface of the drink like the veneer of a crystal ball, watching for literal or symbolic images to appear and suggest an answer.

Oath Taking and Magical Unity

There is no bridge so difficult to cross as the bridge of a broken promise.
—Hosletter's U.S. Almanac, 1897

Words have power. Our ancestors knew the truth of this, and they also knew that few individuals are honest or forthright 100 percent of the time. Therefore, to insure compliance with a promise or oath, they developed simple rituals using beverages. In this respect, the taking of a drink magically sealed the agreement with one's lips. It also meant an acceptance of dire consequences from the Gods should the pledge be broken. With this as a model, the contemporary magical coven could use a special cup to welcome newly initiated members.

Another depiction of this custom comes to us from Germany, where legend calls the cup used for love magic the *Minne* cup. Originally, "minne" meant remembrance. It also was the name of an early Goddess figure. People usually raised the Minne cup, filled with sacrificial beer, in memory of a loved one. Later, the meaning changed so that if two drank from the Minne cup (first the man in honor of affection, then accepted by the woman), it bound them in love.

Here, and in similar marriage observances around the globe, wine becomes the symbol for love's sweetness. A glass symbolizes of the fragility of human devotion. Either way, once the cup is shared, the Gods, friends, and family all witness and recognize the union. As such, the gift of a cup at handfasting could be a potent symbol of the couple's pledge in the years to come.

Besides showing unity or to link "destiny," partaking from one cup indicated trust. In Germany, for example, proper etiquette dictated that a host always offered a freshly filled goblet to honored guests first. To refuse the cup from one's host was an insult. Accepting it acknowledged welcome and acted as an unspoken pledge, on the guest's part, to be thoughtful. Similar customs appear in Arabia.

Chapter Five

From the Cauldron
to the Cup

*T*here is a right and wrong handle to everything.
—Rudolph E. Raspe

The most important part of the inventive process, both spiritually and physically, is having a clean work area. Remove anything which could become distracting. As you prepare, visualize white, bubbly light pouring from your hands into the kitchen. Burn a little incense or create a simmering potpourri for cleansing and purification. A perfect choice of pantry herbs for this purpose are basil and sage. Blend one teaspoonful of each herb in one cup of water, simmering over low heat and replenishing as needed.

Next, bring your tools and ingredients together and say a brief blessing over them. Your kitchen is about to become a sacred space, and your cooking utensils the magical tools to blend ingredients into harmony and power. Use comfortable, meaningful words, and welcome your chosen Divine presence for sanctification. If you live in an area where negative energies could hinder the positive outcome of your magic, or to enhance and focus your energies, set up a protective magical circle at this time.

Now you can start cooking! Keep your intentions firmly in mind while you blend and stir. Visualize the appropriately colored light filling the beverage (see notes in Chapter 4). Chant and sing, or play uplifting music. Continue in this mindset until the beverage is ready to be bottled, aged, or consumed, depending on the recipe.

Last, but not least, remember to mark your storage vessels with labels indicating the date of preparation and their functions. You might choose names that suggest the beverage's purpose. Good examples are abundant:

For love: Raspberry Romancer, Passion Fruit Fervor
For joy: Happiness Harbinger, Peachy-Keen
For insight: Prophetic Punch, Oracular Orange

This is where you really get to have some fun with your metaphysical brewing, so enjoy!

Choosing Additives and Ingredients

Observe moderation. In all, the fitting season is best.
—Hesiod

The painter chooses from various colors, textures, and backgrounds. A musician looks to notes and instruments for his or her Divine expression. In a similar manner, the Kitchen Witch surveys the pantry to discover delectable, magical potential. Anyone reading an herbal book by Scott Cunningham or other authors will be amazed by the supernatural applications for the spices commonly found in almost every home. This understanding and knowledge make brewing magical. Not only spices may be contemplated; flowers, fruits, vegetables, the type of sweetener, yeast, and so forth can be appropriate to your purpose.

In Appendix A is a list of some common components for beverage making, their magical associations, and a little data about their uses in brewing. This serves as a quick reference guide. For additional information, I recommend investing in a detailed magical herbal or food book.[1] These resources help you decide which aromatics and flavors are best for achieving your magical goals.

Combine the ingredients gently so that the resulting energy is balanced, and the taste pleasant. A magical brew for internal transitions will do little good if you

---

1. Many such books are available through Llewellyn. *Magickal Herbalism* and *The Magic in Food* by Cunningham, *Jude's Herbal Home Remedies* by Williams, *The Kitchen Witch's Cookbook* and several others come immediately to mind. For a catalogue of books, call 1-800-843-6666 and ask for the customer service department.

can't "stomach it." On the other hand, preparations specifically made for libations or symbolism can contain anything you like. In this case, clearly mark the bottle with a warning that states in bold lettering "NOT FOR CONSUMPTION," to avoid mishaps.

When creating compounds, consider their color, the total number of items mixed together, the herbs, spices, and fruits, the final storage container, or whatever else you can imagine to enhance the symbolic impact. This affords tremendous creative freedom, since every ingredient has more than one metaphysical application! Add to that your own vision and you suddenly come up with a wealth of options that function well in a variety of settings.

This is the beauty of kitchen magic. It requires few tools, few expensive items, only a little time, and blends wonderfully with any tradition you happen to follow. Throughout this book recipes have been tailored to convey specific magical energies. These are guideposts only. Use them as they are, or change them to suit more personal goals. Remember, what is meaningful about an ingredient to me may be quite different for you. Always use what is most pleasurable in taste and personally significant for best results.

Magical Concocting

When the wine goes in, strange things come out.
—Johann Christoph Friedrich Von Schiller

Time, temperament, and technique; these are the three things to keep in mind for magical beverage formulation. First, let's look at timing. We have already seen that certain phases of the moon were used to help mystical efforts, so when making a drink to help encourage weight loss, begin the process during a waning moon for the "shrinking" symbolism. If preparing something to help conception, the waxing or full moon is best.

In magic pertaining to physical strength, mental faculties, leadership, logic, education, reason, and legal matters, work during the daylight hours. The rays of the sun are strongly aligned with these energies. Conversely, night and lunar influences bear energies for insight, fertility, mysteries, emotions, etc. Additionally, days of the week and every hour of the day have certain planetary aspects that can figure into your magical "formula." To discover what these traits are, consult a reliable astrological calendar, moon sign, or sun sign book.

Another dimension to timing is the aging process necessary for most fermented beverages. It is very easy to adjust the making of a wine or beer, and the aging period, to create something more meaningful. Some examples include:

- Making wine with fire-related fruits and herbs on the night of Beltane, over a gas stove (for fire), and storing it for next year's celebration.

- Starting a brew early enough to present it as a special birthday gift to a friend (including a list of ingredients and their meanings).

- Aging wine for a year and a day, to share at a handfasting or initiation.[2]

- Preparing a beverage on the day of a family member's marriage, and presenting it on his or her anniversary, to celebrate and renew love.

Holidays present a third consideration in timing. Some festivals are centered around beverages or use them as a central element to the celebration. You could prepare in advance an appropriate beverage for the observance, or make it on the day of the celebration to honor the occasion. Below are some examples.

- **Rosalia** (June 4, Ancient Greece): The Greeks celebrated this date in many ways. Primarily it was an opportunity to litter the temples of Aphrodite with rose petals. Additionally, women bathed in rose water to increase their attractiveness, and burning rose incense improved luck.

  Try making rose water today to use in cooking, or make a sparkling rose wine to celebrate the spirit of beauty and love. Leave water with fresh rose petals on the altar to welcome Aphrodite and encourage romantic energies in your home.

- **Winegrower's Fete** (August 29, Old France): In the sixteenth century, a guild formed among the winegrowers of Vevey, France. Each year, until 1889, they held a special festival that had many similarities to Cerealia in Roman times.

  This event was attended by thousands of people in Louis XV-era costumes. A parade was guided by a depiction of Pales, the Goddess of flocks, wearing a robe of blue. She was followed by white oxen, children dressed as shepherds, and yodelers. Next came Ceres, in a flowing red gown, accompanied by harvesters and bakers. People costumed as fauns and satyrs danced merrily around all this. Afterward, everyone enjoyed a night of feasting and drinking in the company of friends and local leaders.

  Today, you can place a cup of any grain beverage (beer) on your altar honoring Ceres, and a grape wine to remember Bacchus. This is also an appropriate day to begin any brewing effort.

---

2. A year and a day (or a full cycle) is a common amount of time in Wicca/Paganism for engagements. It is also recommended as an appropriate study period before an initiation takes place.

- **Allan Apple Day** (October 27, Cornwall, England): The unmarried men and women of this region purchase an Allan Apple on this day. At nightfall, they place the apple under their pillow. Before dawn, the fruit must be eaten without a sound. The participant then goes outside, dressed just as he or she is, to sit beneath a tree. The first person to pass by is believed to be his or her future spouse. Also, if the participant feels no cold while waiting, he or she will remain warm all winter (possibly thanks to the new mate)!

  Come October 27, consider drinking a fresh glass of apple juice, or making another beverage using apples. This will help bring love into your life.

- **Hodening** (Wales): Taking place sometime during the Yule season, Hodening was an odd custom also known in parts of England. Part of this celebration included young men going to various households, improvising poems that demand they be let in. The person at the door also replied with a rhyme. This competition of bardic skill went on until one party ran out of ideas. If the Hodeners won, they came in for Yule ale, cakes, and a gift. Otherwise, they had to go on their way.

  This is an amusing tradition that could be enacted with friends and family. Be sure to have ale and snacks prepared, as you will probably want to lose this competition!

Next comes temperament. I do not recommend doing any magical brewing if you are tired, out of sorts, harried, sick, or otherwise ill-disposed. It is difficult to concentrate when you aren't feeling well. Also, excess negative energy can accidentally flow into your beverage instead of the positive magic you intend. Treat the creation of ritual beverages as any other spiritual endeavor—with compassion, insight, and sensitivity—and you can't go wrong.

Finally, consider the whole method—what kind of spoon(s) you use, the cooking pot, and even the direction of stirring. For bringing positive, encouraging energies, mix your brew in a sunward motion (clockwise). For banishing bad habits, negative energy, or to reverse ill fortune, stir the liquid widdershins (counterclockwise).

Stoneware or seasoned iron pots and wooden spoons are recommended over plastic and aluminum. These are more natural and yield a better-flavored drink. Consider keeping these utensils set aside just for brewing. This is not necessary, but it helps to encourage the exact sympathy (see Chapter 4, pages 39-40, for example of sympathetic magic) desired in your magical beverages to slowly become part of the pot and spoon. Just as with any magical tools, the more you work with them, the more they absorb personal energy.

Another variation to consider is the order in which you add the base ingredients. While yeast must be added at specific points in the cooking process, other ingredients aren't so sensitive. Adding ingredients at a particular planetary hour, or in a unique progression, are two ideas along these lines.

To illustrate, let's assemble a beverage to encourage love, then have that romance blossom into something more permanent. First add pink rose petals to the cauldron to stimulate feelings of excitement and friendship in the "right person." Follow this with cinnamon, sacred to Aphrodite, for growing love. Here, the progression of the ingredients follows the natural flow of relationships. The only difference is affixing magical energy to encourage that flow.

Practical Considerations

*Practicality is common sense mingled with frugality, humor,
creative insight and a little fortitude for good measure.*
—Marian LoreSinger

This section acts as a foundation to any type of brewing effort. While some brewing instructions are recipe specific, or distinctive to a particular category, some sensible suggestions are universal. More specific matters will be discussed in their appropriate sections later.

First, I suggest that you collect glass bottles in many shapes and sizes. Do not, unless absolutely necessary, use plastic. Plastic retains scents and flavors that can ruin your beverages, and it is more difficult to sterilize. If you must use plastic, please throw away the container after the second fermentation[3] to eliminate increased chances of bacteria. As you collect containers, keep in mind that screw tops and corks are valuable to the brewer. Both of these can be loosened during the initial stages of fermentation to bleed off excess pressure ("burping"

---

3. Second fermentation takes place in an airtight container, using fermentation locks or balloons to release pressure. During this time, sediment forms on the bottom of the bottle, while clearer, sparkling liquid remains on top. This liquid is poured off after the second fermentation for final bottling. The sediment, consisting of dead yeast and fruit bits, is thrown away.

the bottles). Also, you can seal both types of lids with wax once the beverage reaches maturity.

> MODERN BREWER'S NOTE: The very thin plastic soft drink bottles with a screw top are referred to as "PET" plastic. This type of plastic is inert and will not contribute off flavors to your brew. PET bottles are permeable to oxygen, however, so don't use them for storing your brew for more than a few months, or oxidation can occur. — J.D.

Keep decorative containers set aside for finished products. Use simpler vessels for fermentation or transportation to social events. Small airline bottles are great sizes for holiday "sampler" packs. Give these to new acquaintances, friends, or family to see which blends they like best before endowing them with larger quantities.

After collecting the bottles, boil them in soapy water and rinse thoroughly. Certain types of fruits attract marvelous insects and molds, and this is not a petri dish experiment. Cleanliness is essential to successful, safe beverages. This goes for all your pots, pans, spoons, and funnels too. Don't skimp on this step.

> MODERN BREWER'S NOTE: It is useful to distinguish between "cleaning," "sanitizing," and "sterilizing." Cleaning is best accomplished with soap or detergent and hot water. Its purpose is to remove organic residue from vessels and utensils. Sanitizing is a process which uses chemicals and possibly heat to kill bacteria and wild yeasts. The most common sanitizing agent is sodium hypochlorite, common houshold bleach. It is so powerful that an effective sanitizing solution can be made using only two teaspoons of bleach in five gallons of cold water. Soaking for 30 minutes to an hour is enough. Sanitizing only reduces bacteria and wild yeasts. Sterilizing completely eliminates bacteria and wild yeasts. Sterilizing is not practical for the home brewer. — J.D.

If you are planning to make fermented beverages, it is worth checking for brewing supply stores in your area. Look under hobbies, crafts, brewing, and malting in the yellow pages. The alternative to these are mail-order supplies—dependable sources appear in the back of this book. Also look for local brewing clubs. These groups provide hands-on, in-person advice for continuing problems, or can be a source of fresh ideas.

When you first begin brewing, try to stick to one category of beverages until that technique is perfected. You will have greater success this way, leading to improved personal satisfaction and the confidence to continue. The brewing process has similarities that carry over from one category to another, so your learning time is not wasted.

There are little idiosyncrasies in fruit and spice combination that surface in practice sessions. For example, knowing that strawberries ferment very quickly and actively affects the entire approach for making strawberry wine, specifically in the quantities of fruit used. Such discoveries are part of the magic of brewing. They teach us much about natures' chemistry lab, so take your time and enjoy them.

In choosing recipes initially, find ones that are simple and inexpensive. Simplicity encourages early success in your attempts. However, if you do fail, being cost-effective from the beginning eases the pain and honest frustration that occurs in figuring out what went wrong. Don't be overly critical with yourself in this scenario; even the renowned European monk-brewers had their "off days"!

For a while, just brew for yourself or family members, choosing recipes that include ingredients you like. If you don't enjoy fresh peaches or allspice, it's unlikely that peach-allspice wine will please you. It will also be difficult to tell if this blend is well-balanced after brewing. By working with pleasurable components, you get honest, valid opinions on quantities of the fruit and spices, until you find the perfect combination.

If you have difficulty locating recipes with personally appealing ingredients, you can experiment. Cinnamon can be substituted for allspice, for example. Do be careful, though, not to eliminate any necessary ingredients. A friend of mine did this once and couldn't figure out why his wine didn't start fermenting. The answer was simple; he'd altered the recipe and decreased the sugar content. The yeast didn't have enough food (sugar) to stimulate its action. Certain spices like ginger root provide essential nutrients (in this case, tannin) that help the fermentation process, so, read the recipes carefully, heeding any cautions from the author.

Cross-referencing sources can be helpful. One author may have a super strategy for wine making, but lousy directions for beer. Then too, many authors write about things according to their personal taste; their choices may not thrill your tastebuds. Once you become adept at beverage making, you will know which items work best together, and can identify the most successful approaches.

Once in a while it is fun to have brewing parties. Gather together all your curious friends, advise them of the basic materialss they need to bring, and watch to see what unique combinations they devise. Like home cooking, sometimes you can get into a brewing "rut"; parties like this can redirect and inspire you. Along the same lines, take an occasional trip to the local library for books on beverage making. The public library is a neglected resource. On those shelves are hundreds of books, some remaining unopened, and many that can be helpful on both brewing and metaphysical topics.

Don't overlook local second-hand book shops and antique stores. We have local booksellers with bargain basements full of treasures for under $5.00. Here, the browsing brewer can discover herb and spice books, old cookbooks, bartender guides, and even a few health tomes with recipes for tonics.

Date everything! Some wines and meads safely age for years, and are better for the time. Others are considered "short" liqueurs and need to be consumed immediately, within two weeks, or up to a few months from preparation. After that period what you have left is something akin to vinegar. If a recipe includes shelf-life information, be sure to mark it clearly on the bottle. This will keep you from accidentally serving an embarrassingly unpalatable beverage (usually after bragging about your home-brewing) to dinner guests.

Many people exhibit odd allergic reactions they may not have mentioned to you. It is considerate to place a list of ingredients on the labels of gift bottles or those from which you are serving guests—it could save someone a bad set of hives, or in worst-case scenarios, even his or her life.

Finally, when preparing beverages for magical effects or rites, remember that not all magical herbs are edible. If a recipe has an unusual ingredient you have not eaten before, let common sense prevail—if you're not certain, don't use it!

Serving Vessels

Drink not the third glass—which thou can'st not tame
When once it is within thee.

—George Herbert

Once prepared, the next thing to think about is presentation of the beverage. Just like laying out a meal, decanters and glasses can be symbolically potent and visually lovely. The finishing touches on any project set it apart.

In reviewing the opulence of medieval and Renaissance table settings, we can see that our ancestors agreed with this notion. Gold and silver, precious gems, and even fine cups carved from whole pieces of jade[4] embellished many banquets. This was a way of flaunting one's wealth, but these exhibits were also remnants from earlier times, when precious substances deserved appropriate containers to honor their sacred function. Many people can't consider gold tableware due to exorbitant prices. Instead, substitute silver plate, stoneware, or handmade pottery. I enjoy using cut glass and treated brass decanters over more costly options. They have an antique flavor befitting the age-old processes I use.

---

4. This was most prevalent in China, where jade was a potent magical stone. Craftspeople fashioned it into everything from statues to musical chimes, the latter of which brought harmony, long life, and joy to the owner.

Local bars may save bottles for you if you ask. Second-hand shops are wonderful places to unearth inexpensive and beautiful decanters and bottles. As you assemble your collection, keep in mind the final use for each item.

Consider their color, shape, and size to equate them to a magical scenario or goal. For example, blue bottles might house beverages encouraging peace or improved meditative states. Use round fluted carafes for fertility or goddess energy, and gold-colored goblets to empower beverages for strength or leadership.

When fortune really smiles on you, use decanters and cups decorated with pastoral scenes. One might relate nicely to the Wheel of the Year with seasonal images; another have the visage of a particular Deity like Athena with her owl; another might depict animal images for rituals pertaining to totems and familiars, or the container might be made in the country where your tradition originated.

The beauty of this approach is that from the first musing about a beverage until the time it is poured out, everything has magical meaning in a magical realm. The pleasure of your guests, the magical energy created, and the end results are truly marvelous to watch.

Creative Toasts

Now fill your glass ane an a', and drink the toast I gie ye.
—D. Henderson

If you didn't already have enough options, here is yet one more! Toasting over beverages is a venerable tradition, in some circles comparable to an artform. People have even been known to have toasting duels to see who had the better talent for crowd-pleasing and flowery flattery.

The term "toast" came into usage around the 1600s in England and neighboring countries, when it was customary to float bits of dry bread in the Wassail bowl. Hosts offered this bread to the most honored guest at the table because it gave the Wassail flavor and zest. More than likely, this dates back to when bread was the main source of yeast for brewing, and thus set fermentation in motion, or the practice may reflect a view of bread and grain as a symbol of providence.

The idea of a "toast" is far older than the Wassail tradition. In Chapter 2, we looked at the religious uses of beverages. Drink offerings were held to the sky to salute the Divine, then poured on the ground, honoring and appeasing that God/dess. When created for a special observance, participants raised their glasses in tribute to that occasion. Eventually, the practice translated itself into toasting achievements, friends, celebrations, and other occasions.

In researching this book, I found a wonderful old text called *Waes Hale* (by Edithe Lea Chase and Captain W. E. P. French, Grafton Press, New York, MCMIII), a collection of literature appropriate for toasts, or actual quoted toasts handed down through family lines. This and other texts helped me assemble a few toasts. Some are amusing, some honor a Pagan deity, and yet others are thematic.

Friendship

Friendship is the wine of life, let's drink of it and to it.—G. F. Handel

Here's to mine, and here's to thine; now's the time to clink it. Here's a flagon of old wine, and here we are to drink it.—Richard Hovry

Bread to feed our friendship, salt to keep it true, water that's for welcome, wine to drink for you.—W. French

Friendship, mysterious cement of the soul! Sweetener of life and solder of society.—Blair

Pagan Tones

Bacchus, God of joys divine, be thy pleasures ever mine.—Anon.

Great spirit of the grape—delirious kiss of lips immortal from the sky, rare nectar of Olympus born of bliss, bright spark of Aphrodite eye.—Madge Merton

Now then the songs, but first more wine, the Gods be with you, friend of mine.—Eugene Field

Here's to the nine muses—they must have been a ball team.—S. Stoppe

Come thou monarch of the vine, Plumply Bacchus with pink eyne, in thy vats our cares are drown, with thy grapes our hairs be crowned, cup us till the world goes round.—Shakespeare

Just for Fun

Here is a riddle most abstruse, canst read the answer right? Why is it that my tongue grows loose only when I grow tight?—De Beers

And wine can, of their wits beguile, make the sage frolic and the serious smile.—Homer

You raised the grapes, you raised the vine, and later you raised, well, a high-old shine!—W. French

Since natures' holy law is drinking, I'll make the law of nature mine and pledge the universe in wine.—Tom Moore

There are five good reasons why I drink, good wine, a friend, because I'm dry ... or lest I should be, by and by, or any other reason why!—John Simmond

Religion

What makes doctrine plain and clear, about two hundred pounds a year, and that which was proved before, proved false again ... two hundred more!—Butler

Love

God made man frail as a bubble, God made love and love made trouble!—Dryden

In terms of magic, the toast equates to a brief spell, incantation, benediction, or invocation. The words can be simple, rhyming, a quote from a book, or whatever seems appropriate. As you raise your glass, imagine the energy being raised. As you speak, release the intentions of that toast with your words, to bless all in attendance.

After a study group meeting, beseech the Gods to impart wisdom and discernment to the assembly. At a handfasting, the passing of the cup denotes support from those gathered to witness the event. Here, a fitting toast is one for joy, peace, and prosperity to the couple. At an initiation, give the new coven member a cup to signal an official welcome. The individual can then present a toast for unity.

No matter the occasion, it is not difficult to find a way to positively express your feelings. If you are not good at public speaking, draw on the marvelous resource of classical authors for aid. Look to parts of your traditional invocations, prayers, and songs. Find words that are comfortable on your lips and mirror the emotion of your heart, and everyone will be touched by the effort.

Summary

You now have all the tools for successful brewing, the three most important of which are two good hands and one keen wit! During the process of creating magical beverages, you will come across "snags," new ideas, and inspiration. Invention is the mother of all these things, including the occasional obstruction.

Be patient with yourself and look upon setbacks as an opportunity to learn something valuable. Throughout the refinement process, not only will your beverages improve, but so should your vision of magic, especially as it pertains to the sacred space of home. Approach your artistic endeavor as though you were walking between worlds with an empty bucket, soon to be filled with the elixir of magic itself; then drink your fill!

Part Two

Enchanted Spirits—
Recipes for
Alcoholic Beverages

He (Osiris) also invented the beverage made
from barley called beer, and which in taste
and flavor is not much inferior to wine. He
taught its preparation to those whose country
is unsuited for the cultivation of the vine.

—Diodor Sic., IV.2

Introduction to
Part Two

Alcoholic Beverages

Eight years ago, with the help of my husband, I worked through the very first batch of home brew our family had ever enjoyed. All things considered, that experiment was very successful and also contagious. We kept finding new combinations of fruits, juices, and spices to try. Slowly this process refined itself into a few favorite recipes, at least one of which is shared with only a handful of close friends.

The ideas and advice offered in this section come from my own experiences. If you are already an accomplished brewer, you may find some of the techniques presented here a little rudimentary. Most have been assembled for folks who do not have access to standard brewing equipment and supplies, or those who prefer using less specialized methods.

There is no reason not to employ these formulas using better accoutrements and tactics should you desire. Most of the methods will result in brews that closely resemble historic wines or beers. More refined procedures and tools produce beverages closer to modern standards, taste, and familiarity.

Tools

- Gallon-sized screw top or cork bottles.

- Balloons and rubber bands for fermentation locks.

- A cool, dark storage area.

- Strainers, cheesecloth, or gauze to filter out sediments.[1]

- Large cooking pans, preferably stainless steel or enamelware, *not* aluminum.

- Funnels in various sizes.

- Large wooden, plastic, or stainless steel spoons or other stirring utensils; a slotted spoon to remove large brewing ingredients (fruit, etc).

- Sharp knife for cutting herbs and fruits.

- Mortar and pestle to macerate root herbs, such as ginger.

- Active wine or beer yeast. (Bread yeast may also be used.)

- Accurate measuring tools.

- A clean, tightly woven, cotton cloth or plastic sheeting to cover beverages during the first fermentation. (Clean dish towels work.)

- A must jar—this is a type of plastic or glass container in which to store brewing (fruit, spices, bits of wine).[2]

Non-Essential Tools—But Fun Ones

- A hydrometer—these are usually available through a home brew supplier (see resources in the back of this book).

  MODERN BREWER'S NOTE: This device measures the amount of sugar in your wine, beer, or mead solution. By comparing the amount of sugar before and after fermentation you can calculate the alcohol content. It can also be used to tell when all or most of the sugar in a solution has been consumed by the yeast and fermentation is complete. — J.D.

- Fermentation locks—these come in various sizes to keep your bottles from accidentally exploding when pressure builds. They are inexpensive

---

1. Nylon, sheer silk, and other thin, clean scraps of material function well as makeshift strainers.
2. Several recipes included in the wine and mead sections call for the leftover must, which serves as a base for a richly flavored, fermented beverage.

(usually under $1.00 each) and keep you from having to clean up a very sticky mess.[3]

- Camden tablets.

  > MODERN BREWER'S NOTE: A sterilizer added to wine must to kill unde-sirable wild yeast and as an anti-oxidant. Each tablet contains 450 mg sodium metabisulphite, and will sterilize one gallon of must. Follow directions when using. Note also that many people are allergic to sulphites. — J.D.

- Yeast nutrients—consist of vitamins and minerals which are essential for vigorous yeast activity. They are available from your home brew supplier. Follow directions.

- Fermentation casks—beautiful wooden casks that make your cellar look like the brewing closets of old. These also give a distinctive flavor to wines and beers often peculiar to the type of wood from which the barrel is made. An alternative is a glass Carboy (about $15.00) with cap and stopper.

- Clarifying tools—these usually consist of a glass jar and special tubing that allows only the clear wine to be siphoned off your fermenting container.

- Corn sugar—makes beverages that ferment more quickly and have clearer flavors.

- Sparkaloid—helps to clarify beers.

- Citric acid—may be used in place of citrus fruit when you want the content but not the flavor.

- Sorbistat—prevents refermentation once a beverage has been boiled to stop the process.

---

3. Pressure in bottles becomes quite volatile in the initial stages of fermentation. This can cause bottles to explode, throwing glass shards everywhere. Either monitor your brews on a daily basis (burping the bot-tles), or buy some balloons or fermentation locks. After having cleaned up more than one explosion in my cellar, trust me when I say this is important.

Say, for what were hop-yards meant,
Or why was Burton built on Trent?
Oh many a peer of England brews
Livelier liquor than the Muse,
And malt does more than Milton can
To justify God's ways to man.

—A. E. Housman

Chapter Six

Bountiful Beers

*W*ork *is the curse of the drinking classes.*
—Oscar Wilde

Known to the Anglo-Saxons as *breowan*, to the Germans as *briuwan*, to the Norse as *brugga*, to the French as *brasser*, and to the Irish as *brach*, by any name, beer is the beverage of "every man." In one account we read, "Beer is in use with a number of peoples, and each one brews it somewhat differently."[1] No matter the process or the ingredients, because of its commonality beer is symbolic of simple pleasures enjoyed with friends, at celebrations, and often at sports events.

In Norse/Germanic cultures, from the Viking era up through the Middle Ages, one of the few places where legal transactions could take place, besides the church, was the beer hall, a place that served for various social and/or ritual functions. In the hall, for example, beer was passed over a central fire by the daughter of the house when serving a special visitor, symbolizing honor and purity. This "common" beverage thus took on a ritual role.

Laborers, servants, monks, and housewives were the beer makers of earlier days. The legacy of common folk is one for the magical brewer to remember and honor. This spirit of enterprise, among an otherwise inconspicuous group, reminds us how meaningful our own creative energy can be.

---

1. Strabo XVII 2.5.

One final note in the contemporary history of beer—at least one German company is considering putting brewing into orbit! At the time of this writing, experiments were underway in the Columbia Space Shuttle to determine if cosmic rays and the lack of gravity can alter yeast to produce a tastier beer. If the yeast proves itself "heavenly," we could potentially see this space-beer on the market by the end of 1995.

Helpful Hints for Beer Making

+ If possible, use dry or liquid beer yeast cultures, rather than a bread yeast.[2]

  > MODERN BREWER'S NOTE: Beer yeast ferments more cleanly with no lingering "yeasty" flavor, and settles better, leaving a clearer beverage. Beer yeast is either top fermenting ale yeast, or bottom-fermenting lager yeast. Ale yeast works best at 60-75°F, while lager yeast requires temperatures of 35-50°F. Most homebrewers ferment at room temperature, so ale yeast is best. — J.D.]

+ Of hops available through brewing stores, Cluster, Cascade, Hallertau, and Saaz are some of the best.

  > MODERN BREWER'S NOTE: Hops have three uses in beer: to add bitterness, hop flavor, and hop aroma. When hops are boiled for a long period, the flavor and aroma are lost, and only the bitterness remains. Some varieites of hops are used primarily for their bittering. Other varities, sometimes called "nobel" varieties, are used for their flavor and aroma. Ask your supplier for information. — J.D.

+ Irish moss, if added to the boiling process for the last few minutes, helps clarify your beer.

+ Bottled spring water may be the best base for your beer if you live in an area with poor quality water. Sediments in the tap water can affect the flavor of the finished product. Usually, any water that tastes good to drink will make good beer. Do not use water that has passed through a water softener.

+ When you notice that the bottom of your fermenting jars look as if they are covered with film, it is time to rack off the clear liquid. Leaving sediment in the bottom of the jar makes for bitter beers. Racking may be done either by carefully pouring off the top portion of the beer and rinsing the bottle or by siphoning.

---

2. The brewer's yeast frequently sold in health food stores *can not* be used for actual brewing. It is inert and will not encourage proper fermentation.

Cherry-Clove Ale

Modern magical practitioners often view cloves as protective, cleansing, and an aid to psychic sight. Cherries call up thoughts of clear spring days and contemplation. Japan's cherry blossom festivals are intended for simply enjoying the beauty of the flowers.

1	pound sweet cherries, pitted	3	quarts strong ale
4	cups sugar	10	whole cloves

Prick cherries with a toothpick or fork, or partially crush them, then place them in a 4-quart container with a lid. Sprinkle the sugar over the fruit, then fill the container with the ale. Cover loosely; fermentation should begin within 48 hours. When rapid bubbling has ceased, strain, cork, and store for 6 months to a year before drinking. The remaining cherries make marvelous pies and conserves.

Magical Attributes: Clear vision, unhindered joys.

Variations: This is a simple brew, easily changed to suit a wide variety of tastes and magical goals. Try strawberries mixed with a stout beer to strengthen love.

Lemon Beer

Lemon brings zest and active energy to any beverage. Because it has a natural purgative quality, it is mostly associated with magic for refinement. Lemon rind has also been frequently used in love sachets and potions.

4	quarts boiling water	⅛	ounce beer yeast
1	lemon, sliced and seeded		Raisins (optional)
1	cup sugar		

Bring water to a boil, turn off heat, and add sliced lemons and sugar. Cover and let cool until lukewarm. Meanwhile, dissolve the yeast in ¼ cup warm water. Stir this into the pot, then allow to age a full 24 hours, until bubbles form on the surface. Strain this into bottles, adding a raisin to each bottle if desired. Chill before serving. This has a short shelf-life; after 2-3 weeks it will become too bitter to drink.

Magical Attributes: Purification, cleansing, refreshed love, ideas.

Variations: Substitute 1½ pounds of currants for the lemons in this recipe and reduce the sugar by 1 cup for a beer empowered for protection and fire magic.

Small Beer #1

This recipe is based on an historical text, referred to in Stanley Bacon's Brewed in America (Anno Press, 1972). The original recipe specified "bran hops," an ingredient unfamiliar to modern home brewing suppliers. "Small" beers were popular on the frontier, as they were only mildly alcoholic and fermented very quickly.

3 cups bran hops	1 gallon unsulphured molasses
3 gallons water	2 teaspoons beer yeast
1 tablespoon malt extract	

Boil the bran hops in water for 3 hours, then strain. Stir molasses and malt extract into the hot liquid. Cool to lukewarm. Suspend the yeast in warm water, adding it to the molasses mixture when properly cooled. Cover with a heavy cloth for 1 full day, then strain again while pouring into a cask or bung. Leave the fermenting container open slightly until fermentation has all but ceased (about 1 week). Bottle and store. Keeps well for about 2 months.

Magical Attributes: Swift decisions and movement, keen sense of timing.

Small Beer #2

Versions of spiced small beers appear in many lands. This recipe is from Wales, a country known for its beauty and solitude.

4 quarts water	1½ cups sugar
¼ cup nettle leaves	½ cup brown sugar
1 inch bruised ginger root	1 package beer yeast
½ teaspoon grated lemon peel	Sugar cubes
½ teaspoon grated orange peel	

Place the nettle leaves with ginger, lemon peel, and orange peel in water. Bring to a boil, then lower heat to simmer for a half hour. Strain. To this add sugars, stirring until totally dissolved. Cool the liquid until lukewarm. While you are waiting, suspend the beer yeast in ¼ cup warm water. Add this to the spiced water and let it work in a warm area with a cloth over the pan until all signs of bubbling seem to stop. Strain again while bottling, adding two sugar cubes to each quart bottle. Let this sit closed securely for 7 days before drinking. Shelf life is another 2-3 weeks.

Magical Attributes: Grace, peace of mind, seclusion.

Variations: For a beer with more cleansing qualities, try adding a teaspoon of freshly ground grapefruit rind and two fruit slices during the boiling. For fuller flavor, substitute honey for sugar in the same proportions. Taste test this, as sometimes more sweetness may be desired to offset the grapefruit.

Dandelion Beer

The most loved and hated plant of all time, dandelions are rich in vitamins and minerals. They are also known to mark the sun by closing their petals when it is dark. They are symbolic of ancient prognostication, and were often used for love augury.

½	quart dandelion blossoms	1	cup brown sugar
½	inch ginger root, bruised	¼	cup white sugar
½	lemon, diced finely	⅛	cup cream of tartar
2	quarts water	⅛	ounce beer yeast (top fermenting)

Wash the dandelion blossoms and place in a large pot along with the ginger, lemon, and water. Boil this together for 15 minutes. In another large container, mix the sugars and cream of tartar together, slowly pouring in the hot liquid to dissolve. Strain and cool to lukewarm. Suspend the yeast in ¼ cup warm water. Add this to the cooled liquid to begin fermentation. Keep in a warm place with a heavy cloth over the top for 3 days before straining and bottling. Age for 1 week, then enjoy. Shelf life on this is short—about 6 weeks before it turns bitter.

Magical Association: Prophesy, psychic visions, dream oracles.

Variations: Strawberries are a good substitute in this recipe. Add about 1 pint during the initial boiling process for a sweeter, slightly pink beer, which is magically good for health and happiness. If you plan to eliminate the dandelions, use the juice of two large citrons instead, to maintain magical significance.

Rhubarb Beer

A favorite farmer's beer, prepared from the produce of a bountiful land. Sometimes nettles were added for nutritional value.

2 handfuls dandelion leaves and roots, freshly picked	2 pounds cane sugar
4 stalks rhubarb	1 teaspoon ground ginger root
1 gallon water	½ ounce beer yeast

Place all the ingredients, except the yeast, in a large pan. Boil for 1 hour. Allow to cool to lukewarm, adding the yeast which has been suspended in warm water. Bottle after 24 hours, sealing tightly. Ready to drink in 3 days, this brew will last 40 days without spoilage.

Magical Attributes: Nature's abundance, providence, the harvest.

Variations: Interesting flavors can be achieved by adding bits of other common fruits or vegetables whose taste you enjoy.

Quick Ginger Beer

Ginger was a widely known spice in the ancient world, written about by Confucius, and used as a flavoring in cookies as early as the time of the Egyptians in Cheops. One version of this particular recipe owes its origins to the American frontier.

3 inch piece fresh ginger root	4 quarts hot water
1½ cups sugar	¼ cup Northern Brewer Hops
1 lemon, peel and juice	¼ ounce suspended beer yeast

Mince and crush the ginger with the flat back of a spoon or mortar and pestle. Put this in a large bowl with sugar and lemon peel, pouring the boiling water over the top. Stir in the hops and steep until lukewarm. Add lemon juice and the yeast mixture. Cover the bowl and allow to set for at least 12 hours before straining and bottling. Ready within 5 days, it retains a good flavor for about a month.

Magical Attributes: Power, success, victory.

Variations: Try adding various fruits to this mixture when the boiling water is added. Strawberries might be included for love, or peaches for wisdom.

Outback Beer

In Australia, recipes similar to this were very popular for home brewers in the Outback, who had little access to bars due to their remote locations, far from villages.

1 gallon water	½ pounds brown sugar
1½ ounce hops	1 pound malt extract
2 pounds sugar	1 teaspoon beer yeast

Place half the water in a pan and bring to a boil, adding the hops (in a cheese-cloth bag or tea ball) to steep. Maintain at a low, rolling boil for 15 minutes. Remove the hops, then stir in the sugars and extract. When the sugar is dissolved, remove from heat, add the other half of the water, return the hops bag to the pot, and allow to cool until lukewarm before adding the yeast.

Leave the pan in a warm area for 7 days, skimming off any froth. It is ready to bottle when the top clears and sediments fall to the bottom. Remove only the clear liquid, pouring carefully into another pan to settle for 24 hours again. Repeat the following day, only this time pour off the clear liquid into bottles, filled three-quarters full, adding fresh water to the top. Cap securely, allowing the beer to age one month before drinking. Best enjoyed cold.

Magical Attributes: Ingenuity, adeptness, quick-mindedness.

Variations: It was not uncommon for other native herbs, roots, and flowers to be added to basic mixtures to vary their flavor. You might also want to try blending in kitchen spices such as cinnamon for prosperity or keen insight in job hunting. Another good choice is nutmeg, considered an aphrodisiac by the Arabs, and which was found whole in ale, as described by Chaucer.

Highland Bitter Ale

Various bitter liquors are served at the Scottish table before meals to strengthen the stomach and encourage good health. Gentian is thought to be a medicinal herb, and was known by the folk name of "bitter root."

2	chamomile tea bags	5	whole cloves
3	teaspoons gentian root, chopped	2	small cinnamon sticks
3	tablespoons coriander seeds	1½	quarts Scottish ale
2	teaspoons orange peel		

Place the tea bags, root, seeds, orange peel, and spices in a large bowl. Crush and mix. Pour this into a large-mouthed jar with a secure lid, and add ale. It is very important that the jar is covered tightly so the froth of the ale is not lost in this process. Leave it set for 7 days, then strain and rebottle securely. May be enjoyed at room temperature, hot, or cold.

Magical Attributes: Vitality, well-being, wholeness.

Variations: For the ale, try substituting in equal portions Scotch, other distilled beverages, wine, or even apple cider for those who prefer non-alcoholic drinks.

Apple Beer

Known sometimes by English countrymen as Lamb's Wool, this drink was often prepared on August 1 to honor the angel who protects fruits, seeds, and all that grows from the land. One cannot help but notice the similarity of this term to "Lamas," or La mas ubal, which literally translates to "day of the apple." Eight is used in this recipe as a number for personal change and improved control.

8	baked apples, peeled and cored	1½	teaspoon ginger root, ground
	Brown sugar to taste	8	cups hot ale
1½	teaspoon nutmeg		

Mix the apple pulp and brown sugar together to taste. Add nutmeg and ginger. Slowly add the warmed ale, stirring until well blended. If desired, float some sweet cakes on top.

Magical Attributes: Earth magics, the harvest, wisdom.

Traditional Mulled Ale

A favorite Victorian treat, mulled ale is a warm, welcoming beverage for cold winter nights in front of a romantic fire. The number two is employed throughout this recipe to encourage positive emotions and communications between two people.

2	cups ale	2	tablespoons butter
2	whole cloves	2	tablespoons sugar
2	teaspoons fresh ginger root, crushed	2	eggs, beaten

Place ale, cloves, ginger, butter, and sugar in a large saucepan and bring to just boiling. Slowly pour this mixture into the beaten eggs, then transfer into a large bottle. Pour this into another jug, repeating several times to build up froth, then return to the pan to reheat. Remove ginger and cloves before serving hot.

Magical Attributes: Partnership, love, romance.

Maple Beer

This recipe was developed in Colonial America where sap was used as a basic sweetening ingredient for beers, yielding a tasty smoky flavor. Maple tree branches have been used for magical wands, or to insure the health of children.

2	pounds dark malt extract, dried	1	ounce hops pellets
½	quart real maple syrup	1	(7-gram) package yeast
2½	gallons water		

Place malt, syrup, water, and hops together in a large pot over medium heat and bring to a boil. Continue to boil for 20 minutes, scooping off any froth. Cool to lukewarm, then add yeast which has been mixed with ¼ cup warm water and allowed to sit for at least 15 minutes. Cover and allow the entire beverage to sit in a warm place for 3 days, then bottle securely for 2 weeks before drinking.

Magical Attributes: Long life, sweet pleasures, guided mystical energies.

Variations: Adding a piece of vanilla bean to this recipe during the boiling process makes for a wonderfully unique blend.

Sunset Ale

This ale, when properly made, has a color similar to amber, which was once thought to be the solidified essence of the setting sun's tears. The old Irish word for malt, Brach, owes its origin to religion. It was the custom to celebrate the middle Sunday of Lent with a glass of beer. This day was known as Bragget Sunday, so the malted beverage for that day was similarly labeled!

1	gallon water	½	package top fermenting beer yeast
½	teaspoon gypsum		
¼	teaspoon salt	⅛	ounce hop pellets
1½	pounds malt extract	½	gallon cold water
4	ounces crystal malt	¼	cup dextrose
½	ounce bullion hops		

Bring the water to a low rolling boil, then add gypsum and salt. Next add malts and bullion hops, and boil for 20 minutes. Remove ¼ cup of the liquid and cool to lukewarm, and suspend the yeast in it. Meanwhile, add the aromatic hop pellets to the rest of the mixture, simmer for 15 minutes, and cool. In a large container place ½ gallon cold water and the suspended yeast. Pour the beer liquid into this and cover loosely. Watch for all signs of fermentation to cease, and siphon the clear liquid into a secondary fermentation vessel. Age for 4-6 weeks, using a fermentation lock. Then add dextrose and bottle. This should be ready in 7-10 days.

Magical Attributes: Fire and sun magic, courage, vitality.

Variations: For a less bitter ale, eliminate bullion hops.

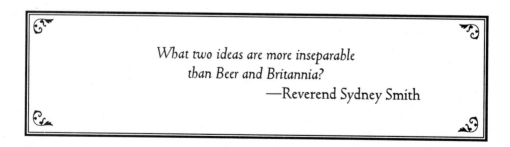

*What two ideas are more inseparable
than Beer and Britannia?*
—Reverend Sydney Smith

Chapter Seven

Cordials, Apéritifs, and Liqueurs

From fumes of wine grown heady, my friends gave hope last eve.
—Hafiz

An old legend says that cordials were originally invented to bring consolation to King Louis XIV in his elder years. As the name implies, cordials are drinks which, when properly prepared, inspire a friendly, favorable atmosphere for conversation. They are usually served after dinner.

Historically speaking, if an aperitif was served before dinner, it had a medicinal application. Flavored brandy, for example, preceded meals to aid digestion and tempt the appetite. In Scotland, whiskey blended carefully with chamomile, orange peel, and juniper berries was considered a "stomach strengthener." The significance in serving times may be kept in mind for your own magical preparations.

Cordials are fruit-flavored drinks that encourage joy. Liqueurs are similar, but can also be flavored with spices. There are many variations on this concept that work well in a social setting, some of which will be covered later.

Elderberry-Blackberry Betterment

Elderberries and blackberries figure heavily in folk remedies, and the tree of the Elder was said to be the only wood acceptable for Pan's Pipes.

2 quarts elderberries	2 cups brown sugar
2 quarts blackberries	Ginger and cloves (optional)
2 quarts water	2 cups brandy

Place the cleaned berries together in a large pot with water. Simmer over low heat to extract the juice, crushing and stirring regularly, for 30 minutes. Strain off juice into another pot. Rewarm the liquid and dissolve the sugar in it. Add any spices you like at this point, and boil for 15 minutes. Cool and add brandy before bottling.

Magical Attributes: Any rite for Pan, connection to nature, health and well-being.

Alternatives: The spices you choose to add to this recipe can aid magical applications. Nutmeg is an option for luck, or allspice to accentuate healthful aspects.

Apricot Nectar

Apricot is considered a love food, sacred to and ruled by Venus. It was a favorite fruit on Elizabethan tables, thought to originate in Western Asia.

1 quart vodka	1 pound dried apricots
1½ cups sugar	1 cup apricot nectar
1 pound ripe apricots, blanched	1 teaspoon vanilla extract

Warm the vodka slightly and dissolve the sugar in it. Slice each whole apricot into 8 pieces. Divide all the ingredients between 2 quart-size jars, cover and seal. This mixture should age 3 months for greatest success, the liquid being served as a cordial, and the fruits as a dessert, with whipped cream.

Magical Attributes: The spirit of Amour!

Variations: To add a little fervor to this beverage, reduce apricot juice by half, then blend in ½ cup passion fruit juice.

Cranberry-Orange Cocktail

This beverage is excellent to make with leftovers from the Thanksgiving table, which are already blessed with the energies of gratitude for Divine providence.

1 pound cranberries, ground	3½ cups sugar
2 whole seedless oranges, ground	2 cups rum

Place all the ingredients, including any juice from the grinding process, into a 2-quart jar with a secure lid. Keep in a cool area, shaking thoroughly once a day for the next 6 weeks. Strain into bottles and seal for use over the holidays.

Magical Associations: The harvest, thankfulness, bounty.

Variations: Use only 1 orange and add 2 apples, peeled and ground. Magically this encourages improved wisdom with one's resources.

Fruit Ratafia

Ratafia comes from a tradition of the Middle Ages where parties accepting any legal transaction or agreement would share a drink to celebrate its "ratification." Figs are used for insight, peaches for wisdom, and pomegranates for luck.

½ pound dried figs	6 ripe peaches, pitted
6 pomegranates, juiced	1 cup sugar (or more to taste)
1 quart distilled spirits (your choice)	

Divide the ingredients in equal proportions between 2 (1-quart) jars. Make sure that peaches and figs are pierced first (use a fork or toothpick). Cover securely, shake daily for 1 month; strain and bottle for later use.

Magical Associations: Commitment, approval, verification.

Helpful Hint: One of the easiest ways to juice pomegranate seeds is to place them inside cheesecloth, and press with the flat side of a spoon in a bowl. Remove the white seeds when expressed, then twist the cloth to release the remaining juice. This is a little time consuming, but well worth the effort for the flavor it produces.

Plum Dandy

This cordial comes to us from the Ukraine where, on cold nights, it is a favorite beverage to share with family or friends. Branches of the plum tree were sometimes hung in the entryway of rural homes as protection from avarice.

1 quart brandy or vodka	2 cups sugar
1 pound ripe plums	

Place all ingredients in a large crock, well sealed. Shake daily for 8 weeks. Strain the liquid off into bottles which should be sealed and aged 6 months before consumption. After straining, the fruit may be used for tarts, pies, or as a spiked dessert with cream garnish.

Magical Attributes: Open discourse among family and friends; kinship.

Variations: Try peaches or pears for similar magical outcomes.

Four Quarter Harmony

Each of the four fruits in this recipe correspond with 1 quarter of the magic circle (or one element). Just as in magic, combining each element in harmony produces some powerful, and in this instance tasty, results! This particular recipe comes from the Ukraine.

1 cup diced quince (earth)	1 quart vodka
1 cup mulberries (air)	⅔ cup honey
1 orange, peeled and sectioned (fire)	⅛ teaspoon cinnamon
1 large apple, diced (water)	⅛ teaspoon ginger

Place the fruits and vodka in a large crock and soak for 4-5 hours. Mix in the honey and spices, covering the crock securely with an oven-proof cover. Place the crock in the oven at 200° F for 10 hours.[1] Cool and strain; serve hot or cold.

Magical Attributes: Balance, symmetry, accord.

Variations: If you cannot find quince, substitute fresh or canned pears (in juice).

---

1.   This technique has a shorter aging period. Be certain your crock is ovenproof, and avoid the temptation to open and check the mixture before it is cool. Frequent opening will decrease the quality of the cordial.

Chocolate Creme du Mint

Pre-Columbian civilizations in South America were known to cultivate chocolate. Mexican chocolate was imported to the European continent as a delicacy.

2 ounces semi-sweet chocolate	1 cup heavy cream, whipped
½ cup sugar	1 pint milk
½ cup cold water	½ liter mint liqueur

Melt the chocolate in a double boiler over medium heat. Stir in the sugar, then add the water, cooking about 10 minutes until thickened. Let this cool, then fold in the whipped cream. Set aside. Heat the milk over low heat until lukewarm. Add the mint liqueur and cream mixture, folding together until well blended. Enjoy hot, or store in the refrigerator, shaking before serving.

Magical Attributes: Pleasure, warmth, fanciful diversions.

Variations: To encourage "sun" energies and health as well as enjoyment, use orange-flavored liquor in place of the mint. As an inexpensive substitute for the mint liquor, use ½ liter vodka and 1 teaspoon of mint extract.

Citrus Tonic

Being high in vitamin C, with a full-bodied aroma, this beverage is wonderful during the winter months to ease the discomforts of colds.

1 cup water	2 cups mixed orange, lemon,
2 cups sugar	and grapefruit peels
3 cups whiskey	

Heat the water and sugar in a small saucepan until the sugar is dissolved. Add to the whiskey and fruit peels (remove as much of the white pith from the peels as possible). Leave the ingredients to set together in a sealed container for 3 months. Strain. Serve warm with a touch of honey and cinnamon sticks.

Magical Attributes: Good health, revitalization, refreshed perspectives.

Variations: For fruitier flavor and increased vitamin benefit, decrease whiskey by 1 cup, add ½ cup each orange and grapefruit juice, and 1 teaspoon lemon juice.

Heather Honey Cordial

This beverage, with but minor changes, originated in Prussia, where it is believed to aid smooth speech and communications. Cloves were a favorite medieval-era breath freshener.

1 cup water	1 small cinnamon stick
1 tablespoon real vanilla extract	1 cup heather honey
1 whole clove (per person involved)	2 cups vodka

In a large saucepan bring the water to a low rolling boil. Add extract and spices, allowing to infuse like a tea while the water cools. If you don't like cloves, remove them before the water reaches lukewarm. Strain, add honey and rewarm to dissolve the honey, skimming off froth on the surface. Add vodka, strain, and bottle securely, aging for 2 weeks before consumption.

Magical Attributes: Messages, rapport, opening the lines of discourse.

Variations: To accentuate the power of speech in this recipe, try replacing the vanilla with either mint or almond extract. Both of these are aligned with the element of air, which helps move messages toward their proper destination.

Mighty Milk

In Chinese mythology, cinnamon was the spice of immortality. Magically, cinnamon is ruled by Venus and considered a fire herb, making it an excellent aphrodisiac.

1 quart milk	4 egg whites
1½ cups sugar	1 teaspoon lemon juice
2 inch piece lemon peel	1 cup cinnamon liqueur
1 small cinnamon stick	

Place the milk in a small pan with 1 cup of the sugar. Add lemon peel and cinnamon stick while simmering over low heat for 3-5 minutes. Cool, strain, and place in the freezer. Meanwhile, beat the egg whites with ½ cup sugar, adding lemon juice when peaks form. Beat this mixture into the chilled milk very slowly, alternating with equal portions of the cinnamon liqueur. Return to the freezer until a slush-like consistency forms. Serve in chilled glasses.

Magical Attributes: Improved potency, passion, fervent energy.

Variation: For success and prosperity, substitute a 1-inch piece of bruised ginger root and ginger liquor for the cinnamon in this recipe.

Currant-Raspberry Delight

Currants were sometimes imported to England by way of Portugal, to grace the Elizabethan table where they quickly became favored for all manner of sweets including jellies, comfits, and sotelties.

1 pound red raspberries	3 cups water
3 cups currants, freshly picked (red or black)	1½ cups sugar (or to taste)
	6 cups currant vodka

Place raspberries and currants together in a pan with water. Simmer over low heat for 2 hours, pressing frequently with the back of a spoon. Remove and strain, reserving the fruit for tarts, ice cream topping, etc. Place the juice back on the stove, slowly adding sugar. Taste frequently, making sure to add a little more than you like because this sweetness will be reduced when you blend in the currant vodka. Bottle and age for one month.

Magical Attributes: Sun and fire magics (note the deep red color achieved in the finished product). If it comes out pink, it might be more appropriate for friendship and improved attitudes.

Variations: For a smoother, more traditional version of this beverage, use honey instead of sugar. This yields a cordial similar to raspberry horilka (recipe on page 210). This particular beverage is also good with traditional "fire" herbs, such as cinnamon and ginger, added during the simmering process.

Russian Vostorg

Shortly after the advent of air freight, many nations found customs, specifically those pertaining to food and drink, changing to meet a new global awareness. In Moscow, this liqueur sometimes replaces vodka. In Russian, the name means "delight."

1	cup cognac	2	cherries (garnish)
2	tablespoons cherry liqueur	3-4	ice cubes
1	teaspoon lemon juice		

Depending on personal preference, this cordial can be prepared one of two ways. You can place all the ingredients except cherries in a blender for a whipped, icy beverage topped with whole cherries, or combine the ingredients in a shaker and serve over ice.

Magical Attributes: One-world perspectives, pleasure, broadening outlooks.

Variation: One especially nice touch with this drink is to add a fresh white gardenia as garnish, to encourage peace.

ཏྠ ྒ

Orange-Vanilla Whip

Vanilla beans were often thought to be a kind of magical charm to ward off weariness. Likewise, oranges are a health panacea, being rich in vitamin C. The number 3 in this recipe is repeated to encourage the triune balance of body, mind, and soul.

3	whole oranges	½	cup water
3	whole vanilla beans	3	cups tequila
2	cups sugar		

Cut three slits in each orange, inserting ⅓ of a vanilla bean in each slit. Place these in a large crock and set aside. Next, in a small saucepan, heat the water and sugar together until a syrup is formed. Pour this over the oranges, along with the tequila. Store in an air-tight container in the refrigerator for 3 months, shaking daily, then strain. Put into blender for a few minutes until frothy, serve in chilled glasses.

Magical Attributes: Health and well-being for the whole person.

Variations: Much the same magical effect can be achieved using 3 apples, with 3 allspice berries each lodged within them.

Chapter Eight

Fantastic Flowers and Vivified Vegetables

O, dewy flowers that open to the sun;
what knowest thou of flowers except,
belike, to garnish meat with?
                    —Shakespeare, *Hamlet*

References to cooking and brewing with flowers first appeared in written histories of China and Japan. Perhaps this was due to the obsession Asians had with cooking as an art. What better to grace any lovely dish or sweet cup than the crowning glory of the natural world: flowers.

In China, flower petals scented some of the most exquisite and highly desired teas. In Japan, the chrysanthemum was the flower of choice, with a special celebration in its honor. On the ninth day of the ninth moon (early September), a wine steeped with chrysanthemum petals was given to the emperor to insure long life and encourage poetic muse. In Feudal times, the Shogun met with all his samurai on this day. Today, the tradition continues with competitive flower shows.

During the Middle Ages, petaled beverages (and foods) found their way to Europe. Flower and vegetable wines and liquors established a place on the table

alongside more traditional fruit preparations. They were a welcome addition to royal gatherings.

In preparing your own fruit and vegetable wines, two factors above all others are crucial for success. The first is freshness. Flowers can be bought dried, but are more effective when freshly harvested. When gathering petals (*only* petals—no green parts), do so just after the dew evaporates, no later than 10:30 A.M. This helps petals retain their essential oils. Handle them carefully, storing in a muslin or nylon mesh bag, and use them as soon as possible. Once wilted, their taste is far less enjoyable.

For vegetables, again dried components can be substituted, but for fullness of flavor nothing beats those freshly harvested. Fresh vegetables have the additional benefit of much higher vitamin content. Their juices may be easily extracted into the brewing pot. Use only those flowers and vegetables that have not been chemically treated.

The second consideration is temperature. Flowers are especially sensitive to heat. When starting a batch of brew with flower petals, you will not be boiling as with many other preparations. To extract the oils, use lower temperatures, heating until the petals turn translucent. Then strain the liquid to prepare it for the the rest of the process. Slower cooking with vegetables yields more pleasant results, as well.

You will notice that I generally recommend ½ package wine yeast, rather than a whole package, as some recipes state. This is because many professional wine yeasts available through distributors make anywhere from 1-5 gallons of finished product. In order to avoid too quick a fermentation, or too much sugar usage, I have decreased the yeast content according to final yield.

~ Vegetables ~

Beet Wine

A wine similar to this is sometimes used in Jewish Passover observances. Beet juice is considered an appropriate magical alternative to blood, and is strongly associated with human emotions, especially love. Five is used repeatedly in this recipe to encourage the energy of insight. The contemporary magician rarely resorts to use of blood in any spell or ritual, but its significance as a symbol should be noted. As the life source, blood was regarded by early mages as one of the most powerful components to truly powerful magics, especially those which protected oneself or one's belongings.

3 pounds fresh beets	5 cups sugar
1 gallon water	½ package wine yeast
Juice and peel of 5 oranges	
5 inches ginger root, bruised and diced	

Remove tops and roots of the beets, then chop the remainder, placing them in a large pot with the water. Bring to a low rolling boil, continuing to cook until tender (about 40 minutes). Reduce heat to simmer, adding orange peel, bruised and diced ginger root, and the juice from the oranges. Let this mixture steep for 15 minutes, then add sugar, stirring until dissolved. Cool to lukewarm and add yeast which has been suspended in ¼ cup warm water. Place in a large container for initial fermentation, using a balloon or fermentation lock, and watching for all signs of fermentation to cease. At this time taste your beverage and sweeten if necessary.1 Put the mixture into a fresh jug, leaving any sediment in the bottom of the old container. Allow to age for another two months before bottling.

Magical Attribute: Versatility and awareness, especially in interpersonal relationships.

~ ~

---

1. Sugar infusions are quite common in brewing. Here, when the fermentation process has stopped, you have the opportunity to add more sweetener to replace what was used up by the yeast in making alcohol. To do this, warm your beverage over low heat, adding a little sugar (or honey) at a time until the flavor is pleasant to you. Cook until the sugar is dissolved, then rebottle the entire mixture. Likewise, if you find the wine is a little too sweet, add water, unsweetened fruit juice, or a bit of lemon to compensate. [MODERN BREWER'S NOTE: Alcohol boils at about 173° F; if you wish to retain the alcohol in your wine, keep the temperature below that. — J.D.]

Tomato Wine

The tomato has its origins in the pre-Columbian regions of Central and South America where the cultures were largely vegetarian. In the mid-1600s, Spanish explorers introduced the tomato to the European continent where it would change the face of cooking forever. The folk name for the tomato is the "love apple."

1	gallon tomato juice	5	cups sugar
2	pounds tomatoes	½	package wine yeast

Warm a small amount of the tomato juice and dissolve the sugar in it. Meanwhile, in another pot, place the tomatoes with the remaining juice in a large pan, boiling until soft (about 7 minutes). Mash thoroughly, returning to simmer for about 1 hour, then strain as much liquid as possible out of the mixture. Blend this with the sugar juice and let sit overnight. In the morning, suspend the yeast in warm water for 15 minutes before stirring into the juice. Ferment for 3 weeks in a large container, then strain off the clearer liquid into bottles for aging. Ready in 9-12 months.

Magical Attributes: Romance, protection, blood mysteries, vitality, fire magics.

Onion Wine

Egyptians worshipped onions, regarding them as one of their most important foods. Hindus made of the onion a symbol of religious mystery and an object of divination. Arab and Chinese people used onions to ward off magic, and among the Greeks it was an appropriate gift to newlyweds to insure they would always be provided for. The onion is sacred to Latona, the mother of both Apollo and Diana.

½	pound onions	1	gallon water
½	pound potatoes	2	pounds sugar
1	pound raisins, diced	½	package yeast

Peel and slice the onions and potatoes, placing them in a large pot, then add the raisins. In a separate container, heat the water and sugar together until dissolved, pouring this over the onion-potato mixture. Next, add yeast suspended in ¼ cup warm water. Leave this to ferment in a warm place with a loose cover for 2 weeks. Strain and bottle. Generally this is a dry wine, with no residual onion scent.

Magical Attributes: Religious study and worship, cleansing and health, foresight, abundance.

Variation: Barley may be used in place of potatoes for improved providence (same proportion).

Carrot Awareness

Diphilus (a third-century philosopher) felt that carrots were indigestible, but were tolerably nutritive and sometimes acted as an aphrodisiac. In Scotland, on a holiday known as Carrot Sunday, the vegetable is gathered, blessed at the churches, and taken home to protect the household. Anyone finding a forked carrot was considered doubly fortunate and safeguarded. For this recipe, the old idea of carrots improving eyesight is the basis for magical connotations.

4 pounds carrots	1 pound raisins, chopped
1 gallon water	½ package wine yeast
4 cups brown sugar, lightly packed	

Boil the chopped, cleaned carrots in water until very tender. Strain, retaining carrots for use in a carrot cake. Return the liquid to the pan, adding sugar and stirring until it is dissolved. Place raisins in a large fermenting jar with the suspended yeast mixture and pour lukewarm carrot juice over the top. Use a fermentation lock or balloon for 3 weeks until fermentation is completed. Strain into another jug with a secure lid, aging the mixture another 2 months before bottling the clear fluid at the top.

Magical Attributes: Keen insight, heightened inner vision, alertness.

Variation: Any herbs you enjoy with cooked, glazed carrots (such as ginger) may be added during the boiling process, for a spicier beverage.

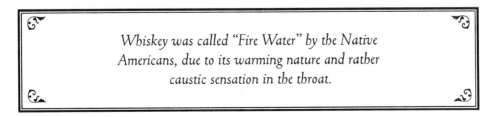

Whiskey was called "Fire Water" by the Native Americans, due to its warming nature and rather caustic sensation in the throat.

Prosperity Persuasion

The luscious green color of this beverage helps encourage growth or improved finances. Serve with a stick of fresh celery.

1½	cups diced broccoli	6	stalks celery
6	large Brussels sprouts		Salt and pepper to taste
1	sprig parsley	1	liter water
1	cup chopped asparagus	1	liter vodka
6	scallions		

Finely chop all the vegetables, placing them in a large pan with water over medium heat. Add salt and pepper. Allow them to simmer for about 2½-3 hours until almost mushy in texture. Strain this through a sieve, pressing the vegetable remnants with a wooden spoon to extract juices. Return the liquid to the pan, mixing in the vodka. Taste the mixture and add spices or sugar if necessary. Bottle and age 1-2 months before using.

Magical Attributes: Abundance, good fortune, success.

Variation: Dilute this beverage with tomato juice for a vegetable cocktail.

Fire Fantasy

This beverage, very appropriate to summer observances, uses the traditional herbs, plants, and colors of fire to ignite transformation in your life.

2	large tomatoes	2	cloves garlic
2	red peppers, bell or hot	1	cup chopped red cabbage
1	teaspoon lime juice	1	teaspoon hot sauce
4	cups water	1	liter whiskey

Finely chop all vegetables and place with other ingredients, except whiskey, in a large pan with the water. Simmer for 2 hours over low heat. Strain the mixture through a sieve, pressing as much juice as possible out of the vegetables. Mix with whiskey and bottle, aging for at least 30 days before use.

Magical Applications: Purification, drastic change, fire- and sun-related magics.

Rhubarb Wine

Rhubarb is a plant under the rule of Venus and the element of earth, making it an excellent choice for giving love strong foundations.

- 4 pounds rhubarb stalks, cut up
- 2 lemon rinds, grated
- 1 gallon boiling water
- 3 pounds sugar (white or brown)

Place the rhubarb and lemon rind in a crock. Pour the boiling water over the fruit, cover the container, and let this set for 3 days. Then strain, returning the liquid to the crock. Let this stand again for 2 weeks, then place in a large, tightly covered container for 1 month. Strain and bottle for use.

Magical Attributes: Commitment to relationships, fidelity.

Variation: Try using 3 quarts water and 1 quart apple juice, and add 1 cup of raisins with the rhubarb and lemon. Magically, this is for wisdom in love.

Hint: If you find the beverage shows no sign of fermentation after the 2-week period (e.g., bubbles), add ½ package of suspended wine yeast, allow this to sit in a warm spot, lightly covered, for 24 hours before aging for 1 month.

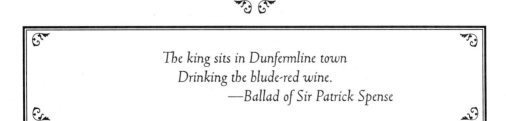

The king sits in Dunfermline town
Drinking the blude-red wine.
—*Ballad of Sir Patrick Spense*

⁓ *Flowers* ⁊

Rose Geranium Oracle

Some Cunning Folk of old would plant specially enchanted geraniums by their door to prepare for impending guests by foreseeing their arrival.

1	quart apple wine	2	limes, sliced
1	cup sugar	2	oranges, sliced
8	rose geranium leaves		

Warm the apple wine, sugar, and geranium leaves for 5 to 10 minutes until sugar is dissolved. Add sliced limes and oranges; cool. Strain and bottle, aging for 1 month before consuming.

Magical Attributes: Prophesy, well-being, insight, love, service to others.

Variation: Replace geranium leaves with 6 bay leaves for similar magical results.

⁓ ⁊

Honeysuckle Serendipity

If you find a honeysuckle plant growing near your home, it is not only a sign of good fortune but a protector of the family's health. The orange in the recipe is for health.

4	cups honeysuckle blossoms		Juice and peel of 2 oranges
1	gallon water	½	package wine yeast
6	cups sugar		

Place the blossoms in a large crock. Heat half the water to just below boiling, then pour over the petals. Allow to sit until blossoms turn almost translucent. Strain and rewarm slightly, then add sugar, orange juice, peel, and yeast. Pour into a fermentation container with a lock and let set until the liquid becomes clear. Strain out fruit, bottle, and store in cool, dark area for use.

Magical Attributes: Luck, good fortune, good health.

⁓ ⁊

Lavender and Spice

This recipe is a version of a medieval Aqua Vitae that knights drank before battle. It was given to those thought to be dead in hope that it might restore vitality.

1 cup dried French lavender	1 inch ginger root, minced
1 inch cinnamon stick	4 whole allspice berries
4 whole cloves	1 teaspoon nutmeg
1 quart water	2 cups honey
1 quart brandy	1 cup raisins
Pinch sage	2 tablespoons rose water

All dry ingredients except the raisins should be ground finely, then put into a large container with the honey, raisins, and rose water. Pour the brandy over the entire mixture. Cover the container and set in the sun (or a warm area) for 20 days, shaking regularly. Strain thoroughly, bottling the clear fluid. Store in cool, dark area.

Magical Attributes: Strength, vitality, recuperative powers, the spirit of life.

Fortune Draught

Dandelions acquire their name from the jagged leaves which resemble lion's teeth (note the French term, dent de lion), which gives this beverage a bit of a protective bite. A four-leaf clover is considered most fortunate, as is dreaming of a dandelion.

2 quarts dandelion blossoms	2 quarts clover blossoms
1 gallon boiling water	3 pounds sugar
2 lemons, sliced	Juice of 2 oranges
½ package yeast	1 cup raisins

Remove stems and leaves from the blossoms, placing them in a large cooking pot. Pour the boiling water over the top, adding sugar, sliced lemon, and oranges. Simmer for ½ hour, then cool to lukewarm. Add the wine yeast, suspended as usual, and stir. This should set, covered with a cloth, for 1 week.

Magical Attributes: Luck, opportunity, windfalls.

Romantic Rose Wine

Greeks considered the rose to be one of the best symbols of love and loveliness, having been born from the blood of Aphrodite. Romans covered festival floors with roses to welcome honored guests. Rose water is called the "dew of paradise" by Arabs.

2	gallon pot half-full of rose petals	½	package champagne or wine yeast
1	gallon water	2	tablespoons rose water
3	pounds sugar	1	teaspoon orange juice

Cover the rose petals with water and simmer over low heat until the petals become translucent. Strain off the liquid and dissolve the sugar in it. Cool to lukewarm, adding champagne yeast (preferably) which has been suspended in ¼ cup warm water. Cover the pot with a cloth for 24 hours to begin fermentation. Then move the liquid to a larger container with a fitted fermentation lock, and add the rose water and orange juice. Allow this to age until fermentation has all but ceased. Rack off the clear pink liquid into bottles with a sugar cube in each bottle. Seal, using champagne corks, and store in a dark, cool area for 1 month. Open with caution as the bottles will have built up a fair amount of pressure.

Magical Attributes: The spirit of love and beauty.

May Wine

Woodruff is called the "master of the woods" in Germany, with a rich smell similar to cinnamon. Its white flowers are sacred to the Goddess and it has often been used in magic to protect against impishness.

½	cup woodruff flowers	¼	pint water
1	quart warm apple wine		Slice of orange per glass
2	ounces sugar		Stick cinnamon

Set the freshly picked woodruff in the warm wine for 30 minutes, then remove. To this add sugar and water. This serves about 6 people and may be prepared warm or cold. Garnish with orange slices and cinnamon.

Magical Attributes: Victory, protection, banishing negativity.

Chapter Nine

Mead, Horilka, and Metheglin

The Druids and Old British bards were wont to carouse
thereof (mead) before they entered into speculations.
—Dr. Howells, Oxford, 1640

In this chapter, I will discuss only wines that use honey as their main source of sweetening. The section on wine (Chapter 14) is restricted to sugar-based beverages. Substitution of sweetening agents in either of these chapters is always an option (in equal proportions), for variations in flavor. The basic mead recipe on page 92 will serve as a good foundation for all your efforts in mead-related drinks. Simply change fruits, fruit juices and spices for different and uniquely flavored results. All proportions given are for one gallon yields. In all instances where a specific type of honey is listed among ingredients, it is because I have tried others and found that particular kind mingles best with the fruit or spices.

Achieving the greatest success with these beverages depends on a little experimentation with flavor components, and on conscientious skimming of the honey sediment that rises to the top of the pot during boiling. A good quality raw honey improves the overall body and taste of the finished mead.

MODERN BREWER'S NOTE: There are four types of mead: melomel is mead to which fruit or fruit juice is added; pyment or piment is mead made with grape juice; metheglin or metheglyn is mead made with herbs and spices; hippocras is spiced pyment. — J.D.

⁓ *Mead* ᛒ

Basic Mead

Since it was honey, not sugar, which was the main source of sweetening for many centuries, simple mead recipes like this show up in almost every nation, with only minor variations appropriate to that culture. (For more information, see Chapter 1.)

- 1 gallon water
- 2 oranges, sliced
- ½ package champagne yeast
- 5 pounds dark honey
- 1 lemon, sliced

Place the honey, water, and fruit in a 2-gallon pot over medium heat. Bring the mead to a rolling boil, skimming off any scum which rises to the top over the next hour. Cool to lukewarm, strain out the fruit, and add the yeast (dissolved in ¼ cup warm water). Allow this mixture to set, covered with a towel, for 7 days, until the first fermentation has slowed considerably. Strain again, pouring off only the clearer top fluids into bottles to age. These bottles should be lightly corked for about 2 months, then tightly sealed for 6 months before using.

Magical Attributes: Vary with ingredients. Basic associations are good health, artistic inspiration, romance, and religious observance.

⁓ ᛒ

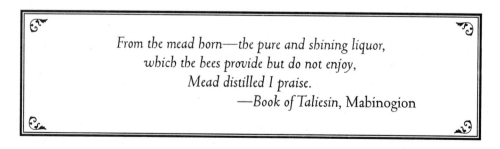

> *From the mead born—the pure and shining liquor,*
> *which the bees provide but do not enjoy,*
> *Mead distilled I praise.*
> —*Book of Taliesin*, Mabinogion

Hops Mead

The hops in this recipe are not added as a flavor, but as a clarifier; this allows the finished mead to be unclouded with a distinctively less dense taste. Hops have many uses, not only to brew beer, but also to make paper and linen. A tea made from hops is sometimes used to improve sleep and encourage a healthy appetite.

1	gallon water	2	oranges, sliced
1	ounce Cascade hops	½	pound white raisins, chopped
4	pounds light honey	½	package yeast
1	lemon, sliced		

Place water, hops, honey, and sliced fruit into a pot, boiling as in the basic recipe (page 92), but only for 30 minutes. Reduce heat and add chopped raisins, stirring for another 5 minutes before removing from heat. Cool, strain, and add yeast as directed in the basic recipe. Place 5 raisins in each bottle before closing. Aging time after secure corking is 1 year.

Magical Attributes: Sweet dreams, smooth versatility, adaptation.

Quick Wine Mead

As the name might imply, this mead is a charlatan in that it is not made from scratch, but prepared when haste is needed. It is similar in flavor to a traditional mead made with grape juice, which in medieval Europe was called "pyment."

1	gallon red wine (medium dryness)	¼	fresh lemon
2	pounds honey		Spices as desired
2	oranges, sliced		

Warm the wine over very low heat, adding honey slowly to dissolve thoroughly. Divide this between 2 (1-gallon) containers, with equal portions of fruit and spices in each. Cork and shake daily for 3 days before using. This should he served warm. The amount of honey can be decreased to suit personal tastes.

Magical Attributes: Expediency, swift action.

Alternative: Try apple wine instead of red wine, and stir with a cinnamon stick.

Apricot-Banana Melomel

Some scholars argue that the Tree of Knowledge in the Garden of Eden was actually an apricot tree because of its abundance in Israel. Persians regard apricots as the "seed of the sun," and in China apricots are considered a tremendous aid to prophets. Hondurans and West Indians believe that the banana is actually the fruit of paradise. In this recipe, the two sweet fruits of Biblical debate are blended together for a marvelous mead!

1½	pounds dried apricots		Juice and rind of 1 orange
1	gallon water	2	cups apricot nectar
6	ripe bananas, peeled	3	pounds honey

Soak the apricots in cold water in a large pan, until they soften and swell a bit. Place the pan on the stove and warm over medium heat as you slice in the bananas. Add the orange rind, juice, nectar, and honey, boiling slowly for 45 minutes, again skimming off any scum. Cool and add yeast as in the basic recipe (page 92), then move entire mixture to a temporary container where it can clear for 3 weeks (cork loosely). Strain off the clarified wine and bottle with secure lids. Age for at least 3 months before serving.

Magical Attributes: The mysteries, insight, oracular vision.

Nutty Mead

In Lithuania, the God Pekun was said to be eating walnuts during the time of the great flood. When one of the shells reached a drowning person, it grew to the size of a boat and brought the person to safety.

1	quart hickory nut leaves	1	lemon
1	quart black walnut leaves	1	orange
1	pound almonds, crushed	1	tablespoon almond extract
1	gallon water	½	package yeast
4	pounds honey		

Be sure the leaves are fresh, with no signs of wilting or infestations. Crush them by hand and place in a large pan with the almonds. In a separate container, heat water with honey and fruit to a low rolling boil, for 20 minutes, skimming. Add extract and follow the basic recipe (page 92), aging the mead for 1 year.

Magical Attributes: Divine intervention, safety, (especially from severe weather), the God aspect.

Varationss: Try adding your favorite nuts in this recipe for different taste sensations. Another leaf which can be added is that of the great oak, sacred to Ceres, Zeus, and the Druids of old. This produces a mead with a sherry-like undercurrent, and engenders energy for fertility and luck.

Pineapple Melomel

A fruit native to the tropical Americas, the pineapple was unknown in Europe until the New World was discovered. The native name was "na-na," which translated means "fragrance." Images of the pineapple, a symbol of welcome, decorate American furniture, architecture, and handicrafts.

- ½ gallon water
- 3 (16-ounce) cans pineapple chunks, in juice
- ½ orange, sliced
- 4 pounds orange blossom honey
- ½ gallon pineapple juice
- ½ package yeast

Place pineapple chunks (juice and all) in a large pan with the water, sliced orange, and honey. Maintain a low rolling boil for 30-40 minutes, skimming any residue off the top, then add pineapple juice, reducing heat to a simmer for 10 more minutes. Cool, then follow basic recipe directions for adding yeast and bottling. Aging time after final corking is about 6-8 months for a sweet wine; 1 year for dry.

Magical Attributes: Hospitality, joyful meetings, discoveries.

Variations: Add 1-2 inches freshly bruised ginger root to this beverage for zealous energy and a rich flavor. For a flavor twist, substitute 2 pounds of brown sugar for half the honey in this recipe.

ᵔᵓ *Metheglin* ᶜʳ

Balm-Mint Medley

Mint is the herb of wisdom, helpful in improving spirits and curing stomach discomfort. The Israelites covered the floors of their temples and homes with mint leaves to refresh guests. Balm helps make one more agreeable and joyous.

1	quart packed balm leaves	1	inch piece vanilla bean
1	quart packed mint leaves	2	pounds dark honey
1	gallon water	½	package yeast

In one pan, crush the balm and mint leaves. In another pan, bring the water to a boil, and pour over the herbs. Let this mixture stand for a day, then strain, squeezing excess juice from the leaves. Place the liquid over low heat, adding the vanilla bean and honey. Stir until the honey is dissolved, continuing to heat for about 30 minutes, skimming residue from the top. Cool the liquid to lukewarm, then follow the basic recipe (page 92).

Magical Attributes: Happiness, rejuvenation, amicable feelings.

Clove Metheglin

Persians used cloves to rekindle relationships gone cold. The potent flavor and scent of the clove gives it associations with energy for protection.

1	gallon water	1	lemon, sliced with rind
3	pounds dark honey	1½	ounces clove (adjust to taste)
2	oranges, sliced with rind	½	package yeast

Place all the ingredients except the yeast in a large pot and boil for 1 hour, skimming as needed. Cool to lukewarm, remove cloves and fruit, squeezing to extract the juice. Next add the yeast, and leave the mixture covered in a warm area for 2 weeks. Siphon off the clear fluid into bottles and age 7 months for sweet wine, 1 year for dry.

Magical Attributes: Protecting marriages, close friendships, and kinship.

Variations: Instead of water, try apple juice, or half water, half orange juice.

Fall Metheglin

This mulled beverage is traditionally made for enjoyment during Lammas, the Fall Equinox, and from Thanksgiving into the Yule season. It has all the scents and flavors of the holidays to inspire magic for the season. Begin this in November to have ready for the next fall's celebrations.

- 1 cup dried apple
- 2 large cinnamon sticks
- 1 tablespoon dried lemon peel (or fresh from 1 whole fruit)
- 12 whole cloves
- 1 teaspoon nutmeg
- 1 gallon water
- 7 bay leaves
- 1 inch bruised ginger root
- 1 tablespoon dried orange peel (or fresh from 1 whole fruit)
- 7 whole allspice berries
- 3 pounds dark honey
- ½ package sparkling yeast

Place all the ingredients, except the honey and yeast, in a 2-gallon pan. Simmer for 1 hour, then add the honey, bringing the entire mixture to a boil and skimming off the scum. Boil for 15 minutes, then follow the basic recipe (page 92). This mead has a marvelously crisp fall flavor and is good hot or cold.

Magical Attributes: The harvest, thankfulness, prudence.

Ginger-Cinnamon Warm Up

A similar Irish beverage, called usquebaugh, flavored with nutmeg and spirits, is used to warm chilled bones.

- 3 pounds clover honey
- 1 gallon water
- 3 ounces fresh ginger root, bruised
- 2 large cinnamon sticks, broken
- 1 cup raisins
- Juice and rind of 1 orange
- Juice and rind of 2 lemons
- ½ package yeast

Dissolve the honey in warm water, adding the ginger root (cut up), cinnamon, and raisins. Simmer for an hour, then strain into a separate container, adding enough warm water to replace the amount boiled away. Peel the lemons and orange, squeeze the juice into the container with the gingered water, and add the rinds. Dissolve the yeast in warm water, then add to mead, stirring well. Follow the basic recipe (page 92), allowing mead to age 8 months to a year before use.

Magical Attributes: Sympathy, cordial feelings, affection, health.

Parsley-Sage Success

In Greece and Rome, parsley was a symbol of victory and success, said to grow from the blood of an ancient fallen hero named Archemorus. Sage translates from a term meaning "salvation," because the Virgin Mary was thought to have used this plant for protection.

- 1 quart pineapple sage leaves
- ½ pound parsley
- 1 gallon water
- 1 orange, sliced
- 1 lemon, sliced
- 3 pounds orange blossom honey
- ½ package yeast

Place the herbs in a large crock. Bring the water to a full boil, then pour over the sage and parsley, allowing it to set for a full 24 hours before straining. Reheat the herb water with the sliced fruit and honey for 20 minutes, then allow to cool; strain off the fruit and add the yeast. Follow the basic recipe (page 92).

Magical Attributes: Protection in new endeavors, preserving prosperity and achievements.

☙ *Horilka* ❧

Grapefruit Rum Horilka

In some rural areas of England, the grapefruit is still called "forbidden fruit," one of many to be thought to be the actual fruit of Eden. The tart yellow juice has a cleansing, protective nature. If your grapefruit are particularly sweet, you can reduce the honey accordingly. However, grapefruit does ferment rather well, so use more honey than you might feel necessary. This recipe is from my friend Yukihanna's kitchen.

12 ripe grapefruit	½ package champagne yeast
1 gallon water	1 liter dark rum
4 pounds dark honey	

Peel the grapefruit, carefully removing the white pith from the peels and the fruit itself. Cut up peels from 4 of the fruit and place in a large pot with the sectioned fruit and water. Bring to a low rolling boil for 20 minutes, then cool. Strain the fruit, juicing carefully, then return the liquid to the pan and add honey. Boil again for 15 minutes to clear residue, then follow the basic recipe for mead (page 92). After 3 months of aging, strain the base liquid again, add rum, and additional honey if necessary for sweetness or flavor. Age for a minimum of 6 months.

Continue to monitor the horilka after the alcohol is added. If it continues to ferment, certain precautions must be taken with your bottling techniques. With screw tops, check at weekly intervals to be certain no pressure is building up. After 3 weeks, if there are no signs of fermentation, you can seal securely for aging.

Magical Attributes: Purification, knowledge, health.

Variations: For richer flavor, try adding one can of frozen grapefruit or pineapple juice at the same time as the honey.

Raspberry-Blackberry Horilka

Native American tribes used blackberries mixed with honey as ceremonial food, and honored the raspberry with its own special ceremony. Upon the first harvest, they would ask the spirit of the fruit for help with all endeavors of peace and war.

1	pound fresh raspberries	2	pounds light honey
1	pound fresh blackberries	½	liter raspberry brandy
1	(16-ounce) can frozen raspberry-cranberry juice concentrate	½	liter blackberry brandy
1	gallon water	½	package champagne yeast

This recipe is prepared by the same method as the Grapefruit Rum Horilka, except that you do not strain out the raspberries until just before adding the brandy. The leftover fruit makes an excellent conserve when mixed with shredded coconut and chopped apples, sweetened to taste.

Magical Attributes: Divine help, messages.

Variation: If the price of brandy is prohibitive, try a fruit-flavored vodka in its place.

Strawberry Surprise

The strawberry is sacred to Freya. In a a country custom as recent as 100 years ago, if strawberry pickers passed a church on their way home, three berries were left on the church doorstep as an offering. Strawberries that dropped on the ground were left there for the poor.

1	pound frozen strawberries	1	quart light honey
1	(16-ounce) can strawberry daiquiri juice concentrate	½	package champagne yeast
1	gallon water	1	liter Scotch or whiskey

Prepare this wine using the same methods as the Raspberry-Blackberry Horilka, leaving the fruit in the beverage for the initial fermentation process, then straining, etc. The leftover strawberries are very tasty for tarts and jams if you don't want to throw them out.

Magical Attributes: Kindness, charity, benevolence.

Variations: If you cannot find the juice mentioned in this recipe at your super-market, use at least twice the amount of frozen strawberries to insure full flavor.

Tropical Fantasy

Something about the smell and taste of tropical fruits calls up daydreams of beautiful beaches and long, relaxing winter holidays beneath the sun. Bring a little vacation time into any day with a sip of this beverage!

1 cup papaya, peeled and diced	1 (16-ounce) can frozen tropical juice concentrate
4 kiwi, peeled and sliced	
1 cup drained, cubed pineapple	1 gallon water
1 cup coconut (dried or fresh)	2 pounds honey
1 cup mango, diced and peeled	1 liter rum
3 ripe bananas, sliced	1 package champagne yeast
1 orange, peeled and sliced	

Follow the directions given for Grapefruit Rum Horilka, straining twice, if necessary, since the bananas make a very thick stock. Aging time is 1 year.

Magical Attributes: Respite, luxury, adventures, travel.

Variations: Many tropical fruits are regarded as love enhancers; this drink might make a good aphrodisiac.

What wond'rous life is this I lead!
Ripe apples drop about my head;
The lucious clusters of the vine
Upon my mouth do crush their wine;
The nectarine and curious peach,
Into my hands themselves do reach;
Stumbling on melons, as I pass,
Insnar'd with flow'rs, I fall on grass.
—Andrew Marvell

Apple-Almond Affection

In the biblical book of Genesis, Israel sent almonds as a gift to show friendship and love. Ancient Phrygians considered this tree to be the father of all life, making this nut sacred to Attis and Cybele. In many lands, the apple is believed to insure both fertility and love, in addition to its healthful qualities.

- 1 gallon apple juice or cider
- 2 ounces sliced almonds
- 2 pounds honey
- 1 tablespoon almond extract
- ½ package champagne yeast
- 1 cup almond liqueur
- 1 liter vodka or white rum

Warm the apple juice with the almonds over a low flame for 20 minutes. Add honey, turning up the heat to boil for 15 minutes, skimming as needed. Cool and add almond extract. Add yeast and allow to set in the open air for 24 hours before straining into a fermentation vessel with a balloon or lock. Clarify for 2 months before siphoning off and adding spirits. Age for 1 year.

Magical Attributes: Pleasant relationships, robust life, fondness.

Final Note on Horilka

When you do not have time for a long fermentation process, it is possible to make a horilka that is ready in 24 hours. This method is probably more traditional than those in the foregoing recipes, which I find provides better flavor and body.

In this instance, combine the fruits, spices, fruit juice and water, adding only enough honey to be pleasing to you. Cook over medium heat for 1 hour, then cool. Immediately add the alcoholic beverages, again taste test for sweetness, and bottle. This mixture will not ferment without the addition of yeast, and can be consumed after one day. However, aging takes a lot of the "bite" away.

Chapter Ten

Spirited Punches

This chapter is similar in form to its counterpart in the non-alcoholic section of this book. In this instance, the recipes add spirits to the punches for flavor. Most can be prepared without spirits by substituting some sparkling water, soda pop, fruit juice, or other flavorings appropriate to the recipe.

In all cases, prepare the punches with the reason for the celebration in mind. Use symbolic themes including color, flavor, and garnishes to accentuate magical goals. In spring, consider punches with pastel colorations and accents of early blooming flowers. Come summer, look to fresh fruits available in the market. Fall is definitely cider season, and winter might inspire the use of canned or frozen ingredients.

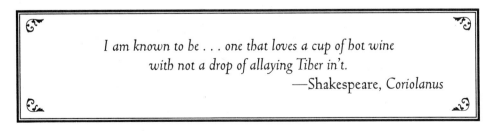

*I am known to be . . . one that loves a cup of hot wine
with not a drop of allaying Tiber in't.*
—Shakespeare, *Coriolanus*

Tea Tot'a-ling

Lemons play an important role in the Jewish Feast of the Tabernacles, when they are brought to the temple so people can enjoy their refreshing fragrance. Tea is a quieter balance to the energy of lemon, offering repose.

½	quart boiling water	¼	cup lemon juice
4	lemon verbena tea bags	4	cups lemon-lime soda
1	cup honey	4	cups vodka

Prepare tea as you usually would, steeping the bags until the water is very dark. Dissolve the honey in the hot tea. Chill. At serving time, combine with lemon juice, soda, and vodka over a bed of ice. Garnish with fresh lemon slices.

Magical Attributes: Paced recuperation, calm adjustment.

Variations: This beverage offers a bounty of options. Match your goal with the flavor of the tea, juice, and soda for an amazing variety of taste and magic!

Ice Cream Passion

The combination of tropical fruit and sherbet makes a powerful vehicle for imagination and flights of fancy, especially in relationships. All the fruits included here have, at some time, been magically associated with love.

1	quart passion fruit juice	1	liter ginger ale
2	cups pineapple pureé	½	liter vodka
1	quart rainbow sherbet	2	cups whole cherries

Mix passion fruit with pineapple pureé until well incorporated. Next, using a hand mixer, beat together the slightly softened sherbet, ginger ale, and vodka. Slowly mix this blend with the juice and pour into your punch bowl. Float cherries on top.

Magical Attributes: Young love, exchange of good feelings, romance, adoration.

Variations: Any "love" fruit or flavor can be substituted. Possibilities include apple, apricot, lemon, peach, pear, plum, and raspberry.

Jumpin' Ginger!

Ginger was one of the nine herbs in the Middle Ages purported to cure plague, and it was heralded by Pythagoras as an antidote for poison.

6	(12-ounce) bottles ginger beer	1	pint ginger liqueur
½	cup honey	2	oranges, sliced thinly
3	cups ginger ale		

Warm the honey until it is dissolved in one bottle of ginger beer. Add ginger ale to this mixture and stir until well blended. Chill the remaining ginger beer and liqueur, pouring this with the honey blend into a medium-sized punch bowl. Float oranges on top. May be served hot, if desired.

Magical Attributes: Improved energy, return to health, fire magic, mental keenness, power.

Variations: To focus the power of this beverage on a specific goal, change the garnishing fruit to reflect those intentions, such as raspberries for love or strawberries for luck. An equal amount of brown sugar may be substituted for the honey.

Hot Orangeade

The orange tree is unique in that it bears leaves, flowers, and fruit all at the same time, making it a symbol of bounty and the triune nature of both Gods and humankind.

1	quart water	½	cup sugar
	Juice of 6 oranges	1	quart rum
1	teaspoon whole cloves	2	whole cinnamon sticks
1	teaspoon whole allspice berries		

Mix the orange juice and water in a 1-gallon-sized pan. Warm over low heat with spices and sugar until a tea-like consistency is reached. Add rum and serve with pieces of cinnamon stick.

Magical Attributes: Balance, fruitfulness, symmetry, abundance.

Variations: For a more purifying beverage, substitute the juice of 4 lemons for the oranges.

Wine and Song

In the late 1600s, sailors landing in India were greeted with this fruity, refreshing concoction. Its potency was deceptive and intoxicating.

½	quart strawberries, hulled	1	cup sugar
3	peaches, sliced	½	gallon sangría
2	cups fresh pineapple, diced	1	bottle champagne

Put both the fruit and sugar in a large bowl, stirring to cover the fruit well, crushing half of the fruit. Let this set for one hour to produce juice. Next add the sangría and champagne (both chilled); serve over ice.

Magical Attributes: Joyful celebrations, cessation of cares and worries, exchange between new companions.

🦉 🦉

Hippocras #1

Use a toothpick to poke holes in the oranges for the cloves. It might be fun to pattern the cloves decoratively, with magical symbols appropriate to your goals. Also known as spiced wine, this version of hippocras was enjoyed by Dutch sailors.

2	oranges, studded with cloves	6	allspice berries
1	cup sugar		Juice of 1 lemon
2	sticks cinnamon	3	bottles sweet red wine

Bake the clove-studded oranges in a 375°F oven about 35 minutes. Then cut each in 4 pieces, placing the pieces in a saucepan with sugar, cinnamon, allspice, and lemon juice. Add the wine and simmer, making sure the sugar dissolves. Pour into a warmed punch bowl, and serve immediately.

Magical Attributes: The deep crimson color of this drink gives it applications for blood mysteries, fire magic, and spells to improve energy and strength.

Variations: Champagne can be substituted for the wine; but only a small amount should be warmed with the spices, then chilled, adding the rest of the champagne at serving time.

🦉 🦉

Hippocras #2

This recipe was popular in the seventeenth century, when various perfumes like musk were often added to improve its aroma.

- 1 quart red wine
- 1½ cups sugar
- 1 teaspoon chili pepper
- 1 large cinnamon stick
- 6 whole cloves
- 1 inch ginger, sliced
- 2 McIntosh apples, peeled and quartered
- 1 tablespoon almond extract
- 1 tablespoon rose water (optional)

Warm the wine to a medium temperature, then pour it into a large bowl with the remaining ingredients, except the extract and rose water. Allow this to set for 1 hour. Strain, add extract and rose water, and serve over ice. Garnish with fresh rose petals, if desired.

Magical Attributes: All the ingredients in this recipe make it an excellent choice for improving friendships and romantic feelings between people.

Mystic Apple Bowl

The apple was not identified as the fruit of Eden until after Milton's epic poem was written. During the time of the Greek Gods, to own an apple tree was to possess supernatural powers. Cinnamon and peppermint enhance this energy.

½	gallon apple juice	3	broken cinnamon sticks
1	cup sugar	3	broken peppermint sticks
2	cups whiskey	2	cups soda water

Heat 2 cups of the apple juice, dissolving the sugar in the juice. Mix this with the rest of the juice and pour into a punch bowl with whiskey and spices. Cover and allow this to set for 30 minutes before chilling, then add soda water and ice just before serving.

Magical Attributes: Occult insight and ability; manifestation of psychic talents.

Old Fashioned Egg Nog

Eggs, one of the oldest symbols of beginnings and reproduction (some even being credited with the birth of gods), make this the perfect beverage for serving at Esotre and other spring festivals.

1	dozen eggs, separated		Dash orange water (optional)
1½	cups sugar	2	pints heavy cream, beaten
1	quart rum		Nutmeg (garnish)
1	quart light cream		

Beat the egg whites until stiff, then set aside. Beat the egg yolks, slowly adding sugar. Pour this mixture into a large saucepan and heat until very warm, but not boiling. Stir in the rum, light cream, and orange water, then pour all into the punch bowl. Fold in the egg whites, then top with whipped cream and a sprinkling of nutmeg.

Magical Attributes: Generation, inception, creative energy, fertility.

Variations: Instead of rum, you might substitute whiskey, brandy, or a combination of all three.

English Ale Bowl

In the Elizabethan era, punches similar to this were thought to encourage free speech among the celebrants, to the point of rumor-mongering!

4 (12-ounce) bottles dark ale
½ cup cognac
4 teaspoons honey

1 orange, peeled
Nutmeg (garnish)

Slowly heat all the ingredients until the honey is well blended, then pour into a warmed punch bowl. Sprinkle the top with nutmeg and a bit of cinnamon, if desired. Makes enough for 8 people.

Magical Attributes: Flowing discourse, free parlay, ease of communications.

Planter's Punch

While the Puritans often balked at beverages such as this as being too potent, variations were a favorite among farmers who found it refreshing during planting and harvesting season.

1½ cups brown sugar
3 teaspoons grenadine
1 cup soda water
1 liter dark rum
1 orange, sliced

½ lime, sliced
1 cup pineapple cubes
3-4 mint leaves
1 maraschino cherry per person

Dissolve brown sugar with grenadine and water in a small punch bowl, then slowly stir in rum, adding an ice cube tray full of crushed ice. Float the fruit slices and mint on top.

Magical Attributes: Completion of projects, fulfillment, following through on aspirations.

Variations: This is a very strong drink, so you may wish to dilute it with a fruity ginger ale, plain soda water, or perhaps pineapple juice.

Bubbling Raspberry Brewpot

In the Philippines, raspberry vines are regarded as very protective. They are often draped near a doorway shortly after a loved one's death, to keep the unsettled ghost from entering.

5 cups fresh raspberries	½ liter raspberry ginger ale
1 liter gin	1 orange, sliced thinly
Juice of 1 orange	Mint leaves (garnish)
5 teaspoons sugar	

Crush 3 cups of the raspberries and place them in the punch bowl. Add gin, the orange juice, and sugar, beating with a wire whisk. Next add ginger ale, floating the remaining raspberries, orange slices, and mint on top. Add ice.

Magical Attributes: Protection, especially from wandering spirits. Boldness in the face of adversity.

Variations: To enhance the raspberry flavor, use raspberry-cranberry juice instead of orange (about ½ cup). Fun to serve with a little dry ice at Samhain!

> *Say how, or when, shall we thy guests,*
> *meet at those lyric feasts made at the Sun,*
> *the Dog, the Triple Tun?*[1]
> *Where we such clusters had, as made us nobly wild*
> *not mad; and yet each verse of thine*
> *out-did the meat, out-did the wine!*
> —Robert Herrick

---

1. A "tun" is a large cask or barrel used as a brewer's fermenting vessel.

Chapter Eleven

Seasonal Brews

*Birth, growth, maturity, and death are but seasons for life
which transform the finite human frame,
yet the learning of spirit is timeless.*
—Marian LoreSinger

All year around, something, somewhere on the earth blossoms, while another falls to seed. This simple cycle is a majestic teacher, if we take the time to watch. It is this subtle movement of the ever-turning wheel, and the symbolism for each season, that this chapter presents. Seasonal significance can vary tremendously, depending on your climate. However, the traditional magical succession has four definitive parts, thus I am writing this in terms of the four seasons.

As the wheel of the year turns steadily on its way, we pause to consider how our holidays and other annual observances can be made more magical and meaningful. In our often-hectic lives, it is sometimes difficult to stop and honor time's passage. The home brews in this chapter reflect seasonal themes, as another option that brings magic into our everyday life.

❧ Spring ❧

Rebirth — The Child

Spring is the dawn of creation. A pale blue light creeps across the horizon to announce a creamy yellow sun. The aroma of fresh rain reaches the window, and a sense of reawakening touches our hearts. This is the time for beverages pertaining to refreshment, fertility, intuitive explorations, and creative work. Commonly associated with the element of air, the energy for growth and vision is abundant, and ready to be poured into each drop of liquid.

Spring Components

- Daisy, pansy, woodruff, dandelion, lilac, and other early blooming flowers.

- Air spices such as almond, anise, hazel, marjoram, pecan, and sage.

- Other flavorings such as maple, citron, lavender, and hops.

- Any beverages which are yellow, pale green, or clear like rain.

- Prepare beverages at dawn, the time of beginnings.

Date-Fig Fertility

The date palm is a tree with two distinct sexes. The Greeks regarded it as a symbol of fertility, and the Israelites often named female children after it, as a symbol of beauty.

2	pounds pitted dates	1	orange, sliced
2	pounds figs	1	lemon, sliced
1	gallon white wine	2	cups sugar (to taste)

Cut up the dates and figs into ½-inch chunks and place them in a large container with the wine. To this, add the orange and lemon slices. Warm the sugar in just a little water to make a syrup, then mix this with the wine-fruit blend. Close tightly and shake daily for 6 weeks before straining and serving.

Magical Attributes: Productivity, child-bearing, resourceful energies.

Flowing Transformation

The number 8 (months) is the number of change. The ingredients here are all aligned with the air element to encourage the winds to bring a refreshing metamorphosis in your situation. Nuts accentuate the symbolism of growth and new beginnings—the seedling.

- 1 liter vodka
- 1 cup maple syrup
- 2 cups pecans, ground
- 2 cups almonds, ground

Warm the vodka and maple syrup, place the nuts in a wide-mouth container (with lid). Pour the warm vodka mixture over the nuts and seal tightly. Leave in a cool, dark place and shake daily for 8 weeks, then strain and enjoy.

Magical Attributes: Personal changes, reversing cycles, modifying habits.

Variations: Replace vodka with 1 liter water, and increase syrup to 3 cups, adding wine yeast as directed in the wine chapter, for a lovely golden beverage with a lower alcohol content.

May Punch

Woodruff is a traditional May decoration. Germans call this lovely white blossom the master of the woods. Its white petals are considered sacred to the Goddess. Magically, woodruff is used to protect against negative energies.

- ½ cup woodruff flowers, freshly picked
- 1 quart warm apple wine or hard cider
- ¼ cup sugar or honey
- ¼ pint water
- 1 orange, sliced
- 1 lemon, sliced
  Stick cinnamon

Allow the woodruff to set in room temperature wine or cider for a half hour, then remove. To this, add sugar and water. Pour into a punch bowl, garnishing with sliced fruit and cinnamon sticks. May be served hot, if desired.

Magical Attributes: Success, safety, relieving a heavy heart.

Variations: Other early blooming, edible flowers such as daisies might be added to the bowl to further encourage vibrant spring energies.

ᘒ Summer ᘓ

Life — The Maiden and Son

Earth is vitally awake now, her senses keen. Every leaf and bud reaches toward a glowing sky as if to praise the sun's return. Summer is the season of fire; a time when the energy of life itself is plentiful. It is a good time to consider cultivating new virtues and enacting fire-related magics. It is also the season for purification and drastic change. The hot solar disk offers the opportunity to burn away the old, so like the phoenix, we can return better than before.

Summer Components

- Rose, marigolds, geranium, hyacinth, nasturtium, violets, and other summer blossoms (check a book on edible flowers before using in a brew).
- Fire herbs such as allspice, basil, bay, clove, dill, fennel, ginger, nutmeg, and peppermint.
- Other flavorings such as cashew nut, lime, orange, pomegranate, pineapple, and walnut.
- Any beverages which are bright red or golden yellow in color.
- Preparing beverages at noon, when the sun is most powerful.

Lammas Tides

Rose, honey, and thyme are all thought to be excellent temptations to persuade the Wee Folk to come for a visit. Since they are active during Lammas, the first harvest festival, the goal is accentuated by apple mead and a little nutmeg for perception.

1 quart apple mead	1 teaspoon nutmeg
1 teaspoon rose water	5 sprigs fresh thyme

Mix the first three ingredients together and chill. Serve in 5 glasses with one sprig of thyme each, on August 1st.

Magical Attributes: Kinship with the Fairy or Devic realms, psychic vision, insight.

Variations: To further improve your sense of inner vision, decorate the glasses with a peppermint leaf, or use one as a breath refresher.

Purification Potion

Anise has been used since the time of Virgil to protect against the evil eye. In medieval Europe, fennel was rubbed on the body to keep mischievous witchcraft away.

2	tablespoons anise	1	quart warm water
2	tablespoons fennel	1	cup sugar
2	inch strip of lemon peel, sliced	1	teaspoon champagne yeast

Place the anise, fennel, and lemon peel in the water and soak for 1 hour. Strain and add sugar to the water, heating until it is dissolved. Suspend the yeast in ¼ cup warm water, and add to lukewarm sugar-water. Bottle and cork loosely, let stand for 10 days. Slowly tighten the cork, then age until clear (about 3 months).

Magical Attributes: Cleansing, turning negativity, safety from malevolent magic.

God Aspect

Nuts have often served as a symbol of male sexuality. An old Phrygian tale recounts how their great God, Attis, was born from an almond nut placed in the heart of the Goddess.

½	cup crushed almonds	1	teaspoon nutmeg
½	cup crushed cashews	1	pint vodka
½	cup crushed hazelnuts	1	pint almond liqueur
1	whole walnut per person		

Combine the nuts, nutmeg, and vodka in a large glass container with a lid, and place in the sunlight for 2 months, shaking daily. Strain. Add almond liqueur and test for sweetness, adding honey if desired. This beverage is quite tasty without the almond liqueur, but the liqueur serves to accent magical aspects and improve flavor.

Magical Attributes: The Huntsman, male virility, Pan, the Horned One.

ᵔᵓ *Fall* ᵔ

Maturity — The Mother and Father

Fall is the harvest of our youthful days. The earth turns on its voyage once more, and grows cooler. Rains fall across the land like a cleansing wave, and slowly trees begin to make the transition from vitality to dormancy. The season is one of fruitfulness; gathering the earth's bounty. It is an excellent time to focus on social activities with family and friends, and to share abundance with those in need.

Fall Components

- Any late-blooming flowers, including squash blossoms.
- Water herbs such as cardamom, chamomile, poppy, mint, and thyme.
- Other flavorings such as berries, apple, avocado, birch, banana, coconut, grape, lemon, peach, pear, and vanilla.
- Preparing beverages at dusk, when the sky fills with the hues of the season.

ᵔᵓ ᵔ

Temperance Tonic

In order of appearance, the ingredients in this recipe have been chosen for their magical associations with restraint, strength, energy, protection, and wisdom.

1 cup coconut juice	2 cups pineapple juice
1 black tea bag	1 pint peach brandy
1 teaspoon ginger	

Warm the coconut juice with the tea bag and ginger, allowing to simmer for 10 minutes. Strain and chill. Add this to the pineapple juice and peach brandy, whipping with a wire whisk until frothy. Serve in chilled glasses with a slice of fresh pineapple as garnish.

Magical Attributes: Moderation, self control, restraint, forbearance.

Harvest Horn

The horn of plenty appears in folklore as an object which unceasingly pours out divine goodness—usually in the form of food or blessings. The magic of this beverage can be accentuated by serving it in a drinking horn instead of a glass.

- 2 cups white grape juice
- 2 cups apple juice
- 1 bottle mixed fruit wine
- 1 orange, sliced
- 1 cup berries (any kind)
- 2 cups ginger ale
- Grape bunches

Mix the juices with the wine, adding orange slices and berries. Allow this to set at room temperature for 30 minutes, then chill. Add ginger ale when pouring into a punch bowl. Garnish the sides of the bowl with grape bunches.

Magical Attributes: Abundance, providence, gathering natural bounty, gratefulness.

Harmonic Draught

Nine is the number of universal law and symmetry. Mint has been honored with such folk names as "heart mint" and "lamb mint" as an indication of its peaceful nature. Greeks and Romans often used mint in baths to help calm tensions. The white flower is added as an emblem of amicable intentions.

- 2 cups boiling water
- ½ cup sugar
- 9 mint leaves
- Lemon slice
- 1 jigger gin

Stir sugar into the boiling water until it is totally dissolved. Steep the mint leaves and lemon for about 10 minutes, then remove and add gin. May also be chilled and served. Garnish with a white flower.

Magical Attributes: Peace, serenity, reconciliation.

Variations: Change the type of flower according to your needs. For example, use a rose to accentuate peace in relationships.

❧ Winter ❧

Death — The Crone and Grandfather

Winter signals a form of death, but it is not one lost in hopelessness. In fact, winter is the time of expectation. Just beneath the surface of the land, seeds and plants rest quietly, knowing the sun will find its way back to them.

Winter is filled with themes of sleep, contemplation, nurturing, economy, and conservation of personal resources, including spiritual ones. It is an excellent season for in-depth meditation and study about one's path.

Winter Components

- Any indoor flowers, or frozen petals such as roses which keep well.
- Earth herbs such as mugwort, magnolia, primrose, tulip.
- Other flavorings such as barley, beet, oats, quince, and rhubarb.
- Any beverages which are white, bluish-white, brown, or black in color.
- Preparing beverages at midnight, when silence and rest fall across the land.

❧ ❧

Visionary Vibrancy

Five is the number for psychic endeavors, combined powerfully with herbs for spiritual awareness, nutmeg and angelica. Onions are thought to produce prophetic dreams, and carrots are said to improve vision.

1 cup boiling water	5 whole nutmeg beads
5 pinches angelica	2 cups onion wine
(about 1 teaspoon)	2 cups carrot wine

Place the angelica and nutmeg in a tea ball to steep in hot water for 15 minutes. Mix with the onion and carrot wines (for recipes, see Chapter 8), which should be chilled and well blended. Serve to 5 people on the 5th day of the week.

Magical Attributes: Psychic awareness, oracles, divination, spiritual insight.

Peaceful Pleasure

Quince insures joy and harmony, especially in relationships. The Greeks sometimes called it the golden apple. Chamomile likewise encourages this tranquility.

3	cups boiling water	2	chamomile tea bags
12	quince, peeled and diced	1	liter brandy

Place the quince and chamomile in the boiling water in a large bowl. Allow to set until cool. Add the liter of brandy and store in an air-tight container for three months. Strain. May be served warm with a cinnamon stick, or chilled over ice.

Magical Attributes: Accord, restfulness, relaxed visits with friends, serenity.

Variations: The flavor of the quince is similar to pear, and can be enhanced by any number of other fruits, such as nectarines, which magically produce a blend of sagacity, peace, and health.

Left-Over Cordial

In older brewing recipes, fruit strainings were used in other wines, meads, and foods. In this way, our ancestors were wont to waste nothing. For the modern magician, this approach represents a chance to live in greater reciprocity with nature.

1	pound leftover fruit	2	cups sugar or honey
1	(12-ounce) can frozen fruit juice concentrate (any flavor)	1	liter vodka

Place leftover fruit and fruit juice (undiluted) in a medium-sized pan to warm. Add sugar or honey and bring to a low boil. Allow this mixture to cool completely, then pour it and the vodka into a wide mouth jar. Cover securely and age for 3 months before straining and serving.

Magical Attributes: Frugality, economy, conservation of resources.

Variations: For those who find this drink a little strong, mix the cordial with equal portions of soda water or ginger ale.

Yule Glogg

A favorite Swedish drink for the holidays, this beverage not only warms the body, but also the spirit of any gathering!

2	cups red wine	⅓	cup white raisins
2	cups brandy	1	teaspoon almond extract
12	whole cloves	1	cup apple juice
2	medium-sized cinnamon sticks	2	cups sugar

Combine all the ingredients except the sugar in a large pan and warm slowly. When the liquid reaches a simmer, but before boiling, light the surface carefully with a match. While it burns, slowly sprinkle in the sugar until expended. Place a cover over the pot to extinguish the flame. Pour the ingredients into a large container to age for 12 weeks before serving; strain and serve hot.

Magical Attributes: Happy celebrations, kinship, joyous parties of old friends and family.

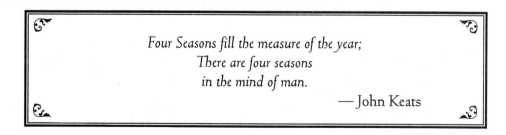

Four Seasons fill the measure of the year;
There are four seasons
in the mind of man.

— John Keats

Chapter Twelve

Tea and Coffee Spirits

After the coffee, things ain't so bad.
—Henry H. Knibbs

To avoid repetition, you may wish to look ahead at the non-alcoholic section on coffee and tea (Chapter 22), where you will find some alternative ideas, both practical and magical, that can be used in addition to the following recipes.

⌁ Coffee ⌁

During the reign of Louis XIV, coffee became the fashionable beverage in aristocratic circles, with elaborate rituals and ceremonies attending its consumption. Even middle-class tables displayed elegant, fine imported porcelainware for serving coffee. Voltaire, a contemporary of the king, was addicted to the drink, consuming as many as 50 cups a day. Modern habits, such as breakfast coffee and after-dinner coffee as a tonic, and in various social settings, are a counterpart of this eighteenth-century custom.

Prosperity Punch

All the spices, nuts, and fruits in this recipe have been chosen for their money-attracting attributes. Oranges were a symbol of prosperity in the Middle Ages, due to their high import cost.

- 2 cups dark rum
- 1 cup coffee-flavored liqueur
- 2 teaspoon sugar
- 1½ quarts orange-flavored coffee
- 2 medium cinnamon sticks
- 4 whole cloves
- ¾ teaspoon nutmeg
- 1 whole almond per person
- 1 orange, sliced

Place rum, liqueur, and sugar together in a large heatproof serving bowl. Light the liquid, using the coffee to extinguish it slowly. Add spices and cool to a comfortable temperature. Place an almond in each cup, and float the orange slices on top.

Magical Attributes: Wealth, abundance, resources.

Variations: Have a little fun with your choice of flavored gourmet coffee in this recipe. For example, if you hope to have an abundance of love, try raspberry.

Coffee Shake for Two

In the tradition of Mohammed, almonds are a symbol of divine hope which can be applied to your relationship, aided by strawberries and chocolate, two wonderful love foods.

- 1½ cups milk
- 1½ cups dark roast coffee
- 1 cup strawberry liqueur
- 1 cup strawberry ice cream
- Whipped cream
- Slivered almonds and chocolate

Place milk, coffee, liqueur, and ice cream in the blender on medium speed and whip until frothy. Garnish with heaping mounds of whipped cream topped with almonds and shaved chocolate. Drink by candlelight!

Magical Attributes: The spirit of true romance.

Variations: For similar magical results, substitute almond ice cream and liqueur for the strawberry.

Coffee Accord

This version of buttered rum is accentuated by mint for reconciliation, catnip to encourage the return of happiness, and lemon for friendship. Coffee functions as the activating energy to promote healing.

4 tablespoons unsalted butter	¼ teaspoon lemon juice
1 cup brown sugar	6 cups hot coffee
½ teaspoon nutmeg	1 teaspoon catnip
¼ teaspoon mint extract	2 cups dark rum

Soften the butter, then mix it thoroughly with sugar, nutmeg, mint, and lemon. Set aside. Brew the coffee, then place a tea ball containing the catnip in the pot. Add the rum. Place 1 tablespoon of the butter mix in each coffee mug, pouring coffee over the mixture and stirring until melted. Garnish with a cinnamon stick.

Magical Attributes: Clearing misunderstandings, truce between people, agreement.

Earth's Winter Wonder

The earth in this recipe is a rich, dark color like fertile soil. This is neatly hidden by a tuft of snow on top (cream and coconut) which protects the sleeping land. This beverage is a good example of how the visual impact of a drink (what it resembles) can be the theme of your magic, rather than the actual ingredients.

2 cups coffee, chilled	1½ ounces dark rum
4½ ounces coffee liqueur	Whipped cream
4½ ounces Irish cream liqueur	Grated coconut

Shake the coffee, liqueurs, and rum together in a large container until well blended. Pour this mixture over shaved ice and garnish with whipped cream and coconut. Serves two.

Magical Attributes: Earth healing or magic, rest, an accent to a winter festival.

Fires of Cleansing

Versions of this beverage are very popular in New Orleans, especially in darkened rooms where it can be exhibited with true flamboyance. Magically speaking, fire is the element of drastic change, purification, and refinement. This beverage is served in a demitasse cup (literally, "small cup"). Yellow, gold, or red cups will accent the magic.

½	pint brandy	1	orange rind, slivered
2	cinnamon sticks	¼	cup curaçao
7	whole cloves	4	cups hot coffee
2	tablespoon sugar		

Heat brandy with cinnamon, cloves, sugar, orange rind, and curaçao until it almost boils. Turn off heat and move to a heatproof serving dish. Carefully light the top of this mixture with a match, allowing it to burn for about 3 minutes before pouring in hot coffee to extinguish. Serve immediately.

Magical Attributes: Purging, total transformation, sun and fire rituals.

South of the Border

A truly Mexican beverage, this drink is dedicated to the southern quarter of the magic circle, which not only represents the sun, but the Devic energy of salamanders—creatures who live and dance in the fires. This is an excellent libation for fire scrying and the power light has to fill any darkness in your life.

½	cup tequila, warmed	Brown sugar to taste
1	cup dark roast coffee	Cinnamon stick (for stirring)

Mix tequila, coffee, and sugar together. Serve with a cinnamon stick, envisioning the element of fire filling your inner wells, sparking creativity.

Magical Attributes: Vision, illumination, divination by fire.

Variations: Consider adding other solar flavors to this beverage: a slice of orange, bay leaf, or a sliver of lime.

Café Exhilaration

Banana is used in this beverage to encourage sexual potency, while vanilla and cinnamon are to improve desire. (See Chapter 18 for more frappé-type recipes.)

3 cups banana-flavored coffee	½ teaspoon cinnamon
1 teaspoon vanilla	1 cup heavy cream
½ ripe banana	5 ice cubes
Sugar to taste	

This is a marvelously easy beverage to prepare. Place all the ingredients in the blender, except for the ice, and whip until thick and frothy. Add the ice, and chop finely so that the consistency is like a frappé. Garnish, if desired, with a cherry!

Magical Attributes: Conception, fertility, sexual pleasure and prowess.

Wishes are Brewing

Ginseng roots, besides being regarded as a tonic, were sometimes carved or tossed into running water to help bring wishes into reality. Dandelion is similarly regarded, its ground roots often acting as a coffee substitute.

4 cups water	½ cup heavy cream
2 tablespoons dark roast coffee grounds	1 egg white
	1 teaspoon vanilla extract
1 teaspoon ground dandelion root	1 tablespoon sugar
½ teaspoon ginseng	

Mix the coffee grounds with the finely-ground dandelion root and the ginseng, then prepare the coffee, using the drip method. While the coffee is brewing, beat the heavy cream and egg white until peaks begin to form. Add extract and sugar. Place a generous portion in each serving cup. Pour the coffee slowly down the side of the cup, allowing some cream to mix with the coffee. The rest will remain on the surface, resembling mountain peaks.

Magical Attributes: Goals and aspirations, hope and fancy.

Variations: To encourage wisdom in your wishful jaunts, fold ¼ peach (peeled and diced finely) into the whipped cream.

ᵔᵔ Tea ᵔᵔ

There is a Chinese tale about how tea came to this country. Daruma, the founder of the Zen sect, retired to meditate in a secluded area. For nine years he prayed, until he unintentionally fell asleep. As he dozed, he began to dream of a beautiful woman who he found attractive. When he awoke from the vision, his longing for her left him deeply ashamed. For that sin, he tore his eyelids off and threw them to the ground. Much to his amazement, and almost in answer to the cry of his heart, the eyelids formed themselves into a tea bush, the leaves of which keep a person awake, even during prayer. Many years later, when Daruma left this world for another existence, his followers honored him by enjoying the leaves of this plant steeped in water (plain tea), drunk from bowls before his image.

Apricot Oracle

The Chinese regard the apricot tree as one of great prophetic power since it was here that Confucius wrote his commentaries. One of the great religious minds of China, Lao-Tse, purportedly born under an apricot tree, was said to be already cognizant at birth.

- 1   cup hot water
- 1   apricot or orange tea bag
- 1   teaspoon apricot jam
- ½   cup apricot brandy
-     Whipped cream (garnish)

Prepare tea as usual, adding the apricot jam while the tea is still very hot to dissolve the jam. Pour in the brandy, then top with a tablespoonful of whipped cream. Sugar may be added for sweetening if desired.

Magical Attributes: Divination, foresight, sagacity, psychic awareness.

Wine Tea

Both wine and tea have a cordial, comfortable appeal. This is a relaxing beverage, perfect for quiet afternoons with friends. In addition, it helps clear the throat during the allergy season.

1	quart strong tea	4	whole cloves
4	tablespoons orange juice	1	slice lemon rind
4	tablespoons sugar	1	pint Sangria
1	stick cinnamon	1	orange, sliced

Heat all ingredients, except the orange slices. Pour into a punch bowl and garnish with oranges. Or, you may chill first, and then serve cold.

Magical Attributes: Kinship, leisurely pursuits, friendly conversation.

Variations: Try dark rum in place of the wine.

Spicy Orange Fitness

The Portuguese believe that the original orange tree that was transplanted from China to Europe, and which birthed all other orange-bearing trees, lives quite hardily today in Lisbon.

2	quarts orange pekoe tea	1	quart mulled mead (page 92)
6	pieces cinnamon stick	1	cup orange juice
6	whole cloves	1	lemon, sliced
½	cup honey (to taste)	1	orange, sliced

Brew the tea and pour it hot into a large container with the cinnamon stick pieces (1-inch piece per cup), cloves, and honey. Warm the mead (recipe, page 92) and orange juice together and add this to the tea blend, mixing thoroughly. Serve hot with a slice of orange and lemon in each cup.

Magical Attributes: Health and well being, vitality, a return of physical balance.

Variations: Try an apple tea with apple juice in this recipe, in place of the orange, for similar tasty magical results.

Rum Maté

Maté is usually prepared with Paraguay tea, which is considered a stimulant and tonic.

- 1 quart boiling water
- ¼ cup maté leaves
- 4 tablespoons honey (optional)
- 2 cups dark rum

To make maté traditionally, pour the boiling water over the leaves in a pot; steep for 15 minutes, then add honey and rum, and serve. The maté leaf is of a goodly size and may be used for tea leaf reading when you get to the bottom of your cup, if you like. Otherwise, strain the tea leaves before adding rum and honey.

Magical Attributes: Return to normal attitudes and manners, improved personal energy.

Variations: Maté is also sometimes flavored with a slice of lemon and kirsch.

Lemon Iced Tea

Lemons appearing in dreams, especially for women, portend good luck in romance and possibly love soon to follow.

- 4 lemon tea bags
- 1 quart boiling water
- 1 cup sugar
- ½ cup orange liqueur
- ½ cup raspberry liqueur
- 2 cups soda water

Steep the tea bags in boiling water for 10 minutes, then dissolve the sugar in the tea (the amount of sugar may be reduced for personal taste). Chill the tea, adding it cold to the liqueurs and soda (both likewise chilled). Pour this over ice, garnished with a lemon wedge. This beverage has a flavor similar to rainbow sherbet.

Magical Attributes: Positive experiences in relationships, especially new romance. Moon magic.

Variations: Try dry champagne in place of soda water on celebratory occasions.

Chapter Thirteen

Spirits for Health

Health alone is the victory. Let all men,
if they can manage it, contrive to be healthy.
—Thomas Carlyle

Using alcohol in medicinal mixtures is nothing new. During the periods of Black Death, typhoid, and other life-threatening infirmities (circa A.D. 1300-1500), alcoholic bases for beverages were used and sold only for medicinal application. These drinks provided relaxation and a momentary flush of heat, regarded as a sign of renewed vitality. Cough syrups and homemade tonics continue to be made from an alcohol base.

Medicine and magic worked hand in hand, sometimes unwittingly. The imagery was abundantly clear to superstitious people (see also, Chapter 3). The spiritual implications of creating healthful drinks are twofold: We can be a primary participant in our own well being, and the process allows us to blend in magical energy, to feed the spirit, soul, and body.

Sniffle Stopper

The remedial value of this beverage can be accentuated magically by working during a waning moon, so the sickness will likewise shrink. This recipe comes from my own "back yard," where I have tried to combine an effective herbal decongestant with other health-ful fruits. This drink helps improve sleep and breathing during cold and flu season.

½	cup warm water	1-2	tablespoons honey
2-3	eucalyptus leaves	1	tablespoon fresh lemon juice
½	cup whiskey		Dash ginger
1	tablespoon fresh orange juice		

Heat the water and eucalyptus until almost boiling. Remove the leaves, add the remaining ingredients, and drink before bedtime.

Magical Attributes: Return to health and well being (more on the physical level than emotional or spiritual).

Whiskey Tea #1

This recipe for relief of coughs and colds is similar to those of Victorian origin. The three mint leaves are used not only for their calming quality, but to represent a return to health for body, mind, and spirit.

1	cup hot black tea	2	teaspoons honey
1	sprig sage	1	teaspoon lemon juice
3	mint leaves	1	shot whiskey

Once the tea is prepared, float the sage and mint in the liquid for about 5 minutes while it cools slightly. Then add honey, lemon, and whiskey. Best if consumed before bedtime.

Magical Attributes: Tea is a lucky plant, associated with money, valor, or vitality.

Variations: Other herbs may be steeped in the tea, (¼ teaspoon each). Recommended for coughs are angelica, anise, bay, fennel, and mullein.

Whiskey Tea #2

Asthma, sometimes caused by allergic reactions, involves lung spasms, which is why early treatments often included vinegar to clear the nose and throat. The other herbs help relax the body and stimulate improved blood flow.

1	tablespoon pennyroyal	
3	whole cloves	
½	teaspoon lavender	
1	teaspoon mullein	

1	cup hot water
2	teaspoons honey
1	teaspoon raspberry vinegar

Steep the pennyroyal, cloves, lavender, and mullein in boiling water for 15 minutes; strain. Dissolve the honey in the mixture; then add the raspberry vinegar.

Magical Attributes: Calming winds, air magic, grounding flights of fancy, the vital breath.

Schnapps Tonic

Most all-purpose tonics are regarded as anything which can improve energy, physical strength, or provide nourishment in order to bring balance back to the body. This recipe combines the traditional tonic herbs in a syrup-like composition. Take a teaspoonful in the morning or at night.

1	pint peppermint schnapps
1	cup honey
½	cup crushed blackberries
¼	teaspoon sage
½	teaspoon yarrow

1	teaspoon chamomile
4	dandelion heads
½	teaspoon catnip leaves
½	teaspoon tansy
3	bay leaves

Warm the schnapps, honey, and blackberries over low heat until the honey is dissolved. Wrap the herbs in a doubled thickness of gauze or cheesecloth, and suspend in the schnapps for 3 months (sealed tightly). Strain before using. If a lighter beverage is desired, mix with equal amounts of water and serve hot.

Blackberry Broth

This recipe is useful for easing restlessness and flatulence. Horehound is one of the five bitter herbs of Passover. It was also used in Europe to cure illnesses thought caused by a magical toxin.

¼	teaspoon angelica root	½	cup hot water
¼	teaspoon dill seed	½	cup warmed blackberry wine
⅛	teaspoon horehound	3-4	whole blackberries
½	teaspoon fennel		

Place the herbs in a tea ball to steep in the hot water for 20 minutes. Add the blackberry wine and a few whole berries as a garnish. Honey may be added for sweetening, if desired. A good beverage to enjoy before bed.

Magical Attributes: Protection from negative magics, purification, atonement.

Variations: If you are not fond of blackberries, try mulberry wine or plum brandy, the fruits of which both have protective connotations.

Ginseng-Angelica Revitalizer

In China, ginseng is used medicinally to reduce tension, improve recuperative powers, and enhance overall mental awareness. It is also used to treat everything from impotence to headaches. Angelica has a similar reputation for easing indigestion, lung problems, PMS, and even allergic reactions. Magically, ginseng is still used by some occultists to improve their talents. The Chinese regarded it as having all the best qualities of earth in concentrated form. Angelica was a popular remedy against enchantment.

1	cup angelica liqueur	½	teaspoon ginseng

A marvelously easy physic to prepare: warm the liqueur with the ginseng and enjoy, or serve over ice during hot weather.

Magical Attributes: Reverse undesired magics, earth magic, mystical pursuits.

Stone Beer

Stone beer, beneficial for intestinal discomfort, was thought to be effective against kidney or gall stones. Birch is a useful tree in that its bark is baked in bread, shaped, smoked, made into wines, used for paper, and carved into canoes. It is said that March is the best month to cut the young branches. Magically, this is the month of success!

1¼	pounds young outer birch bark		1	teaspoon mace
1	gallon water		1	cinnamon stick
2	pounds sugar		⅓	package yeast

Follow the basic directions for beer on page 64. Be sure to strain out the bark and spices.

Magical Attributes: Versatility, adaptability, achievement, mastery.

Cold and Flu Relief

The medieval physician or cunning person might have labeled this a potent "consumption water," naming the beverage after the disease it was expected to alleviate. Take in quantities of 1 or 2 teaspoons, as needed.

1	quart brandy		2	whole cloves
1	cup honey		1	teaspoon sage
½	ounce peppermint leaf		3-4	eucalyptus leaves
2	teaspoons cinnamon			Juice of ½ lemon
½	inch bruised ginger root		½	ounce orange rind

Warm the brandy and honey together until the honey is melted. Add the rest of the herbs and fruit, placing in a closed container for a full 2 weeks, then strain. For colds, eucalyptus is recommended; when severe stomach problems accompany the cold, substitute chamomile, which is gentler.

Magical Attributes: Improved prosperity, centering and calming the nerves.

Beneficent Balm Blend

Arab tales suggest that balm has the ability to make an individual more agreeable and easier to love. Beyond this, it was a favored herb for fevers, headache, and cooking, its minty-lemon scent generally improving sad spirits. Elder is mentioned in medicinal texts from early Egypt, and was most popular for treating throat infections at the turn of the last century. Raspberry brings a soothing effect to blend the lot together. Use this for treating digestion, moodiness, or colds.

1½	quart balm leaves	2	gallons water
1½	quarts elderberries, pressed	4½	pounds sugar
1½	quarts raspberries, pressed	1	package wine yeast

Place the herbs and fruit in the water in a large pan over medium heat. Press the berries frequently to extract as much juice as possible. After about 30 minutes, add sugar, stirring until dissolved. Cook for another 30 minutes. Turn off heat and cool to lukewarm. Strain well. In a small container, mix yeast with ½ cup of warm water, stirring once. Let set for 15 minutes, then add to lukewarm fruit juice. Cover the pan with a towel for 24 hours, then strain again into a loosely covered container. Watch the wine for signs that fermentation is finishing (a decrease in bubbles). Strain once more, then bottle and rack (see also wines in Chapter 14). Age 8 months.

Magical Attributes: Lifting heavy spirits, amiableness, cheerful countenance.

Variations: Some recipes call for a slice of lemon or orange added to this mixture, both of which are tasty and healthful. This beverage may also be made directly from balm, elderberry, and raspberry wine, mixed in equal proportions.

Allergy Formula

Beverages like this were popular among early German settlers in America, especially those who did a lot of hay harvesting, which often left the throat and sinuses raw.

1	quart water	½	cup (real) maple syrup
1	inch ginger root, bruised	¼	cup white vinegar
1	teaspoon anise seed	1	pint ginger liqueur

Warm the water, ginger root, anise, and maple syrup together until fully blended. Remove ginger slices. Combine all ingredients in a glass pitcher. Chill.

Magical Attributes: Cleansing, purification, health, vital energies.

Variations: Instead of using ginger liqueur, for a non-alcoholic alternative substitute 1 pint orange bergamot tea, which is considered quite effective against bronchial discomfort.

Metamorphosis Punch

A version of an ancient Persian beverage considered to be very healthful, this drink gets its magical potency from Greek mythology. Persephone, in a moment of jealous rage, crushed the nymph Minthe under her foot. Pluto, in sadness, transformed her into one of the most favored herbs of history.

5	cups sugar or honey	2	lemons, sliced
1½	liter water	2-3	whole cloves
1	cup wine vinegar	1	pint mint liqueur
3	tablespoons dried mint		

Boil the sugar and water until the sugar is completely dissolved. Add vinegar, mint, clove, and lemons. Simmer for 20 minutes. Strain, mix with liqueur, and chill before serving.

Magical Attributes: Refinement, well-being, love, poise, personal change.

Variations: If vinegar is deleted, this beverage will help settle the stomach, especially if enjoyed after dinner.

Liquor of Life

This recipe is a variation of ones dating from the early 1700s that were thought to assure health and longevity.

5 bay leaves	1 teaspoon chamomile
1 teaspoon cardamom	1 teaspoon anise seed
1 teaspoon angelica	1 inch ginger root, bruised
Rind of one lemon	1 teaspoon nutmeg
1 teaspoon fennel seed	1 cinnamon stick
1 teaspoon licorice	½ teaspoon mace
5 whole cloves	½ teaspoon sage
½ liter brandy	2 cups boiling water

Place the herbs together in a fine cloth bag or large tea ball. Steep the herbs for 30 minutes in the boiling water, remove, and then combine the liquid with the brandy. This mixture was often recommended by the tablespoonful before bed time. Another recommended technique for preparation was to suspend the herbs directly in the brandy for several months, then remove the bag. This yields a slightly stronger flavored beverage.

Magical Attributes: Long life, well being, improved physical energy.

Variations: Whiskey is an appropriate option for a base in this beverage, being used widely for folk remedies. If you wish to make this without alcohol, prepare the herbs like a tea, substituting equal amounts of water for the brandy, or steep the herbs in warm apple juice.

Final Notes on Medicinal Liqueurs

While I have suggested many beverages to treat illness at home, a drink is not a substitute for a doctor. Use caution and common sense with folk remedies, and follow the advice of your physician.

Chapter Fourteen

Wine and Wine Coolers

When they drink this barley wine, they sing and dance!
—Dio, *Athenaeus* 1.61

Of all the chapters in this book, this is my favorite. Wine is a simple pleasure, but a divine one.

As with meads and melomels, the procedure for wine is fairly simple. There are some hints that can help you become increasingly proficient at the art.

First and foremost, use quality ingredients. Once you refine your talents, it stands to reason that better quality components yield more pleasant wines. At first, using less costly ingredients is sensible. Once you get past that point, allow your budget to stretch a bit and you won't be disappointed by the results.

Second, take extra care when straining wines. The more sediments you eliminate, the easier it is to clarify your beverages. When trying to separate clearer wine from its sediment after the first fermentation, either siphon it off or pour very carefully so that the fruit and dead yeast does not enter the new container. This is also a good time to check the flavor and add more sweetener if desired.

Next is care with corking. If you tighten the tops or corks too soon and leave the bottles unattended, they will explode from fermentation pressure buildup. That is why I recommend the use of a balloon secured with a rubber band, or daily "burping," to release some of the carbon dioxide.

The final step is the process called racking, which is somewhat connected to straining. After the second fermentation, bottle the wine in its final containers. Lay these so that they tilt slightly downward toward the neck, keeping the corks damp. In the first month or so, a certain amount of sediment will appear in the bottle. Because of this, many brewers like to pour off the clear wine, rinse the containers, and re-bottle on a regular basis.

If you choose this method, keep one spare bottle of each batch of wine to refill any air spaces left after siphoning and rebottling. As you follow this procedure, the need to rack the wine decreases and your wine will clarify and look and taste more like commercially prepared products.

Basic Wine

Since the procedure for wine making is pretty standard, instead of including a lot of repetitious directions in this chapter, this recipe will serve as a foundation for all those which follow. Any variations distinct to a particular recipe will be noted. All proportions are for 1-gallon yields. Recipes may be halved or doubled.

	Spices to taste	1	tea bag
1	gallon water		Slice of lemon or orange
1-2	pounds fruit	2-3	pounds sugar[1]
1	(12-ounce) can frozen juice	1/3	package wine yeast

If using spices, place these first in the water and simmer for 30 minutes (not in an aluminum pan), until a tea-like liquid is formed. For spicier drinks, leave the herbs in the water, adding fruit, juice, tea bag, lemon and orange slices, and sugar. Hold at a low rolling boil for 15 minutes, then reduce heat for another 15 minutes. Cool to lukewarm. Meanwhile, in a small separate container dissolve the wine yeast in 1/4 cup warm (not hot) water. Let this set for a minimum of 20 minutes to work before stirring it into the cooled juices.

Leave the entire blend in the pan overnight, with a heavy cloth or towel over the top. In the morning, strain the fruit (and herbs if they were left in) out of the juices and let the juices set covered in a warm area for another 24 hours. Strain again and move to a loosely covered glass container for 1 month. As fermentation

---

1. If you taste your wine before the initial stages of fermentation, it will have a very sweet fruit juice flavor. Don't dilute it more just because the sugar content seems high. Sugar is food for the yeast, and the sweetness will diminish with time.

slows, activity in the container will decrease (less bubbles), and you can move the beverage into smaller bottles for racking. Strain or siphon the wine into containers to further clarify it, corking loosely for another 2-3 weeks. If the corks pop out frequently, you know it is too soon for final capping.

All wines should be stored in a dark, cool place. Depending on how dry you like your beverages, 8 months to 3 years aging time produces tasty wines. You will have to experiment to find exactly when you are content with the flavor. At this point, to stop fermentation you may either refrigerate your wine, or bring it to a low rolling boil, then bottle again in air-tight containers. I usually age wine for about 8 months, which yields a sweeter, but not too heavy-bodied beverage.

At first, match ingredients by flavor, such as apples, apple juice, and apple tea. Apples and grapes are two excellent fruits to start with, almost always yielding positive results. Later, once you feel more certain of the procedure, try mixing and matching fruits and juices such as in several of the following recipes.

Magical Attributes: Changes with fruits and herbs used.

Blueberry Repose

Blue is associated with joy and harmony. When we see a blue sky, our hearts rejoice; bluebell flowers are considered lucky, and of course there is the famous "bluebird of happiness."

5	quarts blueberries	1	slice orange
1	gallon water	2½	pounds sugar
1	fruit tea bag	⅓	package yeast

Wash the blueberries thoroughly, then mash them in a large container. In another pan, boil the water; then pour it over the berries and allow to stand for 24 hours. Strain this juice back into your cooking pot, pressing to extract as much of the berry nectar as possible. Follow the basic recipe on page 138, allowing open fermentation for 15 days, then strain thoroughly. Move to a second container with loose corking until liquid is a bright, bluish-red hue, then refine again and bottle for aging.

Magical Attributes: Happiness, peacefulness, contemplation.

Pink Grapefruit-Strawberry Surprise

While strawberries are a traditional love fruit, the light pink color of this wine turns its energy toward matters of friendship and simple pleasures.

4	pink grapefruit (large)	8	cups sugar
1	pound seedless raisins	1	slice lemon
2	quarts fresh strawberries	⅓	package wine yeast
1	black tea bag		

Juice the grapefruit. Place the juice in a large container with raisins and water, then leave overnight in a warm area. Add the strawberries, tea bag, sugar, and lemon, and follow the basic recipe on page 138, except allow cloth-covered fermentation for 6 days before straining off berries and raisins. This will produce a fuller-flavored wine. After first fermentation, allow wine to set for 4 months, then strain and age an additional 6 months before serving.

Magical Attributes: Kinship, leisure, positive attitudes.

Variation: For a wine with cleansing qualities, try 1 pound fresh or canned pineapple in place of the berries.

Happiness Wine

In the East, the orange is an emblem of satisfaction and pleasure. The strawberry is sacred to Freya, the Norse Goddess of love and beauty.

3	quarts strawberries	¼	inch ginger root
3	large seedless oranges	1	gallon water
3	pounds sugar	⅓	package yeast

Hull the strawberries and peel all but one of the oranges. Slice the strawberries and oranges into the brew pot, then follow the basic recipe on page 138. Extra straining may be required.

Magical Attributes: Revitalization, health, happiness.

Variations: Other berries are tasty substitutes for the strawberries here, and as the found bounty of the earth, they offer magical energies for prosperity and joy.

Mulberry Wine

Shakespeare gives us some food for thought when, in A Midsummer's Night's Dream, Thisbe and Pyramus die tragically beneath the mulberry tree. The innocent blood of this couple stained the once-white berries forever purple. The Chinese believe this berry can eliminate the need for food and eventually transform the consumer into a being of light!

1	gallon water	½	lemon, sliced
3	pounds sugar	⅓	package yeast
5	pounds mulberries	1½	inch slice ginger root, bruised

Mash the mulberries and stir them into the water, allow to set overnight. Follow the basic recipe on page 138, allowing open-air fermentation for 1 week, followed by a straining, then another week of open-air working. Pour into glass containers to let set for 3 more weeks, then strain again into final containers. Age 2 years for best flavor.

Magical Attributes: Remembrance, honor, memorials.

Cherry Almond Delight

As early as 8 B.C., herbalists in Assyria were acclaiming the cherry for its wonderful smell and value to health. Magically, cherries, apricots, and almonds are all associated with the energy of love and romance.

1	(12-ounce) can frozen cherry juice	1	orange slice
1	pound pitted cherries	1	tea bag
6	cups apricot nectar	1½	gallons water
2½	tablespoons sugar	⅓	package yeast
½	teaspoon almond extract		

Follow the basic recipe on page 138, allowing a 2-day, open-air fermentation before straining off fruit. Cherries ferment slowly and steadily.

Magical Attributes: Productivity, love magic, sexual equilibrium, harmony.

Variation: Substitute 3 pounds strawberries for the cherries for similar magical results. Strawberries are active fermenters, so watch for excess pressure.

Currant Vitality

This wine turns a beautiful bright red color, reminiscent of life's blood, making it an excellent vehicle to internalize that vital energy.

3½	pounds red currants	3	pounds sugar
1	raspberry tea bag	¼	pound raisins
¼	orange, sliced	⅓	package yeast
1	gallon water		

Place the cleaned currants in a large bucket with the orange slices. Heat half the water to boiling and pour over the berries. While hot, crush the fruit, then leave the mixture to set covered for 2 days. Strain the currant juice and heat, adding the remaining water and sugar. Simmer, stirring constantly until the sugar is dissolved. Follow the basic wine recipe on page 138, allowing 4 days of open-air fermentation. Strain again and bottle, placing 3 raisins in each vessel, then age.

Magical Attributes: Energy, bounty, courage, fire magic.

Variation: Reduce the currants by half and add an equal amount of raspberries for an abundance of love.

Potion of Love

Find deep red apples for this recipe and leave the skins on. All the herbs and fruits have a long-standing association with love. The number of slices of fruit were chosen to represent partnership (2), the union of two people (3), and devotion to the relationship (6).

6	small apples, sliced	1	gallon water
3	cups strawberries	⅛	teaspoon ginger
2	oranges, sliced	⅛	teaspoon cinnamon
2	small slices lemon peel	2½	pounds sugar
3	cups raspberries	⅓	package yeast

Follow the basic recipe on page 138, then remove oranges and lemon peel after the liquid has cooled to lukewarm, and continue as directed.

Magical Attributes: Spirited romance, dedication, fervor, compassion, sagacity.

Plum Passion

In Eastern lands, the plum is an emblem of friendship. It also represents immortality because it is the first tree to show signs of life in spring.

15	large ripe plums		1	strand saffron
1	gallon spring water		1	teaspoon rose water
3	pounds sugar		⅓	package sparkling yeast

Slice and pit the plums, and simmer in the water 30 minutes until the water turns very red. Add the sugar, saffron, and rose water, then follow the basic recipe on page 138. Watch the wine closely. When it begins to get tart, return the entire batch to the stove, adding more plums and sugar until the taste is slightly sweeter than you might like. Age again, and repeat this process 1 more time for an almost liqueur-like wine. At this point, sweeten to personal taste, boil, strain, and rebottle.

Magical Attributes: Long life, kinship, companionship.

Variation: A combination of plum and apple is very refreshing. Magically, the two blend nicely for overall well-being and wisdom in relationships.

> ### Wine Coolers
>
> To make any wine into a "cooler," mix equal portions of wine
> with soda water or ginger ale, and add a few fresh pieces of fruit as
> a garnish. If you prefer a fruitier-flavored cooler, mix 1 part wine
> with 1 part soda and 1 part matching fruit juice.

Finnish Fantasy

In Finland, wines like this one are called Sima. The citrus fruits add precision to magical efforts, and raisins encourage psychic dreams. This wine has a low alcohol content.

2	small lemons	2	cups brown sugar
2	medium oranges	1	gallon water
1	cup raisins	¼	teaspoon yeast

Peel the fruit, setting aside the rind. Remove as much of the white membrane as you can from both the fruit and rind. Slice the lemons and limes into a large bowl with the sugar and cleaned fruit skins. Pour the boiling water over it, allowing to cool to lukewarm. Add yeast as directed in the basic recipe on page 138, allowing open-air fermentation for 24 hours. Finally, place the raisins in the bottoms of the bottles and pour in the liquid, capping tightly. Ferment at room temperature until the raisins move to the top of the bottle, then refrigerate for use.

Magical Attributes: Vision, predictions, oracular power.

Pleasing Peaches

In China, the peach is a symbol of matrimony and longevity. Its blossoms announce the arrival of spring, and peach-handled brooms are used to sweep away undesired magic.

12	large peaches	1	teaspoon vanilla
1	apple tea bag	1	gallon water
1	orange slice	2½	pounds sugar
⅓	package yeast		

Peel the peaches, remove the pits, then slice them into the pot. Follow the basic recipe on page 138. If you find the peach flavor is not strong enough, add some peach nectar for improved taste. Mix this in during the initial cooking process, and strain carefully after open fermentation.

Magical Attributes: Wisdom, discernment, judgment, protection, long life.

Variation: Since this is a very simple recipe, almost any fruit may be substituted to better accentuate your magical goals.

Amendment Wine

This recipe originated in Russia, where orange water symbolizes faithfulness. Almond is used for rejuvenative energy.

1	pound sweet almonds	1	teaspoon cinnamon
1	gallon water	½	ounce orange blossom water
1	pint cherry juice		(optional)
2	pounds sugar	⅓	package yeast
2	teaspoons almond extract		Pinch lemon rind

Finely crush the sweet almonds. Meanwhile, bring half the water to a boil, then pour this over the almonds. Let the nuts soak for 48 hours, then move to the stove and follow basic recipe on page 138.

Magical Attributes: Restoring relationships, reconciliation, forgiveness.

Tropical Temptation

These fruits of warm regions offer a refreshing change from apples and grapes. In Honduran legend, it was the banana leaf which covered Adam and Eve, not fig or apple. Pineapple is the fruit of welcome, and coconut shells figure predominantly in protective magic.

16	ounces pineapple juice	1	gallon water
3	pounds sugar	1	(8-ounce) can Mandarin oranges
⅓	package yeast	1	large ripe banana
2	cups papaya juice	5	kiwi fruit, peeled and diced
2	cups coconut		

Follow the basic recipe on page 138, making sure to boil this beverage before cooling and adding yeast. (Boiling helps to incorporate the different weighted fruit juices.) Shake daily during fermentation and strain well before bottling.

Magical Attributes: Repose, luxurious retreat, safety from the elements.

Here with a loaf of bread, beneath the bough,
a flask of wine, a book of verse
and thou beside me
singing in the wilderness.

—Omar Khayyam

Part Three

The Magical Brew Pot— Recipes for Non-Alcoholic Beverages

Such epithets, like pepper
give zest to what you write,
And if you use them sparely,
they whet the appetite
but if you lay them on too thick
you spoil the matter quite.

—Benjamin H. Hill

Introduction to
Part Three

Non-Alcoholic
Beverages

So shall your wits be fresh to start again.
—Aristophanes

In a world where people are increasingly aware of health and safety, magically prepared, non-alcoholic beverages have an important function. Many people in the metaphysical community choose not to imbibe, feeling that such practices distract from spiritual pursuits. In the mundane world, we hear the term "designated driver" used frequently. This means that we need to find alternative beverages to offer. No matter your personal reason for trying your hand at "normal" beverages, the one thing that will set your efforts apart is the magic you place in each drop.

The following recipes give brief magical associations based on the ingredients, directions, history, and folklore. This information broadens the significance of each component added to your brew. The magic will be more productive because of this understanding. These associations are compiled from common interpretations in three unrelated sources. If you identify the ingredients with something different, follow your inner voice. Let these recipes act like a blank canvass to which you bring intuitive sensitivity and ultimately produce true art.

Tools

Well knows the mystery of that magic tool . . .
—John Pierpont

The best part about non-alcoholic beverages is that they are simpler to make than wines, meads, etc. All the tools needed for this job can usually be found in most home pantries. Besides bottles for storage and ingredients, you need:

- A good set of measuring cups and spoons.

- Mixing bowls; preferably stoneware or pottery.

- A blender or food processor; wire whisks.

- Sharp knife and wooden spoon; if you don't mind, you can certainly use your athame[1] for magical cooking efforts. Wooden spoons aren't essential, but they absorb personal energy better than plastic or metal.

- A strainer, sieve, or cheese cloth; the latter is best when filtering beverages with fine particles.

- Various sized funnels (so they fit in different width bottle necks).

- Non-aluminum pots and pans.[2]

- Freezer-safe pans or glasses for chilled beverages.

The Bluebell is the sweetest flower that waves in summer air
its blossoms have the mightiest power to sooth my spirit's care.

—Emily Bronte

---

1. For those unfamiliar with this term, an athame is the ritual dagger used by many people in magic to draw the lines of energy for sacred space, or as a "pointer" for directing power to a paticular goal.

2. Aluminum has a tendency to leave a funny taste in many fruits which can really ruin your beverages. I suggest seasoned ironware, stoneware, and even crock pots instead.

Chapter Fifteen

Blossoming Beverages

*S*he be fairer than the day, or the flowery meads in May.
—George Wither

In all ages, three groups stand out among the rest as flower fanciers: the ancient Chinese, medieval Europeans, and Victorians. Chinese artisans fashioned transparent cups to highlight the beauty of the beverage within, often flavored by and accented with chrysanthemums. Marco Polo noted in his travels that the Chinese also loved roses, jasmine, and orange blossom; the last two were popular for flavoring and scenting teas.

In the Middle Ages, the nobles adored flowers; with roses most favored over all others. Cookbooks from the period reveal hundreds of uses for roses, including as a base for wines, beer, facial waters, conserves, pottage, meat and poultry flavorings, candies, perfumes, and many other applications to tantalize the imagination. Two examples which list many of these uses are *The Closet Opened* and *Delights for Ladies* (see bibliography).

It should be noted, however, that roses were not the only blossoms to shine upon the medieval table. The alchemists, herbalists, and cunning folk of this period knew every edible bloom, and made practical use of that knowledge.

Moving forward into our own century, the Victorians, being a romantic lot, used a floral language to express their feelings. While a few flowers remained in culinary or medicinal use, flower petals became objects for self-care and pampering. The perfume industry was well established, and pot-pourri and scented water adorned nearly every boudoir.

For the most part, we must search older sources for flower beverages. Herbalists today are reawakening the public to the healthy benefits flowers can provide. Bach's flower essences (basically vitamins) are one good example. These essences draw on the natural nutritive power of petals (roses, for example have more vitamin C than oranges). They may be purchased at many health food stores and cooperatives (see Appendix D).

Black Currant Compassion

Currants get their name from Corinth, Greece, where they were first discovered. In the language of flowers, they mean "your frown will kill me." Raspberry branches have been regarded as protective (due to thorns), while the fruit itself is one of happiness.

1   quart raspberry juice   Sugar to taste
⅓   pound budding black
      currant shoots

Combine the ingredients and simmer for about 20 minutes. Remove from heat and cool. Strain, tasting and adjusting for desired sweetness, then enjoy!

Magical Attributes: Joy, relief from depression, sympathy, charity.

Variation: By adding about 6 cups sugar to this mix after removing the flowers and bringing it to a slow boil until liquid is reduced by half, you can make a tremendous syrup for ice cream, pies, tarts, and even poultry glaze.

Violet Liaison

Both violets and cloves are strongly associated with human passions, thus in this recipe two cloves are used to symbolize a couple. Violets are ruled by Venus, symbolizing enchantment in the language of flowers.

1	lemon, sliced	2	whole cloves
1	orange, sliced	½	cup violet petals, packed
1	quart spring water		

Place all ingredients, except the violet petals, in the simmering pan. Heat the liquid until tepid, but not hot. Add the violets and simmer until they are almost transparent. Strain and serve hot or cold in one glass with two straws.

Magical Attributes: Romance, love, keeping a cool head and warm heart, protection in relationships.

Variation: Try adding two chamomile tea bags to the simmering liquid to bring peace in a home where tensions have discouraged the spirit of romance.

Carnations of Capability

Carnations were the favorite flower of Henry IV of France. Pliny recommended carnations were best picked in July. This may be why one of the folk names for carnation is gillyflower (July-flower).

1	quart hot water	1	cup sugar
2	cups carnation petals		Peel of 1 lemon
½	cup rose petals	2-3	whole cloves
¼	cup lavender	1	stick of cinnamon

Steep carnation petals, roses, and lavender in water for 24 hours. Strain, then rewarm this liquid, adding sugar, lemon peel, cloves, and cinnamon. Simmer for 20 minutes, strain, and serve warm.

Magical Attributes: Skill, expertise, proficiency.

Variation: Substitute lime rind for lemon for competence in matters of love.

Dandelion Delight

This lovely spring tonic makes good use of pesky weeds to rejuvenate the body with Earth's reawakening. Dandelions are high in vitamins, and legends claim that Hecate once entertained Theseus with dandelion water.

3 cups dandelion petals	¼ cup sugar
1 gallon orange juice	Ginger ale (optional)
Juice of 1 lemon	

Clean off the dandelion petals with cool water. In the meantime, warm the orange juice and lemon together, then add dandelions. Make certain you only have petals (no green parts). Add the sugar, stirring constantly until dissolved; strain and chill. To ¾ glass, add ¼ glass of ginger ale for a light, bubbly drink.

Magical Attributes: Divination, wind magic, wishes and goals, communicating with the Spirit world.

Variation: Prepare this recipe with lemonade instead of orange juice, and the juice of one orange instead of a lemon. This has a refreshing, purifying quality and, poured over crushed ice, is wonderful on a hot summer day.

Bouncing Borage

Francis, Lord Bacon wrote that the borage leaf has "excellent spirits" to repress "dusky melancholy and so cure madness." For health, borage is high in both potassium and calcium, and is regarded as one of the four principal flowers among ancient civilizations. Borage is a vibrant blue flower which was revered for its sturdiness. A Latin saying, "Ego Borago, Gaudia semper ago," seems to sum up the spirit of this plant best. Translated, this means "Borage, bring always courage!"

1¼ cups water	1 allspice berry
1 cup mulberry juice	1 tablespoon borage flowers
Pinch vanilla bean	1 teaspoon honey

In a small pan or crock, heat the juice and water to boiling. Pour this over all other ingredients except the honey. Let steep for 15 minutes, strain, and add honey. Enjoy hot or chilled.

Magical Attributes: Energy in abundance, vitality, endurance, spunk.

Variation: Replace vanilla with juice of ¼ lemon, and ¼ orange for allspice, adding a slice of ginger root for energy in love or purification before magic. Borage is thought to aid psychic insight.

Divination Draught

John Gerald felt meadowsweet brought joy to the senses. Marigolds, pansies, and meadowsweet have all been used as components in love divinations. Marigolds follow the sun, lighting the way for psychic insight.

½ quart marigold petals	1 pint water
½ quart pansy flowers	2 slices ginger root
1 ounce meadowsweet	1 pint cherry juice
½ orange, sliced and peeled	Honey to taste

Place all ingredients, except cherry juice and honey, in a large pan, and bring to a low, simmering boil. Allow to simmer until flowers are almost transparent, then cool and strain. Add cherry juice and honey. Best served cold.

Magical Attributes: Psychic abilities, insight, oracles, prophecy.

Variation: For additional oracular power, add a cup of dandelion and a sliced apple for wisdom. Marigolds were once known as calendula (calendar), because they had flowers which blossomed in every month of the year.

Solitary May Bowl

White woodruff blossoms are considered sacred to the Goddess. In pre-Christian times, the bouquet of this flower was used to scent a variety of drinks. In the Middle Ages, woodruff was thought a good tonic for sickness, fever, and to purge the blood.

½	handful fresh woodruff	2	teaspoons sugar
2-3	whole strawberries	1	orange slice
3	cups cider or apple juice		

Rinse the woodruff and strawberries thoroughly. Place all ingredients in a bowl and mix well. To increase the flavor, warm the cider or juice first. Chill the mixture for a minimum of 1 hour before straining and pouring into a large glass to enjoy. Garnish with the berries. A great spring-time refresher!

Magical Attributes: Success, prosperity, protection, especially in "battles."

Variation: For a drink with greater cleansing quality, add a slice of lemon in place of the orange and add 1 to 2 whole cloves.

Honeyed Honeysuckle

In the language of flowers, honeysuckle symbolizes brotherly affection. In the Middle Ages, a syrup of honeysuckle was used to fight fever.

1	gallon grape juice	1	jasmine tea bag
2	cups honeysuckle blossoms	¼	cup honey
1½	cups orange juice		

Simmer all the ingredients in a large pot, warming very slowly over low heat until honey is fully dissolved. If the petals turn translucent before the honey is mixed, remove them and continue warming. Cool to room temperature, remove tea bag, strain, and chill. Shake well before serving.

Magical Attributes: Awareness (especially psychic), good fortune, financial stability, protection of health, friendship.

Variation: Prepared with apple juice instead of grape juice, this beverage is magically appropriate for wisdom in relationships.

Chapter Sixteen

Dessert Drinks

As sweet and musical as bright Apollo's lute,
and a perpetual feast of nectar'd sweets.
                                        —John Milton

I think that there is a little bit of child in all of us. Some of my dearest memories of my father are those when he was either savoring a bit of gourmet candy (especially jelly beans) or baking luscious holiday treats, swearing all the while that he would never bake again. Yet every year we found him in the kitchen, working furiously on some new confection with which to surprise the family. It is this memory, combined with an inherited sweet-tooth, that inspired this chapter.

How often during hot summer months have you longed for a homemade dessert, but hated the idea of turning on the oven or fussing? In the case of dessert beverages, you don't need to worry about either! Instead, with a blender and simple ingredients, you can quite literally "whip up" a little magic with your drinks!

Sparkling Vitamin C

Tea has long been considered not only a social drink, but one which helps calm and relax. By adding the orange juice, noted for its healthful effects, and a little soda for energy "bubbles," this becomes a wonderful magic tonic when you need a pick-me-up.

1	cup orange pekoe or orange spice tea	1	cup ginger ale
1	tablespoon honey	3	strawberries (garnish)
1	cup orange juice	1	orange slice (garnish)

Prepare the tea. While it is still warm, stir in honey to dissolve. Cool, then blend together with orange juice and ginger ale. Serve chilled or over crushed ice with sliced strawberries and orange slice for a bright, invigorating drink.

Magical Attributes: Energy, health, vitality, strength, rejuvenation.

Variations: Change the flavor of this beverage by trying other herbal tea bases. For improved energy for health, for example, use an apple-cinnamon tea.

Orange Joy Juice

Lemons are thought to encourage pure-hearted feelings. In Voodoo traditions, the empty lemon is often used as a magical container or cup. Oranges keep us happy through sound bodies and spirits. In the Orient, oranges are sometimes given as a token of joyful wishes. The best part about this beverage is the simplicity of preparation.

	Juice of 1 orange	1	teaspoon maraschino cherry juice
1	teaspoon sugar	1	cherry (garnish)
1	lemon slice, squeezed		

Pour the ingredients into a glass, swirl with a spoon, and enjoy.

Magical Attributes: Happiness, pleasure, satisfaction.

Variations: Substitute lime for lemon if you feel your happiness is being impeded by negative energies from others. Some traditions use lime twigs to protect from the "evil eye," a common superstition.

Orange-Pineapple Purifier

This drink is an excellent prelude to a ritual fast or bath, both of which have purgative qualities. In the case of the latter, lemon, orange, and pineapple rind might be added to the bath water. The reason these three fruits have been magically linked to cleansing is fairly easy to discern when their juice touches any dirty or sticky area!

5 cups orange juice	1 teaspoon sugar
3 cups pineapple juice	1 vanilla cookie
Juice of 1 lemon slice	Orange whipped cream (garnish)

Pour orange, pineapple, and lemon juices into a large covered container and shake well. For simple purification rites, nothing else should be added. For dessert, however, I recommend a teaspoon of sugar, a gourmet vanilla cookie, and orange-flavored whipped cream as garnish.

Magical Attributes: Cleansing, health, psychic and physical purification, change.

Variations: Lime, guava, and mint can be substituted for lemon, orange, and vanilla. In this case, the mint leaf is used for garnish, the magical effect being much the same.

> *She believed he had been drinking too much of Mr. Weston's good wine.*
> —Jane Austen

Banana Split Spritz

Banana splits bring out the romantic idealist in almost everyone. In India, the banana leaf was an important part of marriage rites. The cherry on top of this creation also encourages love, being ruled by Venus.

- 1 pint ice cream (any flavor)
- 1 cup soda water or ginger ale
- 1 banana, sliced
- 2 teaspoons maraschino cherry juice
- 2 teaspoons topping (any flavor)
- Whipped cream (garnish)
- 1 cherry (garnish)
- Sprinkles (garnish)

Place ice cream and ½ cup soda water in the blender on a low setting. Slowly add the remaining soda water with the other ingredients, then garnish. You may need to add more ginger ale to achieve a texture smooth enough to drink.

Magical Attributes: Love toward self and others, spiritual compassion, courtship and romance.

Variations: Change the ice cream flavor to more directly relate to your magical goals; for instance, Neapolitan to build tolerance among different people, or cookies n' cream to encourage the innocent love of children to be born in your heart.

Raspberry Romance

Pineapple juice is thought to hinder stray passions, while berries in general are "love" foods. In some lands, brides carried lemon flowers as a symbol of purity and tenderness.

- 1 cup fresh raspberries
- 1 cup pineapple juice
- ¼ cup grapefruit juice
- 1 lemon slice

Blend or mash the raspberries until very smooth. Slowly add the other juices and a touch of sugar, if needed, to offset any tartness. Garnish with a slice of lemon.

Magical Attributes: Faithfulness, loyalty, and commitment in relationships.

Variation: For a more erotic drink, substitute passion fruit juice for the pineapple. This mixture is a nice choice to try before conception rites.

Turtle Tenacity

The name of this drink is based on a popular candy, and the symbolism of the turtle is important here. Visualize yourself as a great sea tortoise, slowly but powerfully emerging from your shell while drinking.

- 1 pint butter-toffee ice cream
- 1½ cups milk
- 1 tablespoon hot fudge sauce
- 1 tablespoon hot caramel sauce
- Nuts (garnish)

Soften the ice cream in the light of the sun. Blend the ice cream, milk, and sauces on medium speed until frothy. Garnish with your favorite nuts.

Magical Attributes: Boldness, assertive speech, self-assurance, building confidence.

Variations: The types of nuts placed on top of your drink can enhance more specific magical ends. Use almonds for healing self-images, cashews or peanuts to improve prospects for personal prosperity, coconut to help you feel secure in your path, or walnuts to provide protection from negative thoughts about yourself.

Apple-Grape Guru

An old superstition claims that eating grapes helps encourage prophetic dreams. This, combined with the "healthy" wisdom of apples, should allow you to interpret your visions sagaciously.

- ½ cup grape juice
- ½ cup apple juice
- ½ cup apple yogurt
- 3 crushed ice cubes

Blend all ingredients together until foamy. Serve cold with a slice of apple or grapes as garnish.

Magical Attributes: Dream divination, spiritual insight.

Variations: For peace in a relationship, delete the grape juice, increasing apple to one cup and adding a slice of fresh peeled apple to the mixture, or as a garnish. Apples are ruled by Venus and have long been used in love divinations.

Pina-Colada Imposter

Both pineapple and coconut are associated with protective magic; the coconut because of its strong, resilient shell, and the pineapple because of its prickly, outer shell. Canned coconut cream seems to work best for this beverage, as it is already smooth.

- 1 cup coconut (or coconut milk)
- 1 cup pineapple juice
- 3 teaspoons sugar
- 1 teaspoon rum extract
- Crushed ice

Thoroughly mix coconut milk with unsweetened pineapple juice, sugar, and rum extract. Serve over crushed ice.

Magical Attributes: Protection from falsehood, improved awareness of deceptive images.

Variations: Add a few strawberries to this drink and substitute honey for sugar, to help you remove your rose-colored glasses regarding a romantic partner.

Strawberry-Banana Stimulation

This is an especially nice beverage to try just before conception rites, or for people who are having problems enjoying physical contact. Plain yogurt encourages the spiritual nature while the banana is the male energies and strawberry, female.

- 1 banana
- 1 cup plain yogurt
- 1 cup milk
- 5 strawberries
- 1 teaspoon honey
- Pinch of ginger or cinnamon

Blend together the first five ingredients (spice is optional). Women pour this into a brandy glass, men into a tall, champagne-style one. As you drink, envision the energy moving to "pleasure" centers to help encourage sexual enjoyment.

Magical Attributes: Sexual potency, stamina, fertility, physical pleasure.

Variation: After drinking, nibble on a spearmint leaf to further encourage sexual interest and cleanse the breath for romantic encounters.

Death by Chocolate

Scientific evidence suggests that eating chocolate gives a special sort of pleasure to choco-holics. I'll whip up this drink instead of eating a hot-fudge sundae.

- I   scoop chocolate fudge ice cream
- I   cup chocolate yogurt
- ¼ cup chocolate chips
- I   cup chocolate milk
- Swirl chocolate syrup (garnish)

Place all ingredients except syrup into a blender on low speed for about 2-3 minutes. Add more milk if it is too thick. Beat on medium for another 2 minutes. Pour into a large glass, swirling a little chocolate syrup on top. Enjoy!

Magical Attributes: Self love and pampering, sweet things in life, simple luxuries.

Variations: Thanks to the booming gourmet ice cream business, there are quite a few themes this beverage could reflect. You could try butterscotch with plain milk and melted butterscotch chips for golden sun energy, or perhaps strawberry ingredients all around for joy and love.

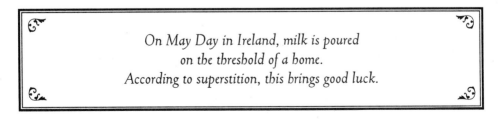

*On May Day in Ireland, milk is poured
on the threshold of a home.
According to superstition, this brings good luck.*

Thanksgiving Day Delight

This drink is based on the traditional cranberry-orange relish so popular at Thanksgiving. This is a marvelously healthful drink with rejuvenating qualities. To maintain the theme of the beverage, before drinking it pour a little on the Earth in thankfulness for the providence of Nature and the Divine. If you are using whole cranberries for this, they must be ground very finely to extract the juice. Otherwise, a frozen concentrate is best.

2	cups cranberry juice	¼	teaspoon cinnamon
2	tablespoons brown sugar	1-2	whole cloves
2	slices ginger root	2	cups orange juice
¼	teaspoon nutmeg		

Warm the cranberry juice just enough to incorporate the brown sugar completely. Add spices and allow to cool. Blend this together with orange juice and 2 ice cubes for a refreshing holiday drink.

Magical Attributes: Joyous gatherings, kinship appreciation, gratitude for blessings.

Variations: Any harvest fruit is a good option here, particularly apples, which will also bring peace and love to your celebration, no matter when it takes place.

The setting sun, and music at the close,
As the last taste of sweets, is sweetest last,
Writ in remembrance more than things long past.
—William Shakespeare

Chapter Seventeen

Joyful Juicing

*F*ill *me with the old, familiar juice.*
—Omar Khayyam

Most of us live in a state of perpetual busyness. Daily duties can leave little time for three square meals a day. This makes easy, healthful beverages very important supplements to our diets. That may be one reason why juicing has become a popular "fad" of the 1990s.

Most fruits and vegetables contain considerable levels of fiber, iron, calcium, potassium, vitamin B and C, and beta carotene, all of which can be beneficial to most diets.[1] These beverages help stave off cravings for candy by supplying our bodies with natural sugars. Thus, juicing can be an integral part of sound weight-loss efforts, with no artificial colors or flavors to hinder revitalization.

You do not have to buy a special juicer for this project. A good blender or food processor and straining equipment will do. The major advantage of juicers is that they are set up specifically for extraction and make your job a lot easier, but a good one can also be costly.

---

1. Beta carotene can reduce chances of lung cancer, and also helps to destroy certain harmful substances which can weaken cell structures. Most of us are already aware of the positive effects vitamin C has on the immune system. Finally, potassium helps restore electrolytes to the body and decreases instances of high blood pressure.

Because the process of juicing is basically the same for most fruits or vegetables, I am going to give general directions here to avoid repetition throughout the chapter. Special instructions will be given as necessary. In addition, each recipe includes basic nutritional information.

General Directions

First, clean the ingredients with warm water. If possible, buy organically grown fruits and vegetables to eliminate the ingestion of pesticides. Remove all leaves, seeds, rinds, and bruised parts before putting the components into your blender/juicer. With the exception of potatoes, fruits and vegetables are usually juiced raw to obtain the highest amount of nutrients. Then all that remains is pulping the ingredients thoroughly.

If you do not want chunky drinks, use a good sieve and strain off only the juice. To recycle the left-over pulp, put it in an equal portion of hot water and bring to a low rolling boil. Boil for one hour and strain again. This juice will not be as high in vitamins or flavor as the first extraction. Be sure to refrigerate any unused portions. The remaining pulp can be composted.[2]

---

2. Before starting a compost heap, be sure to check your local ordinances. Some areas have very strict rules to protect against insect or rodent infestation, especially in densely populated, urban districts.

Cranteloupe Enchantment

Melons and strawberries are strongly associated with love, being round, juicy fruits. This energy is balanced by the Mars energy in cranberries for protection, and orange for purity.

½ pound cranberries	½ orange
1 pint strawberries	Honey to taste
½ cantaloupe	

Follow general directions given on page 166.

Magical Attributes: Well-balanced relationships with others or the self. Proper motivations for long-term commitments.

Nutritional Value: Rich in vitamin C, beta carotene, potassium, and fiber. An excellent choice to help clean out the urinary tract.

Variations: Black or red raspberries can be substituted for strawberries in this recipe to improve happiness.

※ ※

Carrot Keen

Remember the old saying that eating carrots will improve eyesight? Take advantage of this on a spiritual level by internalizing the beneficial qualities.

3 large carrots, scrubbed	2 cups cabbage, diced
3 stalks celery	1 teaspoon thyme
6 radishes	

Follow general directions on page 166, taking extra care in scrubbing your carrots. Fresh thyme, if available, is preferred and best added into the cup after straining.

Magical Attributes: Psychic awareness and insight.

Nutritional Value: High quantities of beta carotene. Fair amounts of sodium, potassium, vitamin C, and calcium.

Variations: Substitute caraway for thyme and parsley for radishes. This potion can help improve sexual desire, fertility, and possibly cure impotence.

※ ※

Lemon-Lime Zinger

Anyone who has used lemon or lime juice and water for cleaning knows first-hand what a terrific cleanser they make. Lemon juice is often used to help purge magical tools of unwanted energies, while lime is considered an effective protection against negative magics.

6	lemons	1	pound sugar or honey
6	limes	2	quarts water

Peel the lemons and limes. Remove and discard the white pith from the peels of 3 lemons and limes. Place the peels in a large pot, covered with 1 quart boiling water and allow to set and infuse like a tea for 10 minutes. Meanwhile, juice all the lemons and limes, adding the remainder of the water, sugar, and the juice from the peels. Taste and add sweetening if desired, then serve over ice.

Magical Attributes: Purification, cleansing, and protection.

Nutritional Value: Lots of vitamin C, potassium, low levels of beta carotene. Consumed hot with honey, this makes an excellent cold tonic.

Variations: For a fruity flair, add the juice of 6 raspberries and 6 strawberries to each glass, or simply float the fruit on top. Another refreshing alternative is to add two whole mint leaves to the rind tea to infuse. The first blend is good for improving joy in a relationship, while the latter can help rejuvenate sexual interest.

Glorious Grape Juice

Sacred to both Bacchus and Dionysus, the grape was a favored symbol of fertility in ancient Rome. Because of their use in wine making, grapes are also associated with celebrations and momentous occasions.

Preparing homemade grape juice is slightly different than other juicing processes described in this book. 1½ pounds of grapes yields about 1 cup of juice.

Begin by washing the grapes (preferably seedless) in warm water. The grapes should be well ripened but still firm. Place in a pan and crush with the flat of a wooden spoon. Cook over very low heat until the the mixture steams. Do not boil. Cool the mixture in a glass container for 24 hours, then strain off the sediment. Reheat the juice and pour into open bottles, which have been scalded with boiling water. Seal the jars and process according to standard canning directions. When sealed properly, this juice will last almost indefinitely. Upon serving, you may find it is too thick or sweet for your taste. At this point, dilute the juice according to personal preference, using spring water, or for more zest, a bit of soda water.

Magical Attributes: Successful end to a project, a welcome windfall, conception, productivity.

Nutritional Value: Beta carotene, iron, potassium, and low levels of vitamin C.

Variations: For a cleansing beverage, to a glass of shaved ice add the juice of ½ lemon, ½ orange, 2 teaspoons pineapple nectar, 1½ ounce grape syrup, and soda water. Decorate with a fresh lemon slice.

Fruit Salad

Apricots had their origins in Asia where they were known as "sun eggs" because of their rich golden color. This magically allows them to become an active energy source for your beverage, on which the symbolism of the other fruits is conveyed like bright beams of sunlight through your body.

2	peaches	1	banana
½	cup apricots	1	cup skim milk or seltzer water
2	kiwi fruit	1	cup vanilla yogurt
½	cup strawberries	1	whole cherry (garnish)
½	cup raspberries		

Juice all the fruits (except the cherry for garnish), then add the liquid to the milk and yogurt, garnishing with the cherry.

Magical Attributes: Abundance of energy, joy, productivity, and love. A good celebratory beverage.

Nutritional Value: A bevy of good vitamins and minerals, a terrific pick-me-up!

Variations: Almost any fruit you enjoy can be added to this blend. Try grapes to enhance the festival spirit or passion fruit for harmony.

Elixir of Health

Because of its spiny exterior and cutting flavor, pineapple is regarded as a shielding fruit. Cucumber peels have long been recommended by folk healers to relieve headaches and the decorative sprig of parsley on our plates dates back to a Roman superstition that it keeps food safe from contamination. Watercress should be refrigerated immediately and used within a day or two of picking due to perishability. It has a slightly peppery flavor, so if you are not a pepper lover, eliminate this ingredient.

1 cup pineapple juice	Watercress (optional)
½ cup cucumber, peeled and seeded	Crushed ice
1 sprig parsley	

Follow general directions on page 166.

Magical Attributes: General well being, physical fitness, and protection of one's vitality.

Nutritional Value: Rich in vitamin C. Good levels of calcium, iron, potassium, and beta carotene. An excellent choice for those watching cholesterol counts.

Variation: A whole, peeled apple may be added to this mixture. The metaphysical effect here is for positive efforts and energy toward magical wholeness.

Prophetic Punch

The scent of roses is thought to encourage prophetic dreams. In the language of flowers, the dandelion means "oracle." Garlic is to purify the visions, and the green vegetables are for growing awareness.

1 cup water or vegetable juice	1 cup romaine lettuce
1 cup dandelion flowers	1 medium onion
2 cups spinach	1 teaspoon rose water or
1 clove garlic	½ cup rose petals, diced

Follow general directions on page 166. Keep rose water or petals out of juicing process. Instead, add them at the end, either by stirring in or floating on top for a garnish.

Magical Attributes: Foresight, divination, oracles, psychic awareness.

Nutritional Value: Large quantities of vitamin C, iron, and calcium. Some potassium, vitamin B, and beta carotene. Garlic contains a natural antibiotic.

Variations: Use red cabbage instead of lettuce, and a tomato in place of the onion. Magically this is to improve one's fortune in matters of the heart.

Fire Festival

The traditional herbs, plants, and colors of fire combine in this drink to quite literally spark your creative source from the inside out! An appropriate beverage for Beltane and many summer observances.

2 large tomatoes	1 teaspoon lime juice
2 cloves garlic	1 teaspoon hot sauce
2 red peppers, hot or bell	Rosemary (garnish)
1 cup red cabbage, chopped	

Follow general directions on page 166. Increase or decrease the hot sauce according to your tolerance. Place a fresh sprig of rosemary in each glass.

Magical Attributes: Fire magic, drastic change, the energy of the phoenix, purification.

Nutritional Value: A good purgative and blood tonic, high in vitamin C. Also some potassium and calcium.

Variations: Fire-related ingredients not listed in this recipe, but which work well for juicing, include carrot, celery, basil, bay leaf, dill, leek, and a dash of curry blended together.

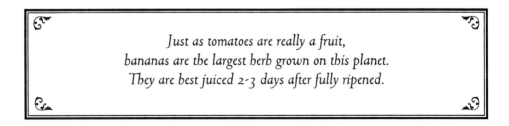

*Just as tomatoes are really a fruit,
bananas are the largest herb grown on this planet.
They are best juiced 2-3 days after fully ripened.*

Green Prosperity

Asparagus was thought to be one of Julius Caesar's favorite foods, contributing to his strength, and celery was used in Rome to prevent hang-overs. In this case, the color of this beverage is a rich green to help encourage growth or improved finances. Visualize your needs while you drink.

1	cup broccoli, diced	2	stalks celery
4	Brussels sprouts	3	scallions
1	sprig parsley	1	cup asparagus
1	cup tomato juice		Salt and pepper to taste
	or 2 whole tomatoes		

Follow general directions on page 166.

Magical Attributes: Abundance, good fortune, success.

Nutritional Value: High amounts of fiber, vitamins C and B. This is a good mix of minerals, most notably iron.

Variations: For prosperity which more specifically pertains to money matters, add a cup of alfalfa sprouts to the mixture.

Let us have wine and women, mirth and laughter,
sermons and soda-water the day after.
—Lord Byron

Chapter Eighteen

Soda Pop, Malteds, and Frappés

With headed bubbles winking at the rim.
—John Keats

One hundred years ago, malted milk shakes and soda pop were dispensed by the glassful, often by the local pharmacist. Soda pop was even prescribed for health problems. Once known as sweet water or fizz water, soda pop has become one of the largest beverage industries in the United States.

Charles Hires, an early producer of soda water, established mail-order sales of homemade beverage kits. Mr. Hires carefully selected 18 ingredients, including roots and herbs, and packaged them with directions for the frugal housewife. The package sold for 25 cents, and made five gallons of root beer. The Hires Root Beer company was established, and other products followed.

People continue to enjoy soda pop, malteds, and other "fountain" drinks. We consume in soft drinks (and related beverages) annually more than we do water.

MODERN BREWER'S NOTE: As of 1991, per capita consumption of soft drinks in the United States was estimated at 48 gallons and rising. By comparison, the per capita consumption of tap water was only 34.1 gallons, and 23.1 gallons of beer. —J.D.

～ Soda Pop ～

Older formulas for soda pop call for forced carbonation or the addition of yeast. Yeast produces an average alcohol content of about 1 percent, which is not acceptable if one is allergic to alcohol. Today, home-brewed soda pop can be much simpler. The basic formula is carbonated water, sweetener, and flavoring. Sweeteners may be adjusted to suit dietary needs, including substituting honey or artificial sweetener for sugar.

General Directions

Make a syrup of the sweetening agent so it will mix well with room-temperature soda water. The proportions are the same for honey or sugar; 2 cups sweetener to 1 cup water, brought to a low rolling boil, then cooled and refrigerated. Then, you can make soda pop by the glass using about 1½ cups carbonated water and 1-2 teaspoons syrup plus fruit, vegetable, or flower essences and extracts. Choose flavorings made by juicing (see the previous section), or those available in the supermarket.

If you don't like the taste of plain soda water, try ginger ale instead. This makes a zestier drink. Also, add the sweetener slowly. Sugars tends to activate the carbonation, to the point where your glass may froth over. The following recipes are examples of creative soda pops to try at home.

> The name soda "pop" quite literally developed
> because of the distinctive sound made by bottles when opened.
> Also, many recipes included sodium bicarbonate, e.g., soda!

Sparkling Mental Might

Eating grapes is believed to improve concentration and mental faculties. The aroma of mint is also supposed to aid these types of efforts.

1 teaspoon grape extract	Sweetener to taste
⅓ teaspoon mint extract	Mint leaf (garnish)
1 cup carbonated water	

Follow the general directions on page 174.

Magical Attributes: The conscious mind, matters of study, education, logic.

Variation: If available, spearmint is the most highly recommended member of the mint family for this recipe.

Blooming Symmetry

All the flowers chosen for this recipe are strongly associated with the energy of agreement and compatibility. This might be a good ritual beverage to mark the acceptance of a new member into a study group or coven.

1 small bundle lilac petals	1 teaspoon violet petals, chopped
1 white rose (no leaves or green parts)	2 teaspoons pennyroyal
2 teaspoons lavender	1½ cups carbonated water
	Sweetener to taste

For this recipe, infuse a floral essence by simmering the cleaned flower petals in a cup of water until their coloration is all but gone. Cool the mixture and add enough to the carbonated water so that your soda has the lovely bouquet of fresh blossoms. Sweeten to taste, and enjoy.

Magical Attributes: Harmony, accord, and peace, especially among families or groups.

Variations: Mint tends to have a calming effect on the human nervous system. An alternative to the flowers in this recipe is to use a cup of warmed apple juice with a fresh sprig of mint.

Sugared Ginger

Ginger is said to accentuate energy toward specific goals. This beverage also tends to set-tle the stomach, allowing you to focus on your magical rites. If you can not obtain gin-ger at a supermarket or an Asian market, try health food cooperatives. Chewing a bit of this makes for a great breath freshener.

1 cup room-temperature carbonated soda	1 lemon balm leaf
2 pieces candied ginger root	Dash of cinnamon (optional)

Follow the general directions on page 174, except place this mixture in an air-tight container for about an hour before serving over ice for best flavor. If time is short, use some sweetener and ginger extract instead.

Magical Attributes: Sweet success, victory, positive culmination of efforts.

Variation: For success, specifically in areas of personal aspirations, add about 2 tablespoons pomegranate juice to this mixture.

⊸ ⊱

Cola Colada

Since coconut is associated with both protection and chastity, when combined with com-mon "love" flavorings, it is a perfect beverage to use in engagement or handfasting rites. While this beverage lacks the caramel coloring of most cola drinks, "cola" really gets most of its flavoring from vanilla and lemon, and not the cola bean, which is produced by an African tree. The extract from cola beans is also sometimes used for a tonic.

⅛ teaspoon lemon extract	⅛ teaspoon vanilla extract
⅛ teaspoon coconut extract	Juice of 1 slice of lime
Juice of 1 slice sweet orange	Dash of nutmeg
1½ cups carbonated water	Sweetener to taste

Follow the general directions on page 174, taste-testing for personal preference.

Magical Attributes: Fidelity, devotion, and integrity, especially in relationships.

Variation: For friendship, float a bit of sweetpea or a passion flower on top.

⊸ ⊱

Malteds

The rich, bubbly taste of a chocolate malted is something truly remarkable on a hot summer day. The first question to come to most readers' minds is exactly what *is* a malted made with? Malt extract, of course. Malt extract is available in both powder and syrup. It is a staple of the baking industry and may be available wherever baking supplies can be found.

A scoop of ice cream can be added to any one of these for a thicker, richer beverage, or for health, add some plain yogurt.

Oriental Rose

Oranges played an integral role in offerings to the Gods of the east, where they were thought to provide joy and abundance to all who receive the oranges. Rose water helps promote health, thus allowing your pleasures to be balanced with judgment.

- 1 orange, sliced and seeded (no pith)
- 1 tablespoon malt extract
- 1 teaspoon sugar or honey
- 4 ounces skim milk
- 4 ounces orange soda
- 2 tablespoons rose water

Process the ingredients together in a blender, first on low speed to dice the orange finely. Then turn to high until an orange-white foam forms on top. Serve over crushed ice.

Magical Attributes: Steady happiness, constancy of good feelings, and physical health.

Variations: This beverage may be warmed over a low flame and served with a cinnamon stick to help settle the stomach and calm nerves. If rose water is not available, use fresh flower petals as a garnish instead.

Chocolate-Covered Cherries

In eastern traditions, the cherry tree is associated with amorous pursuits, and chocolate is a food which inspires passion in most people I know (if only for the chocolate itself!).

8 ounces cherry soda	1 tablespoon chocolate syrup
1 teaspoon cherry extract	1 tablespoon malt extract
Dash cinnamon	Cherries (garnish)

Place ingredients together in a blender and whip until frothy. Pour into a glass, sprinkling cinnamon on top and decorating with fresh cherries.

Magical Attributes: Sweet, romantic love. Please use two straws!

Variations: For orange and mint lovers, either of these extracts can be substituted for cherry in this recipe for similar magical effects. Mint, however, is a little less romantic and a bit more "lusty."

Very Berry

When properly prepared, this malted has a lovely violet hue, the color most commonly associated with spiritual pursuits and metaphysical learning.

3 whole strawberries	6 blueberries
6 raspberries	10 blackberries
1 teaspoon sugar	1 tablespoon malt extract
6 ounces skim milk	2 ounces soda water

Rinse the fruit thoroughly, then blend all ingredients until frothy. Serve as is, or over ice. Sundae sauces can be used in place of fresh fruit; about ½ teaspoon of each is adequate.

Variations: Float a fresh violet on top of this drink to further accent the magical energies. These flowers are often grown in the home to promote sacred pursuits. Also, try adding a scoop of raspberry sherbet.

Malted Milk

Milk, the first source of food for all humankind, has always been sacred to the Goddess. In her Mother aspects, She teaches us about nurturing ourselves and others, healing, and self-awareness. Slice the apple horizontally so the pentagram design of the seeds shows.

- 1 teaspoon vanilla syrup
  or ¼ teaspoon extract
  and ½ teaspoon sugar
- 2 tablespoons heavy cream

- 1 tablespoon malt extract
- 8 ounces milk
- 1 apple slice (garnish)

This is also excellent with vanilla ice cream. Garnish with the apple slice over the rim of the glass.

Magical Attributes: Goddess energy, maternity.

Variation: Substitute chocolate and mint flavorings for vanilla to magically refresh romance.

Toffee Coffee

Coffee beans originally were made into wine in some African nations. It was not until nearly A.D. 1000 that Arabs began making the hot beverage we know today. The stimulating result quickly became popular and also gave us its natural magical associations.

- 8 ounces milk
- 2 tablespoons heavy cream
- ¼ teaspoon vanilla extract
- 1 tablespoon sugar

- 1 teaspoon instant coffee, dissolved
  in 1 teaspoon water
- ¼ teaspoon butterscotch
  flavoring

Beat the heavy cream to the soft peak stage and spoon into a large glass. Separately, blend the other ingredients until bubbly, then pour over the cream. This may also be prepared warm.

Magical Attributes: Energy, vigor, initiative, stamina.

Variation: Try substituting an herb-spice apple tea bag infused in ¼ cup water in place of the vanilla.

⁓ Frappés ⁓

Frappés are semi-frozen drinks served in iced cups. Usually, frappés are made from fruit juices or flavored waters and sweetener, which are blended, then frozen to a snow-like consistency. To quote modern commercials, with this beverage "the thrill is the chill!" Frappés are light enough that they can be served before a meal, or can be prepared as dessert. If desired, small amounts of liquor can be used for toppings, but this impedes proper freezing.

General Directions

In the following recipes, except where noted, use the following basic directions. As was the case with soda pop, it is best to use a sweetener in syrup form to mix evenly with the juice(s). Combine the syrup with hot juice and flavor with any additional ingredients desired. *Add these components slowly, taste testing for personal preference.* Cool and pour into a shallow pan for freezing. Stir this occasionally so the liquid freezes evenly.

When the entire batch has frozen to the soft-crystal stage, remove it from the pan and crush it with the flat side of a wooden spoon. Then fluff with a fork in the same manner you would beat an egg. The beverage can be placed in a tall, chilled glass at this point and garnished with fruit, flavored whipped cream, some sundae syrup, or whatever seems appropriate.

Mellow Yellow

Yellow is associated with the energy of inventiveness and the air element, allowing our dreams to take flight. Bananas are for fertility of efforts, and lemon for clarity in goals. The star fruit is a wonderful addition here, already bearing the shape of the magical pentagram.

	Juice of 4 lemons	¾	cup sugar syrup
1	teaspoon vanilla	1	egg, beaten
2	scoops lemon sherbet	2	bananas, mashed
1	cup heavy cream	1	star fruit, sliced (garnish)

Place lemon juice, vanilla, and sherbet in a pan to warm. Meanwhile, beat cream until fluffy. Slowly mix this with the warm liquid adding sugar and the egg. Freeze to snow stage, then combine the frozen crushed beverage with the bananas in the blender. Pour from the blender into glasses decorated with star fruit. Serves two.

Magical Attributes: Divination, prophesy, creativity, and any air-related magic.

Variations: For air magic, garnish with a paper fan or umbrella instead of fruit.

Honey Licor-Ice

Bees were considered messengers of the Gods. When their byproduct, honey, is combined with licorice, which is believed to relieve hunger, the message sent to the universe is for immediate aid during times of severity.

2	tablespoons licorice extract	2	tablespoons honey (or to taste)
3	cups hot water	2	licorice twists (garnish)

Warm the extract, water, and honey together until honey is dissolved. Add more honey or extract to taste. Follow the general directions on page 180 for freezing and serving. Place one licorice twist in each glass before filling.

Magical Association: Providence, especially with regard to essentials.

Variation: Try a little mint with this recipe to help refresh your outlook.

Pineapple Passion for 2

Just the name passion fruit, elicits certain expectations. Pineapple is the balancing point to this recipe, allowing our desires to be centered on one special individual. This is a nice love potion to serve at weddings or anniversary parties.

1½	cups pineapple juice	2	teaspoons sweetener syrup
1½	cups passion fruit juice	1	teaspoon vanilla extract
½	cup crushed pineapple		Dash cinnamon

Follow the general directions on page 180.

Magical Attributes: Desire, affection, romantic passion toward one person.

Variations: For even more sensual vigor, try using blackberry or mango juice instead of the pineapple.

Fall Frolic

This is a wonderful autumn beverage, which is also good warm, by the way. It tastes of the traditional flavors of fall and is especially nice for Thanksgiving gatherings.

6	cups hot apple juice		Dash nutmeg
2	tablespoons maple syrup		Dash ginger
2	teaspoons honey	2-3	whole cloves
2	bay leaves	2-3	whole allspice
½	stick cinnamon		Juice of 1 orange

Mix the syrup and honey with the apple juice until dissolved. Add spices and allow to infuse like a tea until cool. Strain off whole spices, adding orange juice, and freeze. Finish by following the general directions on page 180. Possible garnishes include rum sauce, a slice of apple or orange, or a little sweet cream.

Magical Attributes: Any fall-related festival, the harvest of labors, outcomes and results.

Variation: Peach juice, sacred to many Chinese deities, may be substituted for apple in this recipe for magical energy to help bring wishes into reality.

Chapter Nineteen

Mellow Meads, Soft Beers, and Wines

Observe when Mother Earth is dry, she drinks the droppings of the sky.
—Tom Moore

Soft wines and beers now appear frequently on our supermarket shelves. How can we recreate these substances at home, adding our own magical vision?

To be honest, it is not always easy. The fermentation process will give your beverage a distinctive flavor, along with an alcohol content. What I'm presenting herein is the closest substitute I could devise through research at home, without the advantage of professional equipment. While the results are pleasant, don't expect them to taste exactly like modern mead, beer, and wine or you will be disappointed.

~ Mead ~

I made an interesting discovery while researching recipes for non-alcoholic mead. Right up through the 1920s, mead was not considered an alcoholic beverage! This is probably because mead was made in a very thick consistency, with more than the necessary amount of honey, fermented only a short time, then drawn off and mixed with juice or carbonated water.

The ratio given in a turn-of-the-century cookbook for the second option was 2 ounces mead to 12 ounces additive. The original preparation was a 1:5 or 1:2 proportion of honey to water. This would yield a beverage with a root beer-like head, and only the very slightest percentage of alcohol.[1]

In the interest of pleasing the purist, I have provided recipes for straight, fruited, or spiced meads without using yeast. This eliminates the need to wait for the beverage to age; however, a little aging (about three weeks) to clarify and rack[2] does improve the flavor. This, combined with careful taste-testing during preparation, is the key to success. Since there is no yeast to eat up the honey, if you make it too sweet, that is the way it will stay unless diluted or infused with juice.

Also, since there is no alcohol to act as a preservative, I do not suggest making any more mead than you will consume in a three- to four-week period. Honey, fruits, and flowers have the capacity to carry wild yeast that can slowly activate and begin fermenting. The other half of this picture is mead gone bad, mold and all. Keep the finished meads in a cool storage space, in air-tight containers, for best results.

---

1. My best estimate on this percentage is based on the idea that most meads were not allowed to ferment much more than three weeks before being consumed. The reason for this is threefold. First, it was an important beverage for many tables. Second, most people could not afford to store large quantities for extended periods. Finally, there was always the risk of contamination in long aging processes. Either way, I assume that this produced, when mixed with a dilutant, a beverage with less than .25% alcohol per glass.

2. Definitions for this can be found in the glossary. Briefly, however, clarifying can be done by letting the beverage sit long enough for the sediment to settle in the bottom of the jar. The clear fluid is then "racked" off (drained) carefully from the top into a fresh bottle. A bit of cheesecloth over a funnel can aid this process.

Basic Recipe

Most nations consider honey a "heavenly" substance because of its many uses in cooking, brewing, and medicine. By partaking of it, we can internalize a bit of that divine energy and allow it to be revitalized within us. This recipe will act as a foundation for the others given in this section. The process is the same, with the exception of the addition of fruits and spices, or minor other variations as noted in each.

1 gallon water	Juice of 1 lemon
½-1 pound honey	Juice of 1 orange

Bring the water to a low, rolling boil in a pan which is NOT aluminum. Stainless steel or stoneware is recommended. Slowly add the honey, allowing it to fully mingle with the water. Taste periodically until a pleasing level of sweetness and honey flavor is achieved. Add fruit juices and bring the mixture to a full boil.

Scum from the honey will start to rise. It is very important that you skim this off until it all but disappears from the top of the pot. Doing this will help your mead to be clearer and less heavy in body. Finally, cool the mixture completely and place in sterilized bottles with secure tops for storage.

The mead can be served hot with a cinnamon stick, or cold over crushed ice with a slice of lemon or orange to refresh the flavor.

Magical Attributes: The God-self within, divine inspiration, sacred visions.

Variations: As mentioned earlier, mead can take on a wide variety of forms, when combined with fruit and/or spices. The options for this beverage are as wide as your imagination. Some samples follow in this section.

Ginger-Rose Mead

Ginger and roses are often combined in Middle Eastern recipes, especially those of Egypt and Asia. These items appeared on altars as offerings and incense to help commune with the gods. Both are considered "love" foods.

- 3 ounces ginger root, bruised
- 1 quart rose petals
- 1 gallon basic recipe

Ginger root and rose petals should be added to the basic recipe (page 185) after honey has been dissolved. Turn off the heat under the pan so the rose scent is not damaged by too high a temperature. Allow both ginger and roses to infuse until flower petals turn translucent.

Magical Attributes: Success in relationships, especially those which are intimate or spiritual.

Variations: For peace and success in the workplace, use white roses (the color of truce) and add a few drops of pecan extract (a nut associated with employment). For a non-flower option, replace rose petals with 1 pound fresh strawberries to retain loving connotations.

Tangerine-Berry

Tangerines, because of their zesty flavor and bright, sunny color, have been associated with protection in Asia and often adorn Buddhist shrines.

- 1 pound strawberries
- 1 pound tangerine fruit, seeded
- 1 gallon basic recipe

Bring the berries and tangerine fruit to a boil with the rest of the basic recipe (page 185). After cooling, strain once before bottling.

Magical Attributes: Safeguarding the sanctity of close relationships. Reaffirming love.

Variations: To protect the accord or serenity of any situation, substitute passion fruit juice for the strawberries in this recipe. You will need one (12-ounce) can frozen concentrate.

Grapple Mead

Here we have combined a cyder-like apple beverage popular in Europe and this recipe, similar to an ancient wine from Egypt, known as "Pyment," for a truly international drink, to encourage a one-world perspective.

1 gallon apple cider	Basic recipe with alterations
Juice of 1½ pounds grapes	given below

Follow the basic recipe on page 185, except replace the gallon of water with cider. Use seedless grapes which have been crushed to extract the greatest amount of juice.

Magical Attributes: Offerings for peace among people. In a group setting, this should be shared from a communal cup.

Variations: Choose the grapes according to your goals. White can be for harmony and purity, or purple for spiritual insight.

Herbal Harmony

Lavender and mint are employed here to promote happiness and harmony. The next two components are for healing. Angelica will aid in dispersing negativity, lemon in building friendships, and sage in increasing wisdom.

¼	cup dried French lavender	3	leaves fresh mint
3-4	allspice beads	¼	teaspoon thyme
¼	teaspoon angelica root	½	lemon rind
¼	teaspoon sage	1	gallon basic recipe

Follow the basic recipe on page 185, adding herbs after the boiling process to create a tea. Lemon rind may require the use of additional sweetener.

Magical Attributes: Accord, agreement, unity.

Variations: For discernment, add a cup of freshly diced peaches to the mixture. If this is going to be consumed in a group setting, add to the pot one allspice bead or mint leaf for each person. Their desire to become unified will literally be cooked right into the brew! In this case, lavender is an optional ingredient also.

ᵜ Beer ᵍ

In actuality, these are "small" beers, in that a minute amount of alcohol content is created in the production. To compensate, prepare your batches slightly stronger than desired, boil them, then serve with a little seltzer water to achieve "fizz."

> MODERN BREWER'S NOTE: To totally eliminate the alcohol, heat the beer to between 180°F and 200°F, and hold for 10 to 15 minutes. Alcohol boils at about 173°F, so it will qickly evaporate. Higher temperatures can give the beer a "cooked" taste. Heating also drives off the carbon dioxide which forms the "head" on beer. —J.D.

These beverages should not be stored for more than 4-6 weeks if you want to keep the alcohol content at a minimum. To alleviate this problem, after the first brief fermentation period, keep the bottles in a refrigerator. This will inhibit the yeast, while extending the shelf life to about six months.

A good way to test beers and wines is to use one bottle with a screw top that is specifically for taste testing. Don't touch this at all for three days, then check for effervescence. If it's not carbonated enough, let it set 3 more days. By then, it should achieve a frothy head when poured into a chilled glass.

Maple Beer

A nice, simple recipe. The maple leaf, having three distinct sections, is representative of the three-fold nature of both God and humankind. Each aspect is bound together in a smooth stream (the syrup) that gives attention to the whole person to encourage balance.

4	gallons water	2	cups hops
1	quart maple syrup	1	package active yeast

Bring the water, syrup, and hops to a low rolling boil and hold there for about 20 minutes. Strain and allow to cool before adding suspended yeast. Set for another 24 hours, strain again, then bottle. It will be ready in one week. See Alcoholic Beverages section (page 64) for information about varieties of hops.

Magical Attributes: Tapping inner wells, centering, peaceful transitions.

Variations: Add berries to this to help encourage self-love and bring well-being.

Birch Beer

The birch is regarded as the queen of the woods, under whose boughs protection from evil or ill luck could be found. Frequently, birch branches have become the base for a witch's broom.

¼ pound black birch bark	3 quarts boiling water
1 quart boiling water	3 pints sugar syrup
½ ounce hops	1 ounce active yeast
⅛ pound ginger root, bruised	5 gallons water

Boil the bark separately in 1 quart water until liquid reduces by half, then strain and boil the remaining liquid rapidly until it is very thick. Meanwhile, simmer the hops and ginger in 3 quarts water. As it boils, add the sugar syrup and the bark extract. Add another 5 gallons of water to the entire mix, and cool to luke-warm (about 100°F). Add the yeast, previously suspended for 15 minutes in warm water. Let this set, covered with a clean, dry cloth, for 3 days. Strain into bottles and cork, storing in a cool area for another 3-5 days before drinking. See Alcoholic Beverages section (page 64) for information about varieties of hops.

Magical Attributes: Rituals for Thor, protection from unseemly weather, Earth and tree magic.

Variations: Another item under Thor's domain is the hazelnut. Adding a few drops of hazelnut extract to this beverage will increase its potency.

Spruce Beer

For this recipe, I have fallen back on the colloquialism, "spruce things up." This originated because the branches of a spruce tree were so dense as to be useful in cleaning, especially sweeping. The only difference here is that we are using the metaphor for improvements or a clean-up in metaphysical terms.

5 gallons water	3 quarts molasses
⅛ pound hops	½ package active dry yeast
½ cup ginger root, bruised	
1 pound fresh spruce needle tips (rinsed), or spruce extract	

Place the hops, ginger root, spruce twigs, and water in a large pot. Cook at a low rolling boil for about 45 minutes, then strain. Slowly stir the molasses into the warm filtered liquid until it is well blended. Cool to lukewarm, then add yeast suspended in warm water. This needs to set for 48 hours before a second straining; secure with caps or corks in glass bottles. Age for 5 days, then enjoy.

Magical Attributes: Getting things in shape, finishing touches, embellishment.

Variations: To further accentuate the spiritual aspects of this potion, add 3 cinnamon sticks, one each to represent your body, mind, and soul.

Dandelion-Mint Beer

Oliver Wendell Holmes said that "these flowers leapt from the kindling sun's fire, and they did so with a bounty as any spring lawn will show." In the language of flowers, they are symbolic of ancient oracles. They are high in vitamins B and C.

6-10 whole fresh mint leaves	4 cups fresh dandelion flowers
½ cup hop flowers	½ lemon, diced
1 mint tea bag	1 pound sugar
1 gallon water	¼ package active yeast

Boil all ingredients except sugar and yeast for 25 minutes, then strain. Add sugar immediately thereafter, stirring in suspended yeast when liquid cools. Follow the method in other recipes in this section for bottling. See Alcoholic Beverages section (page 64) for information about varieties of hops.

Magical Attributes: Growing awareness, improved clarity of psychic gifts, vision, foresight.

Variations: A whole orange or 1 cup pomegranate juice can be added to increase its effectiveness for divinatory work. To eliminate the dandelions, add two peeled, sliced citrons in their place for similar magical applications.

᠗ Wines ᠖

Wines, like beer, can not be properly prepared without some amount of fermentation. Since wine, by definition, is fermented fruit juice, somehow the effect in taste just wouldn't be the same. Because of this, I have employed a similar method in preparing wines as those which are used for home-made soda pop. As with the beers, you can eliminate any alcohol content by heating the mixture to between 180°F and 200°F for a short period, then rejuvenate the bubbles with carbonated water. Also, one part soda to one part soft wine makes an effective non-alcoholic wine cooler where the bubbles help carry your magic to the surface!

Basic Recipe

1	tablespoon extract or flavoring	¾	cups sugar
9	cups juice	¹⁄₁₆	teaspoon yeast

Heat the juice(s) in a large kettle until lukewarm. Dissolve the sugar, feeling free to add more if you want a sweeter wine. Likewise, dissolve the yeast and add any flavorings. It is a good idea to test the beverage now for full-bodied flavor, adding more extract, if needed.

Move the wine into clean glass bottles and either cap (like pop), cork, or secure with a screw top. Keep the bottles in a warm (not hot) area for about 4 days. Open one carefully to see if it is bubbly enough for your tastes. If not, allow to sit about 2 days more. When wine is ready, store in the refrigerator to inhibit further fermentation (and possible explosion of the bottles due to pressure). Makes 6 (12-ounce) bottles.

Below is a sample recipe for you to try.

Grape Ape Wine

Grapes are a celebratory fruit. This concept, combined with the fact that bananas often adorned Hindu temples during marriages, makes this a good choice for the communal cup at handfastings or vow renewals.

36	ounces each white and purple grape juice	2	tablespoons banana extract

Follow basic recipe directions, using the above ingredients.

Magical Attributes: Commitment, adoration, freely given love.

Variations: For a more passionate approach, eliminate purple grape juice, adding instead an equal amount of strawberry-kiwi juice.

Chapter Twenty

Seasonal Beverages

The poetry of Earth is never dead.
—John Keats

In the interest of not repeating the information given in Chapter 11, I suggest you skim that chapter first to see which recipes might be reused for non-spirituous drinks. For example, any apple mead or wine may be replaced with apple juice or cider. Also consider how the non-alcoholic meads and wines can fit comfortably into a seasonal role. In this scenario, apple mead or fall mead are terrific for autumn observances, being filled to overflowing with harvest's bounty.

Depending on your viewpoint, summer drinks should be hot to honor the sun, or cold to bring down your body temperature. Conversely, winter beverages might be frosty to honor the cold hush falling across the earth, or warm, giving strength to the sun who sleeps. I couldn't find a preference so, in the tradition of a true peacemaker, both hot and cold beverages are included for all seasons!

Also, since each season has a central theme, the beverages in that section pertain, in some manner, to that focus. The magical application is the "title" of the beverage in this instance, instead of a separate listing.

⤳ Spring ⤳

As early blossoms grace gardens, woods, and lawns, consider the magics you can work with the element of air. Spring is a time of movement and transformation for the earth and for our spirits, and the winds also carry those changes. Look to the land for the colors of newness, daybreak, and unfolding revitalization. In your wine cellar, check for beverages created for fecundity, productivity, creativity, and new beginnings. Fertility does not only pertain to the personal reproductive process. Apply it to any project where you need resourcefulness, or perhaps the dawning of fresh ideas.

Clover and Daisy Tea

The daisy is a flower which represents youthful innocence and wishes. Clover enhances this with a bit of luck and the power of protection to keep our goals plausible.

- 1   teaspoon dried clover flowers
- 1   teaspoon daisy petals
- 1   cup hot water

Honey to taste
1   daisy bud with leaf (garnish)

Place the petals in a gauze wrap or tea ball and steep in the hot water for 15 minutes. Remove and sweeten with honey. The daisy bud should be snipped so that it barely appears over the edge of your cup, like a young spring sprout.

Magical Attributes: Beginnings, inceptions.

Variations: A stick of cinnamon can replace the daisy garnish in this recipe for successful energies.

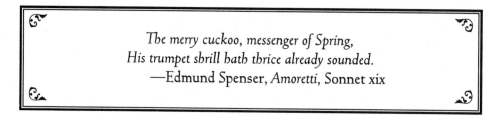

The merry cuckoo, messenger of Spring,
His trumpet shrill hath thrice already sounded.
—Edmund Spenser, *Amoretti,* Sonnet xix

Pansy and Borage Bounty

Borage has often been thought to sooth melancholy after long, arduous winters. Pansy is known by the folk name "heart's ease" and is considered beneficial to restore one's wits. This beverage is full of healthful minerals, including calcium.

- 1 handful each, pansy and borage flowers
- 4 cups water, warm

Juice of 1 lemon
Sugar to taste

Leave the pansy and borage flowers in warm water for 12 hours to infuse. Strain, adding lemon juice and sugar. Garnish with a slice of lemon or fresh, cheerful petals.

Magical Attributes: Refreshment.

Variation: To specifically promote physical strength and health, delete flowers and add 2 tea bags each of apple and orange to this recipe.

Fertility

In this recipe, I have used the banana to represent masculine energy, the peach for feminine, the milk for maternity, almond for love, and a little vanilla to aid desire. Fertility does not always have to pertain to conception of a child. It can, instead, be the growth of ideas, productivity of labors, etc.

- 1 banana
- 1 cup milk
- 1 teaspoon almond extract

- 1 teaspoon vanilla extract
- 1 peach, peeled and diced
- 2 tablespoons heavy cream

Dice the banana and place it in a blender with the milk, flavorings, and peach. Mix this until frothy. Meanwhile, using a hand mixer or wire whisk, beat the heavy cream until thick. Pour the juice into a tall glass, one inch at a time, alternating with layers of cream until topped off.

Variation: At present this drink may be consumed by either sex. You can, however, change the beverage slightly by eliminating the banana for a woman and adding avocado instead. For a man, delete the peach and add a mint leaf.

In the Pink

Pomegranate encourages fertile ideas while both ginger and cinnamon add energy for achievement. The carbonated soda is for effervescence.

2   cups pomegranate seeds, juiced
1   cup ginger ale or soda
     Dash ginger
     Dash cinnamon
1   lemon balm leaf (garnish)

Juice the pomegranate seeds by placing them in a bowl and pressing with the back of a spoon. Strain this off, adding it to the ginger ale with the spices sprinkled on top and the leaf perched on the edge of your serving glass.

Magical Attributes: Creativity, inventiveness.

Variations: For spontaneity in love, try passion fruit juice or raspberry juice, instead of pomegranate.

Glorious Greenery

The pale green color of this beverage looks much like the healthy first blades of grass in spring. It is a color which, along with the mint, promotes consistent, but paced, maturing.

¾   cup white grape juice
     Juice of 1 lime
1-2 drops green food coloring
     Sugar to taste
8   seedless green grapes
1   peppermint leaf (garnish)

Mix grape juice, lime juice, and food coloring together. Add sugar to taste. Chill and serve in a tall glass to show off the green grapes. Garnish with mint leaf.

Magical Attributes: Growth.

Variations: In the summer use red fruits and coloring, such as cherries or strawberries. For spiritual growth, move to purple grape juice and grapes—the color of metaphysical pursuits.

❧ Summer ❧

Roses have come into their full glory, along with a plethora of other wonderful flowers, many of which can add their aroma to your brews. Hot and dynamic herbs mingle powerfully with these or other fire-related fruits and berries for truly energetic results. Consider the symbolism of the sun in all your creative projects and check your supplies for libations that accent the mind, masculinity, strength, intense cleansing, and personal vitality.

Summer Sunset

While berries are generally considered a love food, we have to love ourselves before we can really incorporate new qualities into our lives. The orange is for a healthy outlook.

8 whole strawberries	1 cup raspberries
2 cups orange juice	1 cup crushed ice

Place all ingredients together in a blender, adding more ice if you desire a thicker beverage. Sweetening is not usually needed.

Magical Attributes: New virtues.

Variation: Garnish this drink with a carnation, symbolizing pride in your progress.

Purification Pottage

The herbs for this tea were chosen for their cleansing effect on both the body and psyche.

To a teapot of hot water add 1 teaspoon each of the following: anise, bay leaf, chamomile, fennel, lavender, lemon juice, peppermint, rosemary, and thyme. Steep for 15 minutes, then serve piping hot before meditation.

Variation: To increase the effect of this tea specifically for divination efforts, add a slice of orange and a bit of onion to the stew. This tastes like a weak soup.

Patriot Punch

In the language of flowers, nasturtium means patriotism, so a bit of creative coloring will encourage energy which supports your native land.

1	dozen white nasturtiums	2	pounds sugar
6	rose geranium leaves	1	quart apple juice
2	limes	½	quart ginger ale
	Red rose geranium petals	½	cup blueberries

Make a paste from the nasturtium petals and sugar. To this, add the juice of one lime. Meanwhile, warm the geranium leaves with the apple juice, cool and strain. Slowly blend this juice with the nasturtium and ginger ale. Garnish with a thinly sliced lime, rose geranium petals, and blueberries for a red, white, and blue day!

Variation: If you live outside the United States, you can substitute, in equal measures, different fruits, sodas, or colorings to match the hues of your national flag.

Papaya Power

This drink suggests the sun in splendor, with yellow rays beneath and bright red in the center. In the West Indies, papaya is known as the medicine tree, and is rich in vitamin A. Raw egg, either the white or yolk, should only be used if the beverage will be consumed immediately. Whipped cream may be substituted for beaten egg white.

1	cup papaya juice	1	egg white, beaten
1	cup milk	4	strawberries, crushed
1	teaspoon sugar	2	tablespoons honey

Blend the juice, milk, and sugar; pour into glasses. Beat the egg white to a stiff peak stage and place a scoop on each glass (or substitute a scoop of whipped cream). Top with a spoonful of strawberries sweetened with honey.

Magical Attributes: Energy.

Variation: Add a dash of cinnamon to this beverage to increase its potency.

ᵇ *Fall* ᶜ

While flowers are slowly giving way to the chill in the air, late harvest fruits are abundant. Apples especially make a fine choice for brewing during these months, accented by the last berries and citrus fruits. Fall's theme is one of balance; abundance measured against frugality, social activities, and care for one's health. Enjoy aged beverages filled with the energy of symmetry, well being, and kinship.

Charity Cooler

Pineapple is a symbol of welcome and warmth, basil is added for compassion. Tarragon is for calm nurturing, and walnut is to improve mental keenness to recognize needs.

- 1 large glass pineapple juice
  Dash tarragon

- 1 teaspoon walnut extract
  Sprig of basil (garnish)

Pour pineapple juice mixed with tarragon and extract over ice. Garnish with basil.
Variation: For empathy, specifically in love, add a few fresh berries to this drink.

Matters of the Heart

In the language of flowers, jonquil means the return of affection, while lavender speaks of appreciation and response.

- 1 cup dried jonquil petals
- ½ cup dried French lavender

- 2 cups warm water
  Sugar to taste

Infuse the petals with warm water for 12 hours, preferably during a waxing to full moon. Strain and sweeten. Serve over ice with a fresh flower to bring hope.

Variation: For a special, memorable occasion, garnish with a fresh sprig of rosemary. Substitute a love fruit such as strawberries, cherries, or oranges in place of the flowers. This creates a hot fruit juice tincture high in vitamins.

Fall Harvest

Most of the fruits chosen for this drink are connected with financial prosperity; however, the energy can be put toward other areas of your life in which some opulence is needed, like creativity.

Juice of 1 cup currants
Juice of 1 cup blackberries
Juice of 1 orange
2 cups apple juice

Juice of 1 cup cherries
1 tablespoon honey
1 small bunch grapes (garnish)

Place all juices and the honey into a blender and mix at high speed until bubbly. Serve in a glass with the grapes as garnish.

Magical Attributes: Abundance.

Variations: Citron or pomegranate juice may be added this drink specifically to aid in energy toward the arts.

Sweet Health

While many people think of rosemary only in terms of remembrance, in the Middle Ages it was lauded as having many restorative qualities for health. The high content of vitamin C in oranges aids this feature.

1 cup orange juice
1 tablespoon rosemary
1 teaspoon vanilla

2 tablespoons whipped cream
1 orange slice (garnish)

Make a tea of the orange juice, rosemary, and vanilla, then strain. Serve slightly warm with 1 tablespoon whipped cream blended in, and one on top for garnish, with a slice of fresh orange.

Variation: This is also good cold, served over chipped ice, with a mint leaf for extra energy.

Winter

The bounty of earth has now moved indoors with dried flowers and herbs. The scents of the holidays linger strongly in the air, with aromas of baked bread, hearty meals, and traditional favorites. Winter continues and accentuates fall's thrifty focus, adding its own tenor of rest and gestation. In the wine cellar, look for beverages that accentuate personal insight, economy, contemplation, and peacefulness.

The Toddy

The apple juice brings wisdom, balanced against the lemon's cleansing clarity. The hot beverage is symbolically immersed in snow, with the cherry on the top to help improve personal focus and balance. Visualize this in the middle of your gravity center.

- 1 cup apple juice
- 1 teaspoon lemon juice
- 1 teaspoon honey
- Cinnamon stick
- 1 cherry
- 1 beaten egg white

Warm the apple juice to the point of almost boiling, then stir in the lemon juice and honey with the cinnamon stick. Spoon egg white over the top of the drink (or substitute whipped cream) with a cherry in the middle (sundae style).

Magical Attributes: Contemplation, rest.

Variation: Eliminate the egg and add a dash of ginger, ¼ teaspoon rosemary, and a shot of whiskey (optional) for a terrific winter cough remedy.

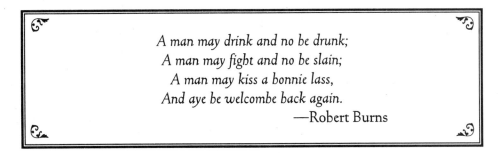

A man may drink and no be drunk;
A man may fight and no be slain;
A man may kiss a bonnie lass,
And aye be welcombe back again.
—Robert Burns

Winter Hope

Persimmon is the fruit of hope, while the other components of this beverage give it a bright yellow color to remind us of warmer days.

- 1 cup white grape juice
- 1 cup persimmon juice
- 1 cup pineapple juice
- 2 cups ginger ale, room temperature

Warm the juices together over low heat. Add this to the ginger ale. Garnish with a fresh flower to remind you of spring.

Variation: For improved outlooks, specifically for finances, add cinnamon and ginger. While this beverage is served warm to bring comfort within, it may also be chilled, if you prefer.

Coconut of Nurturing

For this recipe I have chosen ingredients and variations which are often associated with the Mother aspect of the Goddess to encourage energy for personal development or the growth of parental instincts.

- 1 coconut, fresh
- 1 cup milk
- 1 cup water
- 1 cup fresh coconut meat

Open a hole in the coconut and pour the milk into a non-aluminum pan. Add the other ingredients. Simmer over very low heat for one hour, strain, and enjoy.

Variation: A vanilla bean or sliced and blanched almonds can be added to the beverage as it cooks for richer flavor and similar magical results.

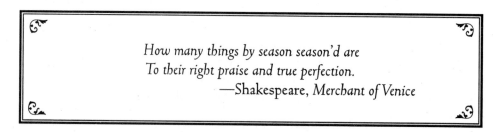

How many things by season season'd are
To their right praise and true perfection.
—Shakespeare, *Merchant of Venice*

Chapter Twenty-one

Pagan Party Punches

Nature never did betray the heart that loved her.
—William Wordsworth

On the many occasions when Pagans, Wiccans, or friends and family gather—be it a ritual, reunion, or festival—magical punches would make a wonderful accent. Match the theme of the beverage to the season, the occasion, or a specific need in the group. Since these beverages can be served from one cauldron, like a communal cup, they link everyone in unity of purpose.

Party punches also are a perfect opportunity for creativity. There are hundreds of ingredients on the market that can replace any of the components in these recipes. One of my favorite twists is to substitute raspberry ginger ale for plain ginger ale, magically bringing joy and abundance. The flavor is subtle, but exhilarating and fun. So, by all means, experiment!

One note of explanation is in order here. While the amounts of sweetener recommended in the recipes are fine for me, you may find them to be too much or too little. Adjusting as you go along will save you time later and provide pleasing results.

Celebration Jubilation

Sparkling waters have long been used in various forms of celebration and were even considered lucky. Raspberry is added for pleasure, and borage flowers for joy.

1	quart ginger ale	1	cup lemon juice
1	quart soda water	2	cups sugar
1	quart white grape juice	1	cup raspberries
2	cups apricot juice		Borage flowers

Mix together the sodas and juices, slowly adding sugar until the taste is pleasing. Float whole raspberries on top of the punch and chill. Place borage around the edge of the punch bowl before serving.

Magical Attributes: Jubilee, merry-making, glad tidings.

Variations: Add a whole strawberry and pineapple chunk on a toothpick as a garnish to celebrate love.

May Day Bowl

The blossoming of woodruff marks the sun's victorious return to the sky and the joyous energy of spring. Woodruff, however, is a masculine herb and since May Day is a festival of fruitfulness, a bit of apple juice is added to honor the Goddess.

½	quart white grape juice	Handful woodruff flowers
½	quart apple juice	Sugar to taste

Mix the chilled juices in the punch bowl. Steep the woodruff flowers in the juice for about 15 minutes, then move them to the edge of the bowl. Add sweetener if desired.

Magical Attributes: Safety during celebration, joy in abundance, flourishing energy.

Variations: Add orange slices to encourage the return to health for all participants who may have been plagued by winter colds. If woodruff is not available, float one or two fresh spring daisies on top of the bowl instead.

Love Glogg

A favorite Swedish drink during winter celebrations, this glogg may be enjoyed hot or cold. For a special treat, roll the almonds after cooking in a bit of honey and offer them to someone special to spark romance. If desired, the beverage may be chilled or even enjoyed as a frappé. The whole spices can be removed before serving, if you prefer.

4	cups apple cider	1	cup raisins
4	whole cloves	½	cup blanched almonds
2	cinnamon sticks		Sugar or honey to taste

Warm the cider and other ingredients over low heat. Once the sugar or honey is dissolved, this is ready to serve.

Magical Attributes: Warm feelings, kinship, the love of friends.

Variation: Add some diced figs during the heating process to improve fertility.

Bowl of Plenty

Representative of the bounty of earth, this makes an excellent beverage for rituals of thankfulness or during holiday gatherings, to bless all in attendance with good fortune.

½	gallon apple cider	1	cup whole strawberries
1	(12-ounce) can raspberry juice	½	peeled grapefruit
	Cinnamon to taste	1	orange, sliced
	Ginger to taste	1	cup whole cherries
1	cup blueberries		Ginger ale (optional)
1	lemon, thinly sliced		

Mix cider with undiluted raspberry juice and spices. If you prefer, use whole cinnamon and ginger root so spices can be removed. Stir in fruit and chill. Add ginger ale just before serving, if desired.

Magical Attributes: Abundance, providence, prosperity.

Variations: Try using this same idea with thematic colors. Add only yellow fruit or juice for rich creativity, or only red fruit and juices for growing passions.

Wee People Nectar

Perhaps best served at Lammas, May Day, and Midsummer when the fey are thought most active. Clover is to help your astral vision, while rose, thyme, and honey are to attract and appease the wee folk. Lots of color is added here, since faeries like gaiety.

1 quart apple juice	Whole cherries
Juice of 2 oranges	Sliced pineapple
2 cups honey	Whole grapes
1 teaspoon thyme	Sliced lemon
1 tablespoon rose water	Clover flowers (garnish)
1 quart soda	

Place the apple juice, orange juice, honey, rose water, and thyme in a blender and mix well. Pour this into a bowl, slowly adding the soda water. Stir in some ice (about 12 cubes) and the whole fruits, and float the flowers on top.

Magical Attributes: Understanding and vision of the "unseen" world; fairy friendship and welcoming.

Variations: Serve this punch near a thorn, oak, or ash tree; where these three grow together fairy homes are likely.

Cool as a Cucumber

The power of the aphorism in this recipe is undeniable. In folk medicine, cucumbers were used to relieve pain, especially headaches, which may have suggested that they ease stress.

1 thinly sliced cucumber	1 quart tomato juice
1 cinnamon stick	6 whole cloves
Salt and pepper to taste	

Mix the spices with juice and cucumber and set at room temperature for one hour. Remove the spices and chill. Serve with a stalk of celery.

Magical Attributes: Calmness, peace, tranquility.

Variations: Add any spices that you enjoy with a vegetable juice, such as basil (for peace in relationships) or rosemary (to bring quiet to a restless mind).

Mulled Ale

We have spoken often about how beer was the common person's offering to the Divine. In this case, pour a bit of the warm brew to the ground first, then lift your cup to toast whatever is appropriate. An excellent choice for winter rituals, and easy to prepare.

5	cups non-alcoholic ale	1 lemon
5	whole cloves	1 cinnamon stick
1	tablespoon brandy flavoring	⅔ cup brown sugar
1	teaspoon ginger	1 teaspoon nutmeg

Simmer all the ingredients over low heat for about 30 minutes. Cool until palatable, then pour in the punch bowl. Please be careful with this last step. Some glassware does not take to drastic temperature changes well, so rinse your bowl in warm water first.

Magical Attributes: Honoring the Gods, or deeds of those close to us.

Variation: This is also very tasty when prepared with non-alcoholic red wine.

Coffee Excitement

This beverage is an especially nice pick-me-up after a long evening of magic. The cream makes for a smooth transition in energy and the ice cream is just for fun.

2	quarts dark coffee	1 teaspoon vanilla
1	cup milk	½ cup sugar
1	cup cream	1 pint ice cream (any flavor)

Brew the coffee and let it cool, adding milk, cream, vanilla, and sugar to taste. Once chilled, float small scoops of ice cream on top of the punch bowl.

Magical Attributes: Abundant energy!

Variations: You can make some luscious punches by matching gourmet coffee with distinctive ice cream flavors. Make sure to whisk the ingredients to whip up the energy!

Apple Beer

In parts of Europe, a version of this drink was often served on August 1 (Lammas Tide) to honor the spiritual protector who presides over fruit, seeds, and the earth's bounty. Lammas was sometimes referred to as "the day of the apple fruit."

6	apples, baked until soft	1	teaspoon ginger
½	cup brown sugar	5	cups hot non-alcoholic
1	teaspoon nutmeg		beer or apple wine

Peel the apples, pulping the fruit with brown sugar and spices (more sweetening may be added, if desired). Mix this with ale or wine and enjoy as a liquid dessert!

Magical Attributes: Earth magic, wisdom, ecology.

Variations: Nice when served with sweet cakes, you can try substituting apple cider or pear juice for the ale. Pear is appropriate to help extend or give life to a living thing which is ailing.

⁓⁕⁕⁓

Esotre Egg Bowl

The egg is a traditional symbol of spring; farmers mark the season by when their hens begin laying. Many myths use eggs as part of the creation story.

12	eggs	1	teaspoon orange juice
2	cups sugar		Lemon peel, grated
2	teaspoons vanilla extract		Orange peel, grated
1-2	teaspoons brandy extract		Nutmeg (garnish)
1	teaspoon lemon juice		

In a double boiler, heat the eggs and sugar over low heat, beating constantly until fluffy. Next, add extracts and juices, continuing to beat until warm. To garnish, place a dab of whipped cream on each cup and a sprinkle of lemon and orange peel and nutmeg on top.

Magical Attributes: Fecundity, fertility, productivity.

Variation: This can also be very refreshing if chilled before garnishing and serving.

⁓⁕⁕⁓

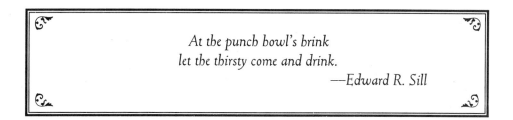

At the punch bowl's brink
let the thirsty come and drink.
—*Edward R. Sill*

Tea Time

Tea was one of the plants sacred to Buddha, and considering all its uses in religion and medicine, it is not surprising. Tea has played a major role in folk remedials for hundreds of years, and during the Victorian era was often associated with quiet moments shared with friends.

1	teaspoon mint tea	2	cinnamon sticks
1	teaspoon apple tea	¼	cup honey
1	teaspoon berry tea	1	orange rind (fresh)
1	teaspoon black tea	1	lemon rind (fresh)
4	cups boiling water	2	teaspoons lemon juice

Steep the tea in hot water using a tea ball or bag, then remove tea. To this, while hot, add the cinnamon, honey, fruit rinds, and lemon juice. This is wonderful hot, or may be chilled and served over chipped ice.

Magical Attributes: Relaxation, healthy leisure, introspection which is rejuvinating.

Variations: Use any herbal tea you like. Some people like to add 1-2 cups apple juice to this mixture.

Divination Draught

Each ingredient in this beverage, with the exception of ginger ale, has at one time been linked with the ability to divine information. Soda adds bubbly energy to your efforts.

- 2 cups cherry juice
- 1 cup orange juice
- 1 cup pomegranate juice
- 1 teaspoon hazel extract
- ½ liter ginger ale or soda water
- Dandelion or broom flowers

Combine the juices and extract together and chill well before pouring in the punch bowl. Add ginger ale and float the flowers, after washing them well, on the surface.

Magical Attributes: Psychic energy, improved insight, foresight, prophecy.

Variations: Try changing the garnish to reflect the goals of the question being asked. For love, use rose petals, or in matters of weather, float heather.

Berry-Mint Medley

Berries have always been regarded as a special gift from the earth, appearing in the most surprising places to bring a smile to our faces.

- 1 liter raspberry ginger ale
- 3-4 whole mint leaves
- 1 (12-ounce) can red raspberry juice
- 1 cup blueberries
- 1 cup blackberries
- 1 cup strawberries

Open the bottle of ginger ale and stuff the mint leaves inside. Close securely and leave at room temperature for at least two hours. Pour the undiluted raspberry juice over ice, slowly adding ginger ale and topping with berries. Float a few mint leaves on top.

Magical Attributes: Joyful gatherings, good feelings, friendship, community.

Variations: Other theme punches are fun to try. Orange juice with orange soda and all orange-colored fruits (tangerines, cantaloupe, etc.) is one example for magic pertaining to warmth, empathy, or consequences.

Pineapple-Ginger Surprise

Both ginger and pineapple are considered protective, the first because of its biting flavor and the second because of its prickly exterior. These are especially protective of health.

- 2 liters sparkling white grape juice
- 1 (12-ounce) can pineapple with syrup
- 1 inch piece bruised ginger root

Drain the syrup from the pineapple and place in a small pan with one tablespoon water. Add ginger root, warm for 15 minutes, then strain. Pour this liqueur into the grape juice; garnish with fresh green grapes or pineapple chunks.

Magical Association: Protection.

Variation: To further accentuate energies for physical well-being, add a little orange rind to the syrup while cooking.

Peachy Keen

The peach is a fruit of wisdom, and its pit (the core of growth) is a good addition to medicine bags. Traditionally, these bags might contain herbs, stones, and other charms to protect, heal, and appease the spirits.

- 1 quart peach juice
- 1 teaspoon rum extract
- 1 cup sugar
- Juice of 1 lemon
- 1 lemon, thinly sliced

Mix the first four ingredients in a blender, then pour into the punch bowl. Float lemon slices on top as garnish.

Magical Association: Sagacity, good judgment, prudence.

Variations: If your group has a particularly difficult time with funding, add pineapple juice or chunks to this punch to encourage wisdom in spending.

Wassail

A traditional beverage for the period between Yule and New Year's, the word Wassail is literally a wish for well-being to all who partake of the bowl.

6	cups apple juice or cider	1	quart non-alcoholic beer
1	teaspoon cinnamon	1	lemon, sliced
1	teaspoon ginger	1	cup sliced apples baked in sugar
1	teaspoon nutmeg		

Warm all ingredients except the apples and lemon over low heat until well spiced. Serve out into cups immediately, adding a thin slice of lemon and 1 or 2 slices of sweet apple to the top. If you like, a little sweet cream is nice on this, too.

Sliced apples baked in sugar: peel and slice an apple. Cover with about ⅛ cup each of water and brown sugar. Cook until slices are tender.

Magical Attributes: Good health, good fortune, happiness, and a prosperous year.

Variation: Instead of beer, try adding various flavors of juices or soft wines which match your magical goals. For example, with health matters use soft apple wine instead of beer.

In a large silver urn, pour Six cups of Kindness
Five cups of Tenderness, Four cups of Affection
Three cups of understanding, Two cups of Good Nature,
One whole cup of Truth, One half cup of Smiles,
One teaspoon of Tears . . . stir well.
—Count De Mauduit

Chapter Twenty-two

Tea and Coffee

Arrayed in the most gorgeous Oriental costumes,
they served the choicest Mocha coffee in tiny cups of egg-shell porcelain
hot, strong and fragrant, poured out on saucers of gold and silver.
—Issac D'Israeli

On a metaphysical level, coffee increases power, energy, or conscious alertness. Conversely, tea is a tranquil plant, full of rest, serenity, renewal of health, and introspection. These intrinsic qualities of both beverages give us some unique variables to consider. I would not suggest, by way of example, using coffee as part of a ritual for peace. Instead, it might be better used to improve mental acuity, which could help in obtaining viable resolutions. This way your ingredients are magically compatible with the desired ends.

❧ Coffee ❧

There is a marvelous story about an Arab goat keeper who was very responsible and sober by nature. One night his goats failed to return home. When he went searching for them, much to his dismay, he discovered the goats dancing with a red-berried shrub. The caretaker quickly surmised that the berries must have been the cause of jubilation, and soon he found himself waltzing, too.

Amid all this merriment, a studious monk came by, observing with far more caution than the caretaker. After some experimentation, he placed the berries in hot water and happily found that he could stay awake during prayers. From this monk, the fame of coffee quickly spread through the religious realms of Arabia, where it is still regarded as holy.

Thus it is not surprising to discover that Arabian traders, or possibly Persians are responsible for advertising the coffee beans' qualities. Back in the desert, where people learned to boil water around A.D. 1000, hot coffee was used in medicines and for the religious observances of the Whirling Dervishes.[1] This also marked the beginnings of coffee houses.

In Arab homes, people extol coffee more than anywhere else on earth. During the Middle Ages (and probably long before) except in the most impoverished areas, one could find a special furnace for preparing coffee in every house. Around this the host and guests sit in a circle, the most honored seated closest to the sacred flames. The coffee is hand ground, roasted, and brewed while everyone chats.

Next, the host adds a bit of cardamom[2] and continues cooking the coffee until it boils three times. Then it is strained into a serving vessel. Next, cups are prepared for each guest by pouring one full of coffee to warm it,

---

1. Whirling Dervishes are members of a Muslim religious order of mystics, vowed to poverty and simplicity. Their dances are renowned as a means for Divine inspiration.
2. Cardamom was much more highly favored in the ancient world than it is today, and was often used in love potions.

then reusing this coffee to warm each cup. When finished, they pour the remainder onto the ground, honoring Sheikhesh Shadhilly, the patron saint of coffee lovers.

Finally, the coffee is served in the same circular fashion, the host and guests each honoring the name of God. The circle is repeated at least once as the cups are small, and this affords more enjoyment. My understanding is that some Arab families still follow this tradition.

No matter where we live, however, we have not completely escaped some of the ceremonial feelings transported with coffee by pilgrims to Mecca. We still find ourselves considering the personality of those who drink coffee sweetened instead of straight. At most formal tables the sugar and creamer dishes hold a place of honor. In many homes some family member has a favorite coffee cup that is not used by other household members unless they want to receive indignant stares.

Coffee Frost

The icy nature of this beverage tends to put a distinctive chill on emotions or energy which has gotten out of control. The innate symbolism of chilling or heating a beverage is very useful in a variety of settings. For example, with teas, you can reverse the meaning of the preparation just by reversing the way it is served (e.g., hot or cold)!

4	ice cubes, crushed	1	teaspoon amaretto flavoring
1-2	tablespoons sugar		Amaretto whipped cream
4	cups strong coffee		

Process the crushed ice with sugar, coffee, and flavoring in a blender on medium speed for 2 to 3 minutes. Pour into a tall glass or cup and top off with whipped cream. Most supermarkets now stock amaretto-flavored aerosol cream, or you can whip cream and add 1 teaspoon extract during the beating process.

Magical Attributes: Calming energies, cooling tempers.

Variations: Orange flavoring is an excellent choice if you wish to sooth undesired feelings of romance or passion, especially those which are ill-timed.

Vienna Holiday

The bay leaf is the ancient Greek symbol of success. The cinnamon stick is linked with passion through ~~Venus~~, an associated Deity. Here, both items are carefully broken in two to help peacefully separate individuals who have an unhealthy relationship.

2	cups Viennese coffee	2	teaspoons sugar
4-5	cloves	1	cinnamon stick (broken in half)
4	allspice berries	1	bay leaf (broken in half)

Brew your coffee according to directions given on the bag or can. Add the spices and let stand 15 minutes to steep. Strain and top with cream and a sprinkle of nutmeg.

Magical Attributes: Victory over lust or love.

Variations: For fuller flavor, leave the bay leaf and cinnamon stick in each cup.

Cafe L'Orange

In the Middle Ages, oranges were a rare and costly commodity in most European homes, and as such were used frugally or to show off one's wealth. Magically speaking, this precious association attached itself to the fruit even after it was readily available.

6	slices fresh orange without rind	1	teaspoon vanilla extract
6	cups hot chocolate	1	cup heavy cream
6	cups strong orange-flavored coffee		Orange peel, grated
			Cinnamon

In each cup place 1 orange slice, pouring over it equal quantities of hot cocoa and freshly brewed coffee. Top with cream, grated orange peel, and cinnamon.

Magical Attributes: Prosperity, abundance, accomplishment.

Variations: This beverage is often enjoyed in Belgium, where sometimes cinnamon and a dash of orange extract are added.

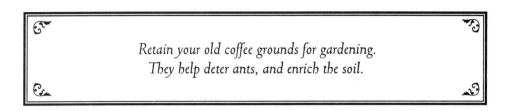

Retain your old coffee grounds for gardening.
They help deter ants, and enrich the soil.

Cinnamon Chocolate Coffee

Cinnamon oil was an important part of many ancient religious rites, including the anointing oils of the Hebrews and the Egyptian mummification process. This, combined with the steadfast nature of nutmeg, makes for an excellent beverage to help keep you consistent in your spiritual studies and goals.

½	cup heavy cream	2	cups strong cinnamon
¼	teaspoon nutmeg		flavored coffee
1	tablespoon sugar	½	stick cinnamon
5	teaspoons chocolate syrup		

Begin by whipping the cream with the nutmeg and sugar and setting this aside. Meanwhile, pour 1 teaspoon of the syrup into each small cup, adding the hot coffee and stirring with a cinnamon stick that can be left for garnish. Top with a teaspoonful of whipped cream.

Magical Attributes: Perseverance, dedication.

Variations: Instead of chocolate syrup, try this with butterscotch to improve your creativity in magic.

Summer Relief

There is nothing which elicits fond, happy memories like going strawberry picking in a wild field. This vision is one of repose and a break from turmoil. The strawberry is a love food, making this beverage especially helpful with overactive imaginations or tempers. This drink cools the body and sweetens the disposition.

3	cups mocha coffee	6	tablespoons strawberry syrup
1	pint strawberry ice cream		

Prepare mocha java according to the label instructions. Chill this in the refrigerator. Mix 3 cups of the coffee in a blender with syrup and ice cream for a marvelous shake.

Magical Attributes: Relief of anxiety, especially in relationships. Energy for accord and love.

Variations: Try pairing other syrups and ice creams for unique results. Chocolate would be for passion, or pineapple for hospitality and protection.

Coffee Shake

This recipe is not so much magical as it is down-right decadent. The rich flavor brings a smile to the face any coffee or chocolate lover. A marvelously easy beverage to make.

2	scoops cappuccino ice cream	1	cup chocolate ice cream
½	cup dark roast coffee, cold	¼	cup cream
	Dark chocolate shavings		

Place all the ingredients, except one teaspoon of the cream, in a blender and mix until smooth. Serve by pouring into a glass, with the teaspoon of cream on top and chocolate shavings for garnish.

Magical Attributes: Rewarding good actions, delight.

Variations: Change the flavors of ice cream for a wide variety of taste combinations, any of which can reflect your magical goals. Cookies and cream might be appropriate for youthful vision, while vanilla is for improved mental energy.

Vanilla Soda

Vanilla is a member of the orchid family, grown in Mexico and Central America. Once discovered, it managed to topple rose water as the favored flavoring of Medieval Europe, and has been used widely as a magical attractant for romance. Magically speaking, it is always best to use natural vanilla extract, rather than imitation. While the latter will have a taste and smell which can encourage symbolism, artificially produced flavorings are spiritually "inert."

2 cups vanilla-flavored coffee, chilled	1 teaspoon vanilla extract
1 cup soda water	Whipped cream
3 scoops vanilla ice cream	

Another cold coffee drink, this is mixed easily in a blender. Serve in soda glasses with the whipped cream for a garnish.

Magical Attributes: Love, rituals honoring Venus or Aphrodite.

Variations: Try adding some almond extract in place of vanilla. Magically, this still accentuates your goals, while adding a lovely, light nutty flavor.

Hazelnut Nog

A favorite wood for dowsers, hazel trees offer their fruit for a number of other magical applications, including increasing fecundity, and as gifts to a young bride for joy in her new life.

4 eggs	1 cup hazelnut-flavored coffee
¾ cup sugar	1 tablespoon hazelnut extract
2 cups milk	1 cup cream

Beat eggs and sugar together until thick and frothy. Heat the milk and coffee, then stir in extract and the sugar mixture slowly. Separately beat heavy cream and fold one tablespoon of this into each cup as it is poured. Serve warm.

Magical Attributes: Fertility, wisdom, luck.

Variations: Replace the milk in this recipe with cream for smooth transitions, especially with regard to attitudes and personal ambition.

ᘒ *Tea* ᘓ

By definition, the word "tea" specifically pertains to the leafy shrub of China and India. In that context, rose hip tea and beef tea are not really teas at all. Instead, they are beverages with tea-like quality. Here is a brief sampling of the herbs employed for tea impostors and their magical or religious significance:

- **Anise**—a popular spice during the time of Virgil, anise wards against the "evil eye" and tastes very similar to liquorice.

- **Basil**—buried with those of Hindu faiths to insure passage into paradise. Rich, spicy flavor.

- **Chamomile**—lauded as the physician's plant, it was sacred to the Egyptians and has a slightly bitter flavor.

- **Cinnamon**—in the mythology of China, this tree grows in paradise, offering immortality to all who eat it. Cinnamon tea is sweet and fragrant.

- **Marjoram**—Venus gave this herb its aroma, and thus it often crowned the heads of newlyweds in ancient Greece and Rome. Sweet taste similar to thyme.

- **Mint**—used by the Hebrews as a strewing herb for sacred temple floors, mint has a refreshing, vibrant flavor.

- **Rosemary**—thought to improve memory by Greek students, it was sometimes worn as a crown. Rosemary has a cool flavor.

- **Vervain**—known to the ancient Druids to improve spell potency; in Persia, an aid to wish magic and an ingredient in many medieval love potions. Vervain has a fairly neutral taste which can be improved by combining it with other herbs.

It would be inappropriate not to take a moment to extol the ancient, dainty art of tea leaf reading. To use tea for divination, choose a hearty leaf tea and brew it loose in your cup. Drain off as much liquid as possible, then tip your cup upside down with a light tap of the finger on the bottom.[3]

---

3 Some instructions direct that the little bit of liquid left in the bottom of the cup should be swirled three times before tipping over (the number of body-mind-spirit). Other instructions indicate that the cup should be turned once around completely while upside down in a sunward direction (clockwise) before the reading. Find an approach that works best for you.

Reverse the cup to see what patterns emerge in the remaining sediment. You can interpret these images symbolically, knowing they often pertain to the questions on your mind at the moment. Designs near the rim of the cup are things closest to occurring, while those in the bottom are in the future. For extra effectiveness, match the type of tea to your question. For example, use marjoram in matters of love.

Besides divination, there are certain social conventions that center around tea. There are formal teas, a social tea, and sick-room teas. There is also the Japanese tea ceremony, Cha No Yu, mentioned earlier. In this ceremony, green tea is whipped in special bowls to form a frothy beverage. The bowl is passed in silence to all in attendance. In the quiet moments, this ritual becomes a group meditation about matters of eternity, the spirit, and universal truths. This makes our ordinary, "generic" tea bag, steeped in the microwave, look rather bland.

These approaches can inspire unique serving arrangements for your own magical teas. If you want to have a Victorian tea, or a thematic oriental-style tea for a special occasion, use these examples as a starting point. However, you do not have to get that fancy. Plain or elaborate, tea is a rich addition to the magical pantry.

Lemonade Tea

The purgative abilities of lemon are well known. Without any sweetener, this tea can be used to aspurge a magical circle, consecrate magical tools, or as the base for a ritual bath before special occasions.

2 quarts water	¾ cup lemon juice
10 lemon verbena tea bags	Lemons, sliced for garnish
1 cup sugar	

Heat the water to boiling, then steep the tea bags for 20 minutes. Remove. Keep the mixture over low heat and add sugar and lemon juice. Especially refreshing when chilled or served over chipped ice.

Magical Attributes: Cleansing and purification.

Variations: Substitute honey for the sugar in this recipe and drink hot for effective cold relief.

Dried Fruit Tea

Drying of food has been a traditional means of preserving it for difficult times in many lands and time periods. In the magical setting, this association can be applied to any situation where you need to conserve energy, or preserve your sanctity or a relationship. This tea must be prepared hot for proper flavoring, but it is delightful served hot or cold.

4	cups hot water	¼	cup dried pear
6	dried apricots	2	fruit tea bags (your choice)
½	cup dried apple		

Bring the water to a rolling boil, add the fruit and tea bags. Simmer for 15 minutes, then remove from the heat and strain. Sweeten as desired.

Magical Attributes: Preservation, sustenance.

Variations: Adding a handful of your favorite nuts during the boiling process would bring greater fertility to your magical effort.

Tea Tonic

This beverage, besides having magical restorative features, is rich in caffeine, vitamins, and physically rejuvenative qualities.

¼	cup Paraguay tea (maté)	1	quart boiling water
1	teaspoon chamomile	1	lemon slice
⅛	cup rose-hips		Honey or sugar

Prepare as you would any tea, using a tea ball or cloth bag for the loose chamomile and rose hips. Lemon and sugar are added in the cup to suit personal tastes.

Magical Attributes: Return to normalcy, adjusting erratic energies, centering and balance.

Variations: The base materials can be reused with other favorite ingredients to make less potent, but magically creative, batches. For example, to help return to well being, add nutmeg to the base. In place of rose hips, use the juice of one orange for high vitamin content.

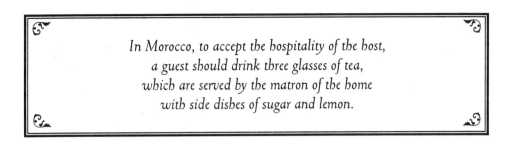

*In Morocco, to accept the hospitality of the host,
a guest should drink three glasses of tea,
which are served by the matron of the home
with side dishes of sugar and lemon.*

Pineapple Mint Merriment

Another beverage which is tasty either hot or cold. An old Greek tale tells us that Zeus and Hermes disguised themselves as travelers and were entertained at the cottage of Philemon and Baucis, who welcomed the strangers by rubbing their table with mint leaves.

1 pint hot water	¼ cup lemon juice
7 mint tea bags	½ cup pineapple juice
2-3 fresh mint leaves	Pineapple bits
½ cup sugar or honey	Mint leaves (optional)

Warm the mint tea bags and leaves in hot water for 15 minutes. Strain. Add the sugar or honey to the warm liquid so that it dissolves properly; then add the lemon and pineapple juices. Pour into cups; garnish with pineapple bits and mint leaf.

Magical Attributes: Joyful hospitality.

Variations: If you use peppermint in this mixture, it can be magically associated with increasing power or virility, as it was to both the ancient Arabs and Romans.

Violet-Anise Ice

In the time of Virgil, anise was considered a potent protection against the "evil eye," as well as an effective deterrent to nightmares. Violets were also used by the Greeks to bring peaceful sleep and safety from spirits.

1	tablespoon anise seed		Sugar
1	teaspoon strong, loose black tea	1	cup cream
1	teaspoon dried violets		Crushed ice
2	cups boiling water		

Bundle the aniseed, black tea, and dried violets together in a tea ball or gauze bag, and steep in the hot water for about 20 minutes, until the water smells heady. Stir in sugar until dissolved, then chill. When cold, add one cup of cream and serve over crushed ice.

Magical Aspects: Safety, protection from negative magic or malignant spirits, peaceful sleep.

Variations: Add one teaspoon of chamomile or valerian root if you are making this specifically for sleep. Both herbs have a relaxing effect on nerves. This beverage can be served hot, adding the cream while the tea is still warm, and eliminating the ice. If dried violets are not available, try a stick of cinnamon or 1 teaspoon fennel for similar magical results.

And Venus, Goddess of the eternal smile,
Knowing that stormy brews but ill become
Fair patterns of her beauty, hath ordained
celestial tea; a fountain that can cure
the ills of passion and can free from frowns,
and sobs and signs the dissipated fair.
To her, ye fair, in adoration bow!
—Robert Fergusson

Chapter Twenty-three

To Your Health

At least you have your health.
—All mothers, everywhere

Many modern researchers help us live healthier lives by instructing us on diet and natural approaches to health care. These are not a substitute for professional help. Instead, they are a means to cure those little aches, pains, and common colds in a positive, non-chemical manner. This is why the recipes in this section are general in nature, designed to help the body's natural immune system to function well.

It is all but impossible for the body to operate at its best when spiritual energies are out of sync. Sickness throws the whole person into an irregular state, meaning that we have to attend to body, mind, and spirit to affect well-being. The flexibility of brewing techniques allow us to add magical vision to the formula while achieving these ends. Older folk remedies commonly added magical elements, even if they weren't called that.[1] From this foundation we can prepare tonics that ease "what ails us," and support spiritual healing, too.

---

1. Usually, the magical aspects of a curative were sympathetic in nature, such as tying one end of a string to the patient and the other to a tree. This "transferred" the disease. Refer to Chapter 3, Medicinal Mixtures, for more information.

"Witches' brews" for health tend to either taste bad and smell great, or vice versa.[2] Eucalyptus and valerian are two of the worst offenders on both counts. Because of this, you may need to add honey or a common aromatic, like mint, for more palatable, pleasing results.

Please remember that not all magical herbs are edible, nor are all old folk remedies safe or effective. If your symptoms persist, don't stubbornly ignore contemporary medicine. This chapter is set up specifically for health-related matters, and all recipes pertain to this on a magical level, too. Any additional magical applications are so noted.

Fever Brew

Bohemian tradition says if children dance in a flax field once every seven years until their maturity, they will grow to be strong and beautiful. Flax seed can generally be found in health food stores.

1 teaspoon flax seed	1 cup hot water
Juice of 2-3 lemon slices	Dash cinnamon
½ teaspoon honey	½ teaspoon lemon jam

Steep the flax seed in hot water for 15 minutes. Strain and add lemon juice, jam, cinnamon, and honey. Drink hot. This also soothes the throat.

Magical Attributes: Vitality, comeliness, prosperity, protection.

Variations: If your stomach can tolerate it, some black pepper or other purgative herb[3] can help cleanse your system.

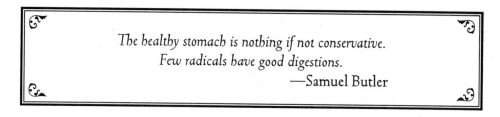

> *The healthy stomach is nothing if not conservative.*
> *Few radicals have good digestions.*
> —Samuel Butler

---

2. This particular observation came about due to numerous complaints from friends and family members who subject themselves to my teas when cold and flu season strikes. For all their complaints, however, they still ask for the tea and drink it!

3. A purgative is similar to a laxative in nature. Another good type of herb is the sudorific (such as cayenne and yarrow), which induces sweating.

Apple Tea

This recipe is favored in France and Australia to help invalids. Apple is also a popular ingredient for love potions.

2-3	apples, sliced	3	cups hot water
1	mint leaf		Honey and lemon (optional).

Steep the apples and mint together in hot water for one hour, then strain. This is excellent warm with a stick of cinnamon, or chilled over ice.

Magical Attributes: Refreshing love. Dreams which teach wisdom, perspective in relationships.

Variations: If serving this drink cold, adding some soda water or ginger ale (about ½ cup) is refreshing.

Vital Water

This is an alternative translation of "Aqua Vitae," as discussed in the chapter on medicinal mixtures. This drink is made from favorite restoratives and tonics of the Middle Ages. Angelica root candied or steeped in vinegar is sometimes used in ritual fasts. This beverage is also excellent protection against colds and negative magic.

1	tablespoon sage	10	comfrey leaves
½	teaspoon angelica		Dash basil
½	teaspoon ginger root, diced	½	teaspoon mint
	Petals from 2 rose buds	½	teaspoon rosemary
1	slice orange rind	1½	pints boiling water
	Lemon		Honey

Another tea-based beverage, the herbs in this should be allowed to steep for about 25 minutes. After straining, re-heat the liquid or enjoy it cold.

Magical Attributes: Life, revitalization, balance.

Variations: The herbalist of the Middle Ages often added some type of spirits to this mixture, which increased the shelf life and was thought most beneficial to health. Suggestions for this include whiskey, vodka, or rum.

Ladies' Tea

Especially good for female discomforts, but not recommended during pregnancy or for nursing mothers. This mixture may help alleviate stomach cramps and general emotional discomfort in men, too. It also may make you drowsy, and should not be used when you need to be especially alert, such as when driving a car or operating machinery. A sprig of valerian tied near your waist helps attract members of the opposite sex.

1	teaspoon raspberry leaf	1	teaspoon valerian
1	teaspoon black currant leaf	1	teaspoon chamomile
1	teaspoon lemon balm	4	cups boiling water

This beverage is prepared as a normal tea. While it can be enjoyed cold, for most effectiveness on cramps it is best served warm.

Magical Attributes: Protection from spirits, purification, quiet restfulness.

Variations: Mugwort and wintergreen are both effective for similar complaints. Use one teaspoon each and increase the water to 5½ cups.

Barley Brew

Barley has been used in many types of prophetic efforts and was often recommended to treat kidney stones. This recipe is especially good for babies with colic, or anyone with flu symptoms.

1	cup pearl barley		Peel of ½ orange
3	cups water	½	cup raisins
4-5	figs	1	slice lemon

Cook the barley in the water. Strain; pour the liquid over the fruits. Return the fruits to the stove, cooking until tender. Squeeze the lemon slice over the top of the whole mixture, cool and strain. Drink only the liquid, reserving the cooked fruit for pie or tarts.

Magical Attributes: Divination, anti-magic protection.

Variations: You may combine this beverage with the base for beef toast (see page 234) for a heartier drink.

Cold Tonic

This tonic eases asthma as well as colds. It keeps well in an air-tight jar in the refrigerator. Magically, bay leaves were sometimes used to write spells on, and were often employed in the preparation of amulets.

½	gallon boiling water		10	eucalyptus leaves
½	teaspoon sage		½	teaspoon rosemary
½	teaspoon anise		½	teaspoon thyme
½	teaspoon valerian		½	teaspoon comfrey
½	teaspoon ginger root, bruised		½	teaspoon yarrow buds
1	teaspoon chamomile		5-10	fresh mint leaves
	Lemon and orange rind		1	bay leaf

Steep for one hour, then strain. I do not recommend drinking it cold—the eucalyptus is far more effective warm. If you let this tincture boil down (using a covered pan) to about 2 cups, it is very strong and can be dabbed on bed pillows or humidifiers to help your breathing at night.

Magical Attributes: Easing rough nerves, rest, cleansing, amulet creation, prophesy, calm understanding.

Variations: Add 1 clove garlic, if you wish.

Rice Remedy

This beverage is wonderful for easing the discomforts of diarrhea.

- 1 ounce rice, rinsed
- 1 pint water
- 1 pint milk

Nutmeg powder
Lemon peel

Soak rice for 3 hours in hot water. Move this to the stove, boiling for one hour, then straining the liquid into another saucepan. To this, add milk and boil again, flavoring with lemon and nutmeg.

Magical Attributes: Fidelity in love. New romance, rain magic, fertility.

Variations: Fennel, a native Mediterranean herb, can be added in the proportion of ½ teaspoon per cup to improve digestion of disagreeable foods.

Strawberry Lemonade

Recommended mostly for cold symptoms, all the ingredients in this beverage are ruled by Venus, making this an appropriate beverage to bring renewed health to love as well.

- 1 pint distilled water
- 1 slice orange
   Juice of 1 lemon

- 1 teaspoon vanilla extract
- 2 teaspoons strawberry syrup

Warm the distilled water and orange slice together, adding the juice of one lemon and flavorings. Serve hot.

Magical Attributes: Luck, especially in matters of study or the conscious mind. Increased energy.

Variations: Raspberry or apple juice could be added to improve the romantic aspects of this drink. Another option is to slowly boil down this beverage until it reaches a syrupy stage, adding a little honey. This makes a good topping for ice cream, or an effective cough reliever.

Vegetable Chicken Broth

Chicken soup or broth has been considered a kind of panacea to folk healers through the ages. This may have developed because it has a soothing effect on nerves, and due to superstitions which claimed a chicken's actions could foretell trouble or victory.

2	quarts cold water	2	pounds chicken, skinned
2	carrots, diced	2	large onions, sliced
2	potatoes, diced	1	cup cabbage, chopped
1	tomato, skinned and diced	1	cup celery, diced
2-3	sprigs parsley, finely diced	2	cloves garlic
1	bay leaf	1	tablespoon lemon juice
1	cup fresh chives, chopped	1	teaspoon thyme
1	teaspoon basil		Salt and pepper to taste

Simmer all ingredients over low heat for 2 hours, adding liquids as needed to keep the level constant. Strain (freeze vegetables to use later in soup). Cook the broth for another hour or until liquid is reduced by half. Enjoy hot.

Magical Attributes: Protection in battles, warnings.

Variations: Add additional chives, if desired, when serving. This recipe makes a good base for wonton soup. Just add noodles and a little soy sauce.

Warm it Up

Often used in cold curatives or to improve an appetite. Magically, Romans used house leeks (a type of onion) to protect their residences from fire, violence, and the evil eye.

2	cups milk	1	sliced onion
1	clove garlic, minced	1	teaspoon butter
1	slice toast, cubed		

Place all ingredients except the toast in your blender, mixing well. Warm over a low flame, add butter, pour over toast cubes and drink. This helps relieve chills.

Magical Attributes: Protection of home, prophetic vision.

Variations: Add a cooked potato for a beverage with the thickness of a cream soup.

Beef Toast

Good for indigestion and fussy stomachs in general; favored in Scotland and during the Victorian era to improve physical strength after long bouts of sickness.

1	piece of toast, broken	2	cups boiling water
2	ounces lean beef, shredded		Salt and pepper to taste

Sprinkle 1 teaspoon salt on the beef and soak it in cold water for 30 minutes. Simmer this in 2 cups of water for about 2 hours, taking care to skim off any fat residue. Strain and add toast pieces and any flavoring you desire.

Magical Attributes: Peace and prosperity.

Variations: After straining, return the liquid to the stove and add a beaten egg, cooking for about 10 additional minutes before serving with toast. This gives a little extra substance to the drink.

Garlic Water

Deemed a kind of cure-all, a recipe similar to this is a favorite part of the French Yule celebrations. This beverage has a purgative quality.

1	quart water		Salt and pepper
15	cloves garlic	⅓	cup grated parmesan and
2	bay leaves		romano cheeses
2	sprigs fresh sage	2	egg yolks
½	teaspoon thyme	¼	teaspoon olive oil
½	teaspoon rosemary		

Boil water with herbs for 45 minutes; strain. Reserve the garlic and press into broth. Meanwhile, beat eggs, cheeses, and oil slowly together. To the egg mixture, add 1 cup broth and beat again. Mix this thoroughly into garlic base over low heat until thick. Serve with bread crumbs or croutons on top.

Magical Attributes: Banishing, protection from malevolent influences.

Variations: Add an onion or two to the garlic broth. In this form the drink can become an appropriate part of magical oath taking or rites of purification.

Part Four

*Appendices,
Glossary,
Bibliography,
and Index*

Is not old wine wholesomest, old pippins toothsomest,
old wood burn brightest, old linen wash whitest?
Old soldiers, sweethearts, are surest,
and old lovers are soundest.

—John Webster

Appendix A

Ingredients, Correspondences, and Magical Associations

Ale and Beer: *fire;* offerings and purification. Sometimes used as a base for punches or spiced beverages. Sacred to Tenemit, Isis, and Hawthor (Egypt), Shoney (Scotland), and Kremana (Slavonic).

Allspice: *fire;* prosperity, good fortune, and health. Use somewhat sparingly, as it can have a "hot" taste.

Almond: *air;* wisdom, financial matters, well-being. Sacred to Artemis in Greece, Chandra in India, and Ptah in Egypt.

Aloe: *water;* the Greeks used aloe as a laxative and also to ward against the plague.

Angelica: *fire;* protection, healing. A gift from the angels to protect one from sickness.

Anise: *air;* safety, vitality, cleansing. A pungent herb which can take over the flavor of a beverage. Add in small quantities.

Apple: *water;* discernment, prudence, love, the soul. Apples are a steady, dependable fruit for fermented beverages. They help to balance flavor without overwhelming it. Sacred to Induna of Norse traditions, Venus and Apollo in Rome and Zeus in Greece. Apple juice makes an interesting base for beer.

Banana: *air;* the masculine element (specifically sexual), commitment, love, protection. Not the easiest fruit to get to ferment properly, it is very heavy and often separates out of wines. Sacred to Kanaloa (Hawaii).

Bay: *fire;* intuition, vigor, protection, victory, power. One bay leaf can be added to almost any drink without noticeable changes in flavor. Bay is a nice addition to mulled beverages. Sacred to Eros and Adonis in Greece, and Buddha in India. Bedouins put bay in their coffee. Considered a good protection against lightning.

Birch: *water;* cleansing, earth magic, banishing. Birch twigs are most often used in birch beer, but also make an interesting augmentation to other creative efforts. Sacred to Thor.

Caraway: *air;* used extensively for love potions, and to improve circulation. This is one of the oldest native European herbs.

Cardamom: *water;* for refreshment, used as early as 4 B.C., being imported from Indonesia. Arabs like it with coffee or as a component in elixirs for romance.

Carrot: *fire;* sexuality, insight, grounding. Carrot juice is best suited to non-alcoholic beverages and is great for personal energy.

Celery: *fire;* mental keenness, weight loss, desire. In early times, the root was used for love potions.

Cherry: *water;* psychic insight, love, whimsy. Cherries ferment slowly and are excellent when blended with vanilla bean.

Cinnamon: *fire;* spiritual pursuits, potency, victory. Another strong aromatic with intense flavor. Unless you really enjoy the taste of cinnamon, add it in limited amounts. Stick cinnamon recommended. Sacred to the altars of Aphrodite (Greece) and Venus (Rome). Mentioned in Exodus, cinnamon has long been considered an aphrodisiac. One of the important oils of the Hebrew Tabernacle.

Citron: *fire;* safety and power, cleansing. Lemon-like fruit, but larger. Can be used in place of lemon in any recipe. Sacred to Ge (Egypt), and Zeus and Hera (Greece).

Clove: *fire;* protection, love, prosperity. Only a few whole cloves are needed in any beverage for a noticeable tang. The first semi-official antiseptic.

Coriander: *fire;* found at many Egyptian grave sites, coriander aided passion and happiness.

Cumin: *fire;* also a very old herb, Isaiah describes how the plant was threshed with a stick for harvesting.

Currants: *fire* (red currants) or *water* (juice); abundance. Currant wine is fabulous if you have the patience to clean all the leaves and branches of this bush.

Daisy: *water;* simplicity, prophesy, youthful energy. This flower most often appears as part of spring wines. Sacred flower of Freya.

Dandelion: *air;* wishes, sensitivity to spirits, divination. A pesky weed which, true to nature's sense of humor, can be made into wine, coffee, and salads. Sacred to Hecate and Theseus (Greece).

Date: *air;* spirituality, strength, vitality. Dates are rather heavy in taste and are best used for liqueurs or purgative juices. Sacred to Ea and Anu (Babylonia), Artemis (Greek), and Isis (Egypt).

Dill: *fire;* used by Saxons to settle children to sleep, and to protect them from negative magic.

Elecampane: *air;* love, protection, psychic powers. Thought by the Greeks to have been born from the tears of Helena. The root was used in early medicines.

Elder: *water;* peace, wholeness, safety, healing. Elderflower wine is a favorite spring creation, especially for magic circles. Sacred to Venus.

Fennel: *fire;* purification, protection from evil, physical well-being. Caution on the amount used due to its strong taste. Sacred to Prometheus (Greece). Chinese, Egyptians, and Europeans considered this a most effective deterrent to Witchcraft.

Fig: *fire;* potency, love charms, fecundicity. Similar in texture and body to dates. Sacred to Amon Ra and Isis (Egypt), Brahma (India), and Juno (Greece).

Ginger: *fire;* success, increasing power, money, romance. Ginger adds a crisp boost to most beverages: use with prudence. Ginger root is much better than powder. According to the Koran, the faithful enjoy a ginger-spiced drink in paradise.

Grains: *earth;* prosperity, good fortune, abundance. Grains are featured as part of health drinks or beer. Barley specifically is Sacred to Demeter (Greece), Taliesin (Wales), and Vishnu (India).

Grape: *water;* the conscious mind, celebration, fruitfulness. The acclaimed base ingredient for most wines also makes a lovely addition to many other juices. The favored fruit of Bacchus (Rome) and Hawthor (Egypt).

Honey: *air;* purification, well-being, happiness, discernment. A prime ingredient in mead, honey is an excellent sweetener for almost any beverage. Sacred to Min (Egypt), Ea (Babylonia), Artemis (Greece), and Kama (India), among others.

Hops: *air;* rest and peacefulness, health. A main constituent in beers. Add hops judiciously or their flavor becomes overwhelming.

Kiwi: *water;* leisure, young love. It takes a fair amount of kiwi fruit to produce a strong flavor in any brewing, but it is well worth the effort for its berry-like flavor.

Lavender: *air;* restfulness, joy, peace, purity. A little French lavender in any beverage lifts the bouquet without overpowering the taste.

Lemon: *water;* freshness, kinship, longevity. A fruit which adds a slight tang and fragrance to everything. An appropriate offering on the Buddhist altar to Jambhala.

Lemon Balm: *air;* recommended by Pliny to calm the nerves.

Licorice: *water;* old wives' remedy to relieve thirst. A favorite snack of Napoleon.

Mango: *fire;* passion and romance. An orange-like undertaste, but richer; the weight of mango juice makes it difficult to mix with other fruits. Sacred to Buddha.

Maple Syrup: *air;* sweet things in life, health, love. Maple syrup is an interesting taste sensation when used in place sugar or honey in wines, meads, and ales.

Marjoram: *air;* happiness, safety, bounty, well-being. Best when used in melomels, metheglin, and tea. Sacred to Venus (Greece) and Ilmarinen (Finland). For joy; in Greece, if found growing on a grave; a sign that the deceased had found peace.

Milk: *water;* the Goddess aspect, maternal nature, lunar energy. Honored by Hawthor, Isis, and Min (Egypt), Zeus (Greece), and Ilmarinen (Finland). Use carefully to avoid spoilage.

Mint: *air;* revitalization, lust, adventure, safety, money. A subtle herb when added to fermented brews in whole, fresh leaves (3-4 at a time). Can be used plain in either iced or hot tea. Sacred to Pluto (Rome).

Mulberry: *air;* sagacity, practicality, psychic awareness, inventive energy. One of the first berries used in wine, and still an excellent choice. Sacred to Minerva (Rome).

Nutmeg: *fire;* good fortune, fidelity, fitness. Good all-around, mild-tasting herb. One of the commonest herbal curatives found in the sacred writings of India.

Orange: *fire;* love, luck, prosperity, health. Orange is an integral part of many fermented beverages, in small amounts, and is a popular breakfast juice, addition to coffee, etc. At one time oranges were thought to prevent drunkenness, which may explain why slices still appear in many mixed drinks.

Passion fruit: *water;* love, peace and friendship. Another heavy tropical fruit, it is best mixed with other heavy liquids, notably mango and banana.

Peach: *water;* long life, fertility, good wishes. Peach is a light fruit which can be used alone or as an accent to other fruits and herbs. Sacred to Hsi Wang Ma (China).

Pear: *water;* passion, zest, love. Pear juice is subtle enough to be mingled with many other ingredients. Its consistency, however, is a little "thick" and it is best when somewhat diluted. Sacred to Athene (Greece).

Pepper: *fire;* a very rare and expensive herb for the medieval home, it paid dowries and taxes. In medicine, used as a stimulant.

Pineapple: *fire;* luck, money, commitment, dedication, protection. The cutting taste of pineapple makes it a good palate cleanser. Its citric content helps it to mix well with other fruits.

Plum: *water;* adoration, respect, protection. Makes a wonderful liqueur or sparkling wine with an oriental flair.

Pomegranate: *fire;* creativity, invention, prosperity. While the juice is difficult to extract, it is well worth the time. Makes a wonderful, deep red wine or mead. Sacred to Dionysus (Greek), Persephone (Phoenicia), Ceres (Rome).

Quince: *earth;* love, protection, happiness, and fulfillment. A pear-like fruit with similar taste and body. Makes a nice blending fruit as it doesn't overcome other flavors. Sacred to Venus (Rome).

Raspberry: *water;* safety and love. Raspberries ferment quickly and always provide hearty, full flavor to beverages.

Rhubarb: *earth;* protection, faithfulness, devotion, health. A rather tart addition, rhubarb can balance out sweeter ingredients.

Rose: *water;* intuitive senses, love, divination, well-being. Rose water is one means of smoothing out the flavor of a beverage. Roses in quantity lend a strong aroma and lovely color to your brew. Sacred to Venus (Rome).

Rosemary: *fire;* mental acuity, cleansing, rest, youthful vigor, memory. Use in minimal quantities, according to personal taste. Sacred to Venus (Rome). For friendship and remembrance; protection from the evil eye. Often used in incense.

Saffron: *fire;* weather magic, prosperity, joy, psychic awareness. Added in small amounts, saffron helps smooth out the body of a beverage. Appeared as an offering in the temples to Eos (Greece), Amon Ra (Egypt), and Brahma (Hindu). The spice of kings.

Sage: *air;* panacea of health, wisdom. Best used in metheglin and other fitness-related drinks. A favored herb by Zeus (Greece) and his Roman counterpart Jupiter. This herb promises long life and many children. One of the most widely used herbs for healing in the Middle Ages.

Strawberry: *water;* light-hearted love and joy, energy of summer. Strawberry is a very active fermenter with a lovely flavor and scent. Sacred to Freya (Norse/Teutonic).

Sugar: *earth;* dispel evil, sweeten ill disposition. Sugar is the key ingredient in most alcoholic beverages, but not recommended for those with weight problems or sugar imbalances. Sacred to Kane (Hawaii).

Tea: *fire;* wealth, courage, strength, vitality, health, rest. Tea is a good substitute for ginger root or other barks/roots to provide tannic acid. Herb teas provide additional flavor.

Thyme: *water;* bravery, fortitude, purification, awareness. Another herb excellent for metheglins and teas. An honored herb among the fairy folk.

Turmeric: *fire;* purification. In Indonesia, the root is used to prepare a yellow-orange wedding paint for the couples' arms. Far Eastern people add this to makeup for a "glowing" complexion.

Vanilla: *water;* mental awareness, love, productivity, zeal. I like a little vanilla bean or extract in almost all my brews.

Watermelon: *water;* love, health. Melons are tricky to use for brewing, being very susceptible to temperature changes. Probably best used to flavor grain spirits. Sacred to Set (Egypt).

Wine: *fire;* observances, offerings. Used as a base for Horilka and certain spiced punch bowls. Sacred to Gestin (Sumeria), Ishtar (Mesopotamia), Osiris and Isis (Egypt), and Bacchus (Rome).

Yogurt: *water;* spirituality, awareness, dietary focus. Yogurt is frequently employed in non-alcoholic drinks for health and weight loss.

Correspondences

The following is a brief list of color and number correspondences which can be used in brewing. For example, include one teaspoon each of green herbs like basil, mint, and bay in mead for abundant energy or accelerated growth.

Red — vigor, fearlessness, endurance, fire
Orange — force, outcomes, warmth, empathy
Yellow — intellect, prophesy, inventiveness, air, activity
Green — development, abundance, confidence, well-being
Blue — water, harmony, restoration, happiness, reflection
Purple — devotion, commitment, perception
White — safety, cleansing, purity
Black — banishing, the void, rest
Brown — earth, nature, groundwork, new undertakings
Pink — relationships, diversion, leisure, positive outlooks

1 — oneness, beginning, agreement, sun magic, energy
2 — symmetry, sanctification, alliance
3 — balance, objectives, body-mind-spirit, trinity
4 — components, time, aspirations, triumph, elements
5 — adaptability, perception, psychic endeavors
6 — protection, devotion, completion of tasks
7 — wisdom, variety, moon magic
8 — power, personal transformation, control
9 — universal law, service to others
10 — dependability, rationality
12 — productivity, longevity, a full year
13 — veneration, forbearance, belief
21 — respect, remembrance, excellence
40 — ascetic states, retreat, revitalizing self, communion

Appendix B

Brewing Deities

Reading the myths and legends of many cultures is an enriching experience. In the process, you get a clearer understanding of the diversity of our world, and insight into why we are who we are. Among these legends, many Divine images appear and reappear, inspiring humanity toward better living. The following are some possible Gods, Goddesses, heros, heroines, and even Saints from which to choose, including their country of origin and spheres of influence. This list could be much longer, but I have limited myself to some of the more interesting and assorted options here. For additional ideas, look at fruits or spices sacred to your patron Deities and check resource books like *The Witches' God*, and *The Witches' Goddess* by Janet and Stewart Farrar, and *Ancient and Shining Ones* by D. J. Conway.

Ahurani: Persian; goddess of water.

Anat: Canaanite; fertility goddess, appropriate for any milk-based beverage.

Aphrodite: Greek; goddess of love. Any beverage with roses, clover, sweet aromas, or apples.

Apollo: Greek; god of science, music, and poetry. Sometimes associated with mead. Combination of science and art attributes; call on him for general brewing efforts.

Athena: Greek; warrior goddess. Any beverage with coconut. In Rome, known as Minerva.

Baldur: Norse; god of sacred wells and light. Good for non-alcoholic beverages used for magic.

Binah: Hebrew; the supernatural Mother, also known as She Who Nourishes. Her cabalistic symbol is the cup.

Blodeuwedd: Welsh; name means "flower face." Any flower-based drinks, especially those with broom or meadowsweet.

Bragi: Norse; keeper of the mead of inspiration, god of eloquence and wisdom.

Buddhi: Tibetan; goddess of achievement. Aids in learning your art(s).

Carmenta: Roman; inventor of arts and sciences; similar in function to Buddhi.

Ceres: Roman; goddess of agriculture. Appropriate for beverages, especially beer.

Cerridwen: Welsh; goddess of the cauldron and grain.

Chicomecoatz: Aztec; goddess of maize and rural abundance; good for corn-based drinks and harvest festival beverages.

Cormus: Greek; god of laughter and mirth. Good for celebratory brewing efforts.

Dionysus: Greek; god of wine and mead. In Rome known as Bacchus or Liber; similar personifications in almost every culture.

Esculapius: Greek; god of physick and all health beverages.

Euphrosyne: Greek; muse who rejoices the heart.

Frigg: Norse; personification of earth. Appropriate for libation beverages.

Gambrinus: Germanic; the inventor of beer and patron saint of brewers.

Ganemede: Greek; the cup bearer to Jupiter; good for hospitality.

Gibil: Babylonian; God of arbitration; good for beverages prepared for oath cups or peace cups.

Gunnloed: Teutonic; god of mead.

Hesperides: Greek; three sisters with golden apples in their magic garden.

Hygeia: Greek; goddess of health.

I: Chinese; God of archery who possesses the drink of immortality.

Idun: Norse; keeper of apples of immortality.

Isis: Egyptian; Goddess whose sacred fruits include figs and dates; offerings often consisted of beer, milk, and wine.

Ivenopae: Indonesian; mother of rice, good to bless sake.

Kanaloa: Hawaii; goddess whose sacred fruit is the banana.

Lares and Penates: Roman; home and hearth gods.

Momus: Greek; god of raillery.

Nikkal: Canaanite; goddess of first fruits; for beverages to be used in offerings.

Oegir: Norse; beer brewer of Asgard.

Omacatl: Aztec; god of delight and celebration.

Osiris: Egyptian; god of cereals and common people; especially for beer.

Pomona: Roman; goddess of fruits and autumn. Fruit-based or harvest drinks.

Shoney: Scottish; god of ale. Mirrored in Egypt by Tenemit.

Thor: Norse; red-fruited drinks.

Vertumnus: Roman; god of orchards.

Wang Mu: Chinese; goddess served the peaches of immortality.

Appendix C

Brewing Folklore

Wherever people gather to share good food and drink, superstitions will likely figure in the conversation. Not all superstitions are silly or outmoded. In recent years, some have been proven correct through scientific study. Accurate or not, however, there is power in the longevity of beliefs held in the common heart of humankind. It is this very power and energy that can be used symbolically in magic (see also *Folkways: Reclaiming the Power and Magic*).

In reading this section, recall some of the lore you heard around the family table, on camping trips, from friends, and the elders in your home to see if they also have some metaphysical applications.

- **Evil spirits are allergic to blessed water**—this basically means that any beverage you create magically helps protect not only you but your living space. Sprinkle some around the perimeter of the magic circle for asperging. Dot your door mantles with a drop of homemade wine or ale. Consider beverages as an alternative to anointing oils that can sometimes be too pungent.

- **Tea and sugar must go into a pot before water or milk for good luck**—in preparing any beverage, make sure that sugar or honey is one of the first ingredients added after the water. This stimulates a little serendipity.

- **Having wine or beer spilled on you is good fortune; breaking a wine glass means happy marriages and affection**—instead of crying over "spilled milk," rinse off your clothing, wipe up the spillage, and dedicate it to one of your favorite gods or goddesses to encourage fortuity. Keep the glass for use in a witch bottle.

- **To prevent drunkenness, drink from an amethyst chalice or eat orange rind first**—carry orange candy and an amethyst crystal as a gentle reminder not to overindulge; even better, give them to the designated driver of a group for strength of conviction.

- To dream of drinking barley beer means long life and joy—the next time you are ill or a little melancholy, sip barley brew or carry barley grains with you to regain well being and happiness.

- Brandy is said to appease and protect one from spirits—anoint yourself with brandy before attempting channeling or mediumship. An appropriate asperger before seances.

- Saki is commonly offered to Japanese gods and ancestors to show gratitude or to attempt appeasement—as such it might be a good beverage to have available at Summerland rituals, or Samhain when the veil between worlds is thin.

- Whiskey is a potent component in early American folk magics—it was rubbed on the skin to attract good energies and remove curses—Whiskey might be a good ingredient in any beverage for banishings or turning mal-intended magic.

- The mead moon is the full moon in October which takes place during the apple harvest. It is considered the best time to make this honey wine beverage—why not try? Apples are inexpensive at this time of year, as is cider, both of which make wonderful bases for mead. The potency, flavor, and magical energy are all enhanced by this timing.

- Warm milk is good for stomach problems—despite more contemporary awareness that this is indeed true, it does not lessen the potential use of warm milk in any drink (or punch bowl) to accentuate health and well being.

- If two women pour from the same teapot, one will become pregnant within a year—this symbolism is fun to use if two friends hope to have children. Also, a teapot might be used as part of a ritual for conception or inventive energy.

- Bottles of wine and champagne should always be passed around a table in sunward fashion lest they be stale or turned sour. This is also the best direction to pass beverages for continuing good fortune—when mixing beverages, stir clockwise to bring good energies and rich flavors. When serving, pour out in the same direction to bless your guests with luck.

Appendix D

Brewing Goods and Services

Brewing Hobbyist Supply Stores

Brewers Emporium
249 River Street
Depew, NY 14043

Hennessy Homebrew
470 N. Greenbush Road., Rt. 4
Rensselaer, NY 12144

Winemaker's Shop
Bully Hill, RFD 2
Hammondsport, NY 14840

Aetna Wine Supplies
708 Rainier Avenue South
Seattle, WA 98118

Milan Laboratory
57 Spring Street
New York, NY 10012

Wines Inc.
1340 Home Avenue
Akron, OH 44310

Publishers of Brewing Books and Related Topics

Please specify the type of book listing you desire when writing any of these publishers for a more timely and focused response.

Mills & Boon Ltd.
17-19 Foley Street
London, England W1A 1DR

Prism Press
Box 788
San Leandro, CA 94577

SCA: Compleat Anachronist
Box 360743
Milpitas, CA 95036-0743

Garden Way
Storey Communications
Schoolhouse Road
Pownal, VT 05261-9988

Culinary Arts
Box 2157
Lake Oswego, OR 97035

General Items, Including Spices and Grains

European Imports
23 N. Bemiston Avenue
St. Louis, MO 63105

Roffman's House of Delicacies
2500 Haney Street
Omaha, NB 68131

Paprikas Weiss Importer
2546 Second Avenue
New York, NY 10028

B. Altmans
5th Ave. at 34th Street
New York, NY 10016

Bloomingdale's Delicacies
340 Madison Avenue.
New York, NY 10017

Aphrodisia
282 Bleecker Street
New York, NY 10014
212-986-6440

Lotus Light
Box 2
Wilmot, WI 53192
414-862-2395

Angelicas
147 First Avenue
New York, NY 10003
212-677-1549

Frontier Cooperative
Box 299
Norway, IA 52318
800-669-3275

General Items, Including Spices and Grains (cont'd)

Pierce
33 Brookline Avenue
Boston, MA 02215

J. Goldsmith & Sons
123 S. Main Street
Memphis, TN 38103

Coffee and Tea Specialists

Coffee Connection
119 Braintree Street
Boston, MA 02134
800-284-5282

McNulty's Tea & Coffee Co.
109 Christopher Street
New York, NY 10014

Peet's Coffee and Tea
Box 8247
Emeryville, CA 94662
800-999-2132

First Colony Coffee & Tea Co., Inc.
204-222 West 22nd Street
Box 11005
Norfolk, VA 23517

East India Tea & Coffee Co. (tea only)
1481 3rd Street
San Francisco, CA 94107

Utensils and Small Appliances

Kitchen Aid
Hobart Corp.
Troy, OH 45374

Magic Mill
235 West 2nd Street
Salt Lake City, UT 84101

Bridge Company
212 E. 52nd Street
New York, NY 10022

Moulinex
1 Montgomery Street
Belleville, NJ 07109

Nutone Scoville
Madison & Red Banks Rd.
Cincinnati, OH 45227

Zabar's
2245 Broadway
New York, NY 10024

Bazar de la Cuisine
160 E. 55th Street
New York, NY 10022

Ronson Corporation
1 Ronson Rd.
Ogletown, DE 19702

Cross Imports
210 Hanover Street
Boston, MA 02113

Miscellaneous

Economy Candy
108 Rivington Street
New York, NY 10002
212-254-1531

Silver Palate
274 Columbus Avenue
New York, NY 10023
212-799-6340

A good collection of dried fruits, almond paste, unique condiments, etc. which can be used as a flavor component in brewing. Catalogue is free. Charge cards welcome. Minimum order $25.00.

A collection of rare, unusual, and interesting jellies, jams, preserves, sauces, and condiments. Charges accepted. Terrific bottling-for-gift items.

Appendix E

Modern Brewing Basics

by Jeffrey Donaghue

It's easy to brew good wine and beer. However, it's even easier to brew bad wine and beer. The purpose of this appendix is to provide information about fermentation, and to outline simple modern brewing techniques that can easily be used. This is not intended as a comprehensive text on wine and beer brewing. To learn more and in greater detail, check your local library for recent books on brewing. Retail and mail-order supply sources and most well-stocked book stores will also have many useful books.

During fermentation, brewing yeasts metabolize or consume organic sugars, resulting in certain by-products. In order for yeast to do its fermentation job, it needs certain things. As its primary food, yeast needs sugar. Yeast also needs oxygen to live in this sugar solution. Finally, yeast needs certain nutrients for a well-balanced diet. Professional brewers call these nutrients "free amino acids."

When yeast is introduced into a sugar solution such as your brew, it begins the respiration phase. It consumes oxygen and gets ready for the next phase. Fermentation is the second phase. During this phase it reproduces and consumes sugar and nutrients. The two most important byproducts are carbon dioxide, seen as bubbles, and ethyl alcohol. As the yeast's sugar food source becomes used up, it becomes dormant and settles to the bottom of the vessel. This is the last phase: sedimentation.

The Process

Some aspects of brewing beer and wine-making are common to both. There are also some things unique to each one, but in essence both processes are quite simple and easy to learn. With very little basic equipment, ingredients, and information, success can be almost guaranteed. We will now go through a general procedure which will work with both wine and beer, pointing out differences as we go along.

The Primary Fermenter

You will first need a container of the right capacity to hold the ingredients. This is your primary fermenter. Food-grade plastic, stainless steel, and enamel ware are all good choices. Plastic should be free of scratches to make sanitizing possible. Avoid iron, aluminum, and copper because the acidity in fermenting beverages will cause metals to dissolve into the brew, giving it a metallic taste. Depending on the recipe, you will either cook the ingredients and then put them into the primary fermenter, or put them in first, adding water later.

In wine recipes where all the ingredients, including all the water, have not been cooked, it is best to mix a crushed Campden tablet with the other ingredients in the primary, to kill wild yeasts, bacteria, and molds. *NOTE: Campden tablets are sulphites; if you are allergic to sulphites don't use them.* In beer brewing, all ingredients are usually boiled, and the addition of sulphites is not necessary. For wine, this mixture is now called "must"; for beer, it is called "wort."

The wine must in your primary should now be covered with a lid, plastic sheeting, or clean cloth, and allowed to cool overnight. This will allow the sulphite to dissipate and the temperature to drop to a safe level. Both sulphites and high temperature would kill the special brewing yeast which you will be adding.

When the must or wort has cooled, you will add the proper yeast. Just as there are many types of wine and beer, there are many types of yeast to make them. Special strains are available for English ales, German lagers, Belgian Wit beers, French Beaujolais Nouveau, sweet and dry meads, and Japanese sake, to name just a few. You can use regular bread yeast, but it tends to stay in suspension and gives the finished beer or wine a yeasty taste. The small extra expense of brewing yeast is worthwhile. Pure liquid cultures can be added directly to the must or wort. Dry yeast must be re-hydrated. To do this, pour the yeast into a cup of water which has been sterilized by boiling and then cooled to 105°F or less. Do not stir. After 15 minutes, this can be added to the primary fermenter.

The primary fermentation will begin within 12 to 24 hours. During this time, the primary container should remain covered as above to prevent insects, such a fruit flies, and air-borne yeasts from getting into the must or wort. Temperature is also important. For beer, you will usually be using ale yeast which ferments best between 60°F and 75°F. Wine can ferment at higher temperatures, but below 80°F. As the temperature drops, the yeast slows down and soon fermentation stops altogether. When temperatures get too high, the yeast "goes crazy" and produces compounds which can add bad flavors. This is especially true with beer yeast. Primary fermentation will be very active, sometimes creating a big foamy head on the must or wort. As the time specified in the recipe passes, activity will decline.

The Secondary Fermenter

After a week or so, fermentation activity will subside and the time will come to transfer the brew into the secondary fermenter. You will do this by either carefully pouring or siphoning the liquid off the sediment in the bottom of the primary. The secondary fermenter should be equipped with a fermentation lock of some kind. The fermentation lock is a simple device that allows the carbon dioxide gas which continues to be produced as the yeast ferments to escape, but does not allow anything else to get in. The locks are inexpensive and very useful. Secondary fermentation will continue from a few days to many months, depending on the type of brew being made.

For still wines, those without carbonation, you will repeat the "racking" process several times, siphoning the wine off the sediment into another clean container, until fermentation has ceased. When fermentation has stopped, the wine is bottled and set aside to age. Aging time for wine will vary depending on the ingredients. Follow the recipe. In general, six months to a year is enough.

Bottling

For a sparkling wine the procedure is a little different. You will either bottle the wine before it has finished fermenting and it still has some residual sugar, or you will wait for fermentation to end and then add a measured amount of sugar to the clear wine. The sugar should have been first dissolved in boiled water. The wine will then continue to ferment in the bottle, but since the carbon dioxide gas cannot escape, it is absorbed into the wine, carbonating it. Needless to say, if too much sugar remains, the bottles could explode from the build-up of excess pressure. Adding a measured amount of sugar will give the best results. Good recipes and experience are the best teachers here, but you should not exceed 1 to 1½ ounces of sugar per gallon. Aging time will be the same as for wine. For sparkling wine or mead, you should use returnable beer bottles or champagne bottles which are made to withstand high pressure. You will notice that champagne bottles can be capped with the same type of capper used for beer bottles. Because fermentation continues in the bottle, a fine layer of yeast sediment will develop at the bottom. Decant when you open the bottle.

The procedure for beer is a little easier. The beer should have completely fermented after a week in the Secondary fermenter. You then add a measured amount of sugar that has been dissolved in a small amount of boiled water. The amount will be based on the recipe, but should not exceed 1 to 1½ ounces of sugar per gallon. You can use returnable beer bottles, cappable champagne bottles, or strong screw-top beverage bottles. The thin plastic "PET" bottles used for soft drinks can be used as well. All types have their advantages and disadvantages. Bottle as for sparkling wine above. Beer will be "conditioned" and ready to drink within 10 to 14 days. Most beer will not improve after a few months. As with sparkling wine, there will be a layer of yeast sediment in the bottle after a short time. Open carefully and decant into a glass or pitcher.

Some of the recipes in this book recommend stopping the fermentation before it finishes. Fermentation will stop naturally, either when all the sugar has been used up, or the alcohol level gets high enough to kill the yeast (about 15 percent). Also, in very sweet wines, the high concentration of sugar will cause the yeast to go dormant after a very short fermentation. There are other methods of stopping the fermentation in wine. As the author suggests in her recipes, you can heat the wine. This will kill the yeast and any bacteria which may be in the wine. There are disadvantages to this. First, since alcohol boils at 172.8° F, you will boil off some or possibly all of the alcohol you have worked to create. Second, heating will change the taste of your beverage. This is especially true of the more delicately flavored wines. If boiled for very long, the wine can take on a cooked taste. Another method of stopping fermentation, or simply assuring that it does not start up again, is to add one of the commercially available wine stabilizers. These are the same as the "preservatives" found in all the processed and packaged food you eat every day. Ask your supplier for advice. You will have to decide if you want to add to the amount of preservatives you are already consuming.

Precautions for Ensuring Success

The process, as you can see, is very simple. It's so simple, in fact, that if left on their own most sugar solutions, such as fruit juices, will naturally begin to ferment with the help of air-borne wild yeasts. Your task as a brewer is to control fermentation, and the single most important tool you have at your disposal to do this is sanitation.

First and foremost, all ingredients that you add to recipes should be of high quality and fit for human consumption. They should be well washed before use. The computer expression "garbage in—garbage out" applies to brewing as well. All fermentation containers and utensils should be cleanable and cleaned. Plastic items should only be made of *food grade* plastic. If it does not say "food grade," don't use it. Non-food grade plastics may have fungicides and heavy metal plasticisers in them which are toxic. All materials, but plastic especially, should be free of cracks and scratches where harmful bacterial can lurk. Glass, stainless steel, and enamelware make the best containers. Wooden containers and utensils will also work, but extra care must be taken to assure that no harmful bacteria remain in this porous material.

Everything that comes in contact with your wine or beer should be sanitized. This can be done with heat or chemicals. Boiling and high temperature drying in a dish washer are two common ways of using heat. When making wine, a strong sulphite solution of several Campden tablets per gallon can be used to sanitize your equipment. Soak all equipment and rinse or air dry. Beer makers shun sulphites, and rely more on chlorine to sanitize. One or two ounces of household bleach in 5 gallons water will make an effective sanitizer. Soak everything for a few hours. Rinse or allow to air dry. Sanitizing bottles and bottle caps is an important step often overlooked.

In general, any water which is good to drink will make good wine or beer. All water which is added to a recipe should be boiled or treated with sulphite to eliminate possible contamination.

We next have to think of safety. When using unusual ingredients such as herbs, check with contemporary sources to make sure they are safe to consume. Many of yesterday's safe home remedies have been found to contain toxins or carcinogens. There are no known harmful pathogens which can grow in wine or beer. That is because wine and beer both contain one of the most potent chemicals known to humanity, alcohol. Women who are pregnant or intend to become pregnant soon should never consume alcoholic beverages. Everyone should treat alcoholic drinks with the same respect that has always been part of the best brewing traditions.

Glossary

Brewing has a fascinating history and interesting terminology. In this list there are many terms which come from the Germanic regions, especially those pertaining to beer. As you might guess, this is because Germany was as famous for its beer as France became for wine. In this manner, an examination of terminology affords some insightful, and sometimes humorous, glimpses of our ancestors and the veritable treasure trove of tradition they have left to us.

Aerobic Fermentation: Known as the first fermentation, this takes place in open air from 2 days to 2 weeks before the beverage is transferred to an air-tight container.

Advocaat: In Dutch, this drink's name translates to something like "a beverage for lawyers." It is a traditional holiday liqueur which has an egg nog-like flavor.

Aging: One of the most essential steps in making good wine is proper aging in an air-tight container. Most wines are best aged for a minimum of six months and meads a year to insure full body, mellow aroma, and well-balanced flavor.

Aiguebelle: A liqueur similar to Chartreuse, made with over 50 herbs and spices at the monastery of Notre Dame.

Ale: Beer brewed at a warmer temperature with top-fermenting yeast.

Amaretto: Originally made in 15th century Italy, this liqueur gets its flavor from almonds.

Aperitif: A before-dinner drink which is usually a dry, high-proof wine.

Applejack: A type of apple liqueur which originated about 1700 in Germany, and is considered as having good digestive qualities.

Arabica: The earliest cultivated species of coffee, which is still widely grown.

Balance: A beverage is considered to be well balanced when the flavor, aroma, and texture all blend harmoniously during consumption.

Beaker people: A small group of individuals in Northern Europe who, as early as 2000 B.C., were producing and selling beer-like beverages.

Benedictine: Dates back to the early 1500s. This liqueur was first made by the monks of Fecamp, using herbs with reputed medicinal value. Each bottle carries the abbreviation of the Latin phrase "to god the most good."

Bilbil: African champagne-like beverage whose name translates to mean "mother of the nightingale," because those who drink it usually break out in joyous song.

Brandy: An alcohol distilled from fermented fruit juices.

Broken grade: A type of tea in which the leaves have been crushed into small pieces for tea bags. This allows the tea to yield its flavor more quickly.

Bussa: Armenian beer known in the 1700s. It was uniquely stored in underground pots and consumed through reeds.

Ch'a Ching: The very first book of tea released in the late eighth century. The title translates to mean "the classic tea," and this text may have been the foundation for the highly complicated Japanese tea rituals. It includes detailed instructions on every aspect of enjoying tea, from growing the plant to proper methods of picking, drying, and steeping.

Cha-no-yu: The carefully choreographed Japanese tea ritual with seemingly hundreds of ground rules for completion. The room for the ceremony must not be repetitious; no line, color, or form should appear twice. No ceremony should allow for more than five guests, each of whom washes his or her hands and face before entering the tea room. Each movement of the host is designed to reflect humility, grace and hospitality as well as certain mysteries of the Eastern religions.

Chartreuse: An herbal liqueur made by Carthusian monks. Its preparation is kept secret to all but a handful of faithful individuals. Two types exists, yellow and green, the green being more potent.

Chicory: Endive root which is sometimes ground and roasted like coffee or added to coffee for textural variance.

Clarifying: To slowly suspend fruit or yeast particles in a beverage to bring about a transparent, light-colored liquid, through straining, racking, and filtration systems when available.

Congou: From a Chinese word meaning "the art of tea," this is a general term for any unbroken black tea blocks from China.

Danzigergoldwasser: A German orange liqueur which contains flakes of gold leaf in the bottom. Originally, gold and silver leaf were used in beverages to help improve the healing qualities.

Demitasse: A favorite miniature cup among drinkers of certain very rich coffees. The term is from the French, translating quite literally to "half cup" or "little cup."

Dolo: A beer made in the French Soudan which was prepared with millet, maize, and bananas.

Drambuie: A personal favorite drink. Its name comes from the Gaelic, meaning a "drink which contents." This is considered by the Scots as the nectar of the gods. The recipe is reported to have begun with Prince Charlie.

European preparation: A phrase among coffee producers which indicates a manner of hand-cleaning coffee beans so that all debris and imperfections are removed before blending.

Fermentation lock: A special device used by home brewers to keep air out while releasing excess pressure from the fermentation process. One creative alternative is a balloon fastened to the top of your fermentation jar.

Fortifying: The process of adding spirits to wine to increase the alcohol content, and sometimes to stop the fermentation process when the wine has reached a pleasing flavor.

French roast: Any coffee bean which has been roasted to a very dark brown or almost black coloration, giving the resulting beverage a bittersweet flavor.

Grasadur: Scandinavian mead spoken of in sagas, flavored strongly with herbs and very intoxicating.

Hippocras: Wines common to the sixteenth and seventeenth century, praised by knights and clergy alike. They were a mix of wine with spices, aged together for 2-3 days.

Kitcha-Yojoki: Written by a Buddhist abbot, Yeisei, in the late 1100s, this was Japan's first collective work on tea, which supported the idea of the beverage as healthful and revitalizing.

Lager: From a German word meaning "store," this is a beer made from bottom fermenting yeast at cooler temperatures, and aged for longer periods.

Lees: The sediment of solid fruit and yeast cells at the bottom of the fermentation vessel. Be careful to keep its sediment out when pouring off wine into clean bottles. Lees can make wine bitter or heavy.

Mead: A wine sweetened with honey. One of the most popular drinks of the Middle Ages.

Melomel: A honey wine whose flavor comes from added fruit or fruit juice.

Metheglin: A honey wine whose flavor comes from added spices, herbs, or barks.

Mocha-Java: Perhaps the first coffee blend, this is a mixture of two parts java to one part Arabian mocha coffee beans.

Must: Wine in its earliest stages where large pieces of fruit, yeast, and juice are present. Most home brewers have a special must jar where bits of left-over honey, sugar, spices, and fruits for wine can be kept and used for a mixed-flavor beverage.

Oegisdrykk: A harvest ale of the Norse gods, described in the older Edda.

Pan frying: A method of drying tea leaves which allows a skilled individual to shape the leaves in a unique manner befitting the tea being created.

Pelusium: Ancient Egyptian beer made with strong aromatic herbs instead of hops and served as an appetizer.

Perrione: Known in the 1600s to be of Guianese origins, this liquor was made from cassai root and drunk only at funeral feasts. The person most drunk after 3-4 days of observance was considered the most honored.

Prewmeister: A municipal authority of the 1300s in Nuremburg, whose sworn official duty was to be present at every brewing to insure proper ingredients, measures, and eventual sale.

Probestecher: A group of beer tasters/testers in fifteenth-century Hamburg, Germany. Any beer which did not meet with their approval was confiscated.

Pyrolysis: A process during the roasting of coffee beans that breaks down the fats and carbohydrates into oils which are the source of coffee's aroma and taste.

Rosé: A wine whose color is usually obtained from grape skins left in the must for the first fermentation.

Rum: A distilled beverage made from sugar and molasses.

Sabaia: A fourth century beer consumed by Illyrians (Rome), especially those of poorer classes. It was made from barley and other cereals.

Sack mead: A honey wine made with greater amounts of honey for increased potency.

Strega: An Italian liqueur made with more than 70 herbs; considered an excellent love potion. Thought by some to have been created by an Italian witch.

Stuck fermentation: When for unknown reasons your beverage stops fermenting before the sugar has been used up to the desired taste. This happens due to imbalance in the ingredients and can be rectified by certain yeasts and nutrients.

Sura: Ancient Persian beverage of millet, water, honey, melted butter, barley, and curds. Frequently made for ritual purposes.

Table wines: Meant to aid the appetite and clear the pallet for improved appreciation of the meal. White wines are thought best for chicken, fish, poultry, and red wines for beef and other red meat.

Tannin: An ingredient found in barks, roots, leaves, and stems; small quantities of tannin improve the balance of wine.

Tea auctions: There are about six tea auction centers in the world where millions of pounds of various grade teas change hands in one day. In older times, the bidding was governed by a one-inch taper candle; when it burned out, the last bid heard won the chest.

Tea vans: Appearing on war fronts after the turn of the century, these vans traveled to any war zone, with hot cups of tea for servicemen. The vans were sponsored by various organizations such as the Quakers.

Tolles bier: A beer made in the region of Cologne around 1600 which was used in trade with nearby towns, often on holidays and sacred days, much to the disconcertion of the clergy. Later in the period, the beer was outlawed as "unfit" with little effect.

Turkish coffee: Made from beans ground to powder, then through a process of repeated boiling, this coffee is sweetened and served, with grounds and all in the cup.

Vodka: A pure grain alcohol with a neutral flavor. While many people associate this drink with Russia, there is strong evidence that it was first made in Poland in the 1500s.

Wax water: A byproduct of brewing processes caused by boiling honeycomb in water to yield as much sweetness as possible. The wax would be removed from the top of the cooled liquid and used for domestic purposes.

Zythos: A barley wine or mead, most likely of Egyptian origin, but written about in Greece. This drink takes its name from the Greek word *zeo* meaning "to boil." This term also has close ties with the Sanskrit expression *yas* and the Anglo Saxon *gist* which have similar connotations. The similarities between these phrases and our modern word "yeast" should not be overlooked.

Bibliography

Arnold, John P. *Origin and History of Beer and Brewing.* Chicago: Wahl-Henius Institute of Fermentology, 1911.

Aylett, Mary. *Country Wines.* London: Odhams, 1953.

Baker, Margaret. *Folklore & Customs of Rural England.* Totawa, NJ: Rowman & Littlefield, 1974.

Bartlett, John. *Familiar Quotations.* Boston: Little Brown & Co., 1938.

Marshall, Mac, Editor. *Beliefs, Behaviors and Alcoholic Beverages.* Ann Arbor, MI: University of Michigan Press, 1979.

Belt, T. Edwin. *Vegetable, Herb & Cerial Wines.* London: Mills & Boon LTD, 1971.

_____. *Flower, Leaf & Sap Wines.* London: Mills & Boon LTD, 1971.

Beyerl, Paul. *Master Book of Herbalism.* Custer, WA: Phoenix Publishing, 1984.

Black, William George. *Folk Medicine.* New York: Burt Franklin, 1883.

Broth, Patricia and Don. *Food in Antiquity.* New York: Frederick A. Praeger, 1969.

Chase, A.W. MD. *Receipt Book & Household Physician.* Detroit: F.B. Dickerson Company, 1908.

Chase, Edithe L. and French, W. E. P. *Waes Hale.* New York: Grafton Press, 1903.

Chow, Kit & Kramer, Ione. *All the Tea in China.* San Francisco: China Books and Periodicals, 1990.

Clarkson, Rosetta. *Green Enchantment.* New York: McMillian Publishing, 1940.

Clifton, C. *Edible Flowers.* New York: McGraw-Hill, 1976.

Compleat Anachronist Guide to Brewing. Milpitas, CA: Society for Creative Anactronsim, 1983.

Conway, D. J. *Ancient and Shining Ones.* St. Paul: Llewellyn Publications, 1993.

Culpepper, Nicholas. *Complete Herbal and English Physician.* Glenwood, IL: Meyerbooks, 1991. Originally published 1841.

Cunningham, Scott. *Encyclopedia of Magical Herbs.* St. Paul: Llewellyn Publications, 1988.

_____. *The Magic in Food.* St. Paul: Llewellyn Publications, 1991.

_____. *The Magic of Incense, Oils and Brews.* St. Paul: Llewellyn Publications, 1988.

Davids, Kenneth. *Coffee.* San Francisco : 101 Productions, 1976.

Digby, Kenelm. *The Closet Opened.* London: E.L.T. Brome, Little Britian, 1696.

Doorn, Joyce V. *Making Your Own Liquors.* San Leandro, CA: Prism Press, 1977.

Elspan, Ceres. *Herbs to Help You Sleep.* Boulder, CO: Shambhala Press, 1980.

Encyclopedia of Creative Cooking. Charlotte Turgeon, Editor. New York: Weathervane Press, 1982.

Every Day Life through the Ages. London: Reader's Digest Association, Berkley Square, 1992.

Farrar, Janet and Farrar, Stewart. *The Witches' God: The Masculine Principle of Divinity.* Custer, WA: Phoenix Publishing, Inc., 1989.

_____. *The Witches' Goddess: The Feminine Principle of Divinity.* Custer, WA: Phoenix Publishing, Inc., 1987.

Foster, Carol. *Cooking with Coffee.* New York: Fireside Books, 1992.

Fox, William, M.D. *Family Botanic Guide,* 18th edition. Sheffield, England: William Fox and Sons, 1907.

Freeman, Margaret. *Herbs for the Medieval Household for Cooking, Healing and Divers Uses.* New York: Metropolitan Museum of Art, 1943.

Freid, Mimi. *Liquors for Gifts.* Charlotte, VT: Garden Way Publishing, 1988.

French, R. K. *The History and Virtues of Cyder.* New York: St. Martin's Press, 1982.

Gayre, Robert. *Brewing Mead.* Boulder, CO: Brewers Publications, 1986.

Gordon, Lesley. *Green Magic.* New York: Viking Press, 1977.

Haggard, Howard W. M.D. *Mystery, Magic and Medicine.* Garden City, NY: Doubleday and Company, 1933.

Hale, William Harlan. *Horizon Cookbook & Illustrated History of Eating and Drinking.* Garden City, NY: Doubleday and Company, 1968.

Hall, Manly. *Secret Teachings of All Ages:An Encyclopedic Outline of Masonic, Hermetic, Qabbalistic, & Rosicrucian Symbolical Philosophy.* Los Angeles: Philosophical Research Society, 1977.

Hardwick, Homer. *Winemaking at Home.* New York: W. Funk, 1954.

Hechtlinger, Adelaide. *The Seasonal Hearth.* New York: Overlook Press, 1986.

Hiss, Emil. *Standard Manual of Soda & Other Beverages.* Chicago: GP Englehand & Co, 1897.

Hobson, Phyllis. Making *Wines, Beers, & Soft Drinks.* Charlotte, VT: Garden Way Publishing, 1984

Honey, Babs. *Drinks for All Seasons.* Wakefield, England: E. P. Publishing Ltd, 1982.

Hopkins, Albert A. *Home Made Beverages.* New York: Scientific American Publishing Company, 1919.

Hosletter's U.S. Almanac. Pittsburgh: Hosletter Co., 1897.

Hunter, Beatrice. *Fermented Foods and Beverages.* New Canaan, CT: Keats Publishing, 1973.

Hutchinson, Ruth and Adams, Ruth. *Every Day's a Holiday.* New York: Harper & Brothers, 1951.

Jagendorf, M.A. *Folk Wines, Cordials & Brandies.* New York: Vanguard Press, 1963.

Kieckhefer, Richard. *Magic in the Middle Ages.* Melbourne, Australia: Cambrige University Press, 1989.

Long, Cheryl. *Classic Liqueurs.* Lake Oswego, OR: Culinary Arts, 1990.

Lorie, Peter. *Superstitions.* New York: Simon & Schuster, 1992.

Lowe, Carl. *Juice Power.* New York: Berkley Books, 1992.

Luce, Henry R., Editor. *Beverages.* Alexandria, VA: Time Life Books, 1982.

MacNicol, Mary. *Flower Cookery.* New York: Fleet Press, 1967.

Magnall, Richmal. *Historical and Miscellanious Questions.* London: Longman, Brown, Green and Longman, 1850.

Mares, William. *Making Beer.* New York: Alfred A. Knopf Co, 1992.

Murray, Keith. *Ancient Rites & Ceremonies.* Toronto: Tudor Press, 1980.

Murray, Michael T. *The Healing Power of Herbs.* Rocklin, CA: Prima Publishing, 1992.

Olney, Bruce. *Liqueurs, Apéritifs and Fortified Wines.* London: Mills & Boon LTD, 1972.

Opie, Iona and Tatem, Moria. *Dictionary of Superstitions.* New York: Oxford University Press, 1989.

Palaiseul, Jean. *Grandmother's Secrets.* New York: G.P. Putnam's Sons, 1974.

Paulsen, Kathryn. *The Complete Book of Magic & WitchCraft.* New York: Signet Books, 1970.

Plat, Hugh. *Delights for Ladies.* London: Hvmfrey Lownes, 1602.

Ryall, Rhiannon. *West Country Wicca.* Custer, WA: Phoenix Publishing, 1989.

Schapira, Joel, David, and Karl. *The Book of Coffee and Tea.* New York: St. Martins Press, 1906.

Singer, Charles J. *Early English Magic and Medicine*. London: British Acadamy, 1920.

Skinner, Charles M. *Myths and Legends of Flowers, Trees, Fruits and Plants*. Philadelphia: Lippincott, 1925.

Tchudi, Stephen N. *Soda Poppery*. New York: Charles Scribner Sons, 1942.

Telesco, Patricia. *Folkways*. St. Paul: Llewellyn Publications, 1995.

_____. *A Victorian Flower Oracle*. St. Paul: Llewellyn Publications, 1994.

_____. *A Victorian Grimoire*. St. Paul: Llewellyn Publications, 1992.

_____. *The Kitchen Witch's Cookbook*. St. Paul: Llewellyn Publications, 1994.

Tillona, P. *Feast of Flowers*. New York: Funk & Wagnall, 1969.

Turner, B.C.A. *Fruit Wines*. London: Mills & Boon, LTD, 1973.

Urdag, George. *The Squib Ancient Pharmacy*. New York: Squibb and Sons, 1940.

Walker, Barbara. *Women's Dictionary of Sacred Symbols and Objects*. San Francisco: Harper Row, 1988.

Webster's Universal Unabridged Dictionary. New York: World Syndicate Publishing, 1937.

Wheelwrite, Edith Grey. *Medicinal Plant and Their History*. New York: Dover Publications, NY 1974.

Whiteside, Lorraine. *Fresh Fruit Drinks*. New York: Thorsons Publishers, 1984.

Williams, Judith. *Jude's Home Herbal*. St. Paul: Llewellyn Publications, 1992.

Woodward, Nancy Hyden. *Teas of the World*. New York: Macmillan Publishing Company, 1980.

Younger, William. *Gods, Men & Wine*. Cleveland: World Publishing, 1966.

Index

On the following pages you will find listed, with their current prices, some of the books now available on related subjects. Your book dealer stocks most of these and will stock new titles in the Llewellyn series as they become available. We urge your patronage.

TO GET A FREE CATALOG

You are invited to write for our bi-monthly news magazine/catalog, *Llewellyn's New Worlds of Mind and Spirit*. A sample copy is free, and it will continue coming to you at no cost as long as you are an active mail customer. Or you may subscribe for just $10 in the United States and Canada ($20 overseas, first class mail). Many bookstores also have *New Worlds* available to their customers. Ask for it.

In *New Worlds* you will find news and features about new books, tapes and services; announcements of meetings and seminars; helpful articles; author interviews and much more. Write to:

Llewellyn's New Worlds of Mind and Spirit
P.O. Box 64383-K708, St. Paul, MN 55164-0383, U.S.A.

TO ORDER BOOKS AND TAPES

If your book store does not carry the titles described on the following pages, you may order them directly from Llewellyn by sending the full price in U.S. funds, plus postage and handling (see below).

Credit card orders: VISA, MasterCard, American Express are accepted. Call us toll-free within the United States and Canada at 1-800-THE-MOON.

Special Group Discount: Because there is a great deal of interest in group discussion and study of the subject matter of this book, we offer a 20% quantity discount to group leaders or agents. Our Special Quantity Price for a minimum order of five copies of *A Witch's Brew* is $79.80 cash-with-order. Include postage and handling charges noted below.

Postage and Handling: Include $4 postage and handling for orders $15 and under; $5 for orders over $15. There are no postage and handling charges for orders over $100. Postage and handling rates are subject to change. We ship UPS whenever possible within the continental United States; delivery is guaranteed. Please provide your street address as UPS does not deliver to P.O. boxes. Orders shipped to Alaska, Hawaii, Canada, Mexico and Puerto Rico will be sent via first class mail. Allow 4-6 weeks for delivery. International orders: Airmail – add retail price of each book and $5 for each non-book item (audiotapes, etc.); Surface mail – add $1 per item. Minnesota residents add 7% sales tax.

Mail orders to:
Llewellyn Worldwide, P.O. Box 64383-K708, St. Paul, MN 55164-0383, U.S.A.

For customer service, call (612) 291-1970.

THE VICTORIAN FLOWER ORACLE
The Language of Nature
by Patricia Telesco

Read the future with flowers! This book tells you how, from creating your own magically charged oracle, to doing readings for yourself and friends. The Victorian peoples loved their "parlor games" almost as much as they loved their flowers, and they devised hundreds of creative ways to glimpse the unknown, whether to discover a future lover or determine when to harvest. It is easy to see why divination by flowers or herbs was developed: the living organisms of nature communicate divine lessons and messages in a unique and beautiful way. This fundamental belief of the divine spark in all things is what gives *The Victorian Flower Oracle* such charm and potency.

With clear instructions on how to create a flower deck with pressed flowers or artwork, or a deck of wood or stone, *The Victorian Flower Oracle* provides the divinatory interpretations of 79 flowers, herbs and trees. The information on the language of flowers also lends itself to herbal recipes, ritual wines, and various home decorating projects which are also included in this charming book. Reconnect with the Gaia spirit as you find answers to the questions nagging at your heart!

ISBN: 0-87542-786-3, 264 pgs., 6 x 9, illus., softbound $12.95

A VICTORIAN GRIMOIRE
Romance • Enchantment • Magic
by Patricia Telesco

Like a special opportunity to rummage through your grandmother's attic, *A Victorian Grimoire* offers you a personal invitation to discover a storehouse of magical treasures. Enhance every aspect of your daily life as you begin to reclaim the romance, simplicity and "know-how" of the Victorian era—that exceptional period of American history when people's lives and times were shaped by their love of the land, of home and family, and by their simple acceptance of magic as part of everyday life.

More and more, people are searching for ways to create peace and beauty in this increasingly chaotic world. This special handbook—Grimoire—shows you how to recreate that peace and beauty with simple, down-to-earth "Victorian Enchantments" that turn every mundane act into an act of magic . . . from doing the dishes . . . to making beauty-care products . . . to creating games for children. This book is a handy reference when you need a specific spell, ritual, recipe or tincture for any purpose. What's more, *A Victorian Grimoire* is a captivating study of the turn of the century and a comprehensive repository of common-sense knowledge. Learn how to relieve a backache, dry and store herbs, help children get over fears of the dark, treat pets with first aid, and much, much more.

ISBN: 0-87542-784-7, 368 pgs., 7 x 10, illus., softcover $14.95

A KITCHEN WITCH'S COOKBOOK
Patricia Telesco

Appetizers • Breads • Brews • Canning & Preserving • Cheese & Eggs• Desserts • Meats • Pasta & Sauces• Quarter Quickies • Salads, Dressings & Soups • Tofu, Rice & Side Dishes • Vegetables• Witches' Dishes

Discover the joys of creative kitchen magic! A Kitchen Witch's Cookbook is a unique blend of tasty recipes, humor, history and practical magical techniques that will show you how cooking can reflect your spiritual beliefs as well as delightfully appease your hunger!

The first part of this book gives you techniques for preparing and presenting food enriched by magic. The second section is brimming with 346 recipes from around the world—appetizers, salads, beverages, meats, soups, desserts, even "Witches' Dishes"—with ingredients, directions, magical associations, history/lore and suggested celebrations where you can serve the food. (Blank pages at the end of each section encourage you to record your own treasured recipes.)

A Kitchen Witch's Cookbook makes it clear how ingredients found in any pantry can be transformed into delicious and magical meals for your home and circle, no matter what your path. Let Patricia Telesco show you how kitchen magic can blend your spiritual beliefs into delectable sustenance for both body and soul!

ISBN: 1-56718-707-2, 7 x 10 • 320 pp., illus., softbound $16.95

THE URBAN PAGAN
Magical Living in a 9-to-5 World
by Patricia Telesco

Finally, a book that takes into account the problems of city-dwelling magicians! When preparing to do ritual, today's magician is often faced with busy city streets and a vast shortage of private natural space in which to worship. Technology surrounds, and fear and misunderstanding still exist about "magic" and "witchcraft." This leaves even experienced spiritual seekers trying desperately to carry a positive magical lifestyle into the 21st century. With the help of *The Urban Pagan*, we all can learn to incorporate earth-aware philosophies of days gone by with modern realities.

The Urban Pagan is a transformational book of spells, rituals, herbals, invocations and meditations that will help the reader to build inner confidence, create a magical living environment, and form an urban wheel of the year. It updates interpretations of symbolism for use in sympathetic magic and visualization, shows how to make magical tools inexpensively, provides daily magical exercises that can aid in seasonal observances, shows practical ways to help heal the earth, and explains the art of cultivating and using herbs, plus much, much more.

0-87542-785-5, 336 pgs., 6 x 9, illus., softcover $13.00

Prices subject to change without notice.

FOLKWAYS
Reclaiming the Magic & Wisdom
by Patricia Telesco

Rediscover a rich legacy of folk wisdom! This fascinating encyclopedia of folk beliefs is an ideal reference tool for magic practitioners or anyone interested in the folkways of our ancestors.
This invaluable resource places a colorful history of superstitions
and customs concerning folk medicine, nature, magic and more
at your fingertips—with definitions, origins of belief and suggested magical usages for over 650 folkways, grouped alphabeti-
cally by subject.

Within each subject category of this book are practical sugges-
tions for applying these folkways in your magical workings. When you're looking for an idea
for creating an effective spell, simply page to the corresponding subject and browse the rele-
vant entries—you will find hundreds of ideas for personalizing and enriching your practice.

In our era, much insightful, earth-centered knowledge—often disguised as old wives' tales
or village customs—has been left by the wayside. *Folkways* will make it possible for you to
gather up this lost wisdom, blend it with a modern sensibility and create a new system of
myths to enrich your magic.

ISBN: 0-87542-787-1, 6 x 9, 416 pp., illus., softcover $14.95

HEALING HERBS & HEALTH FOODS
OF THE ZODIAC
by Ada Muir, Introduction by Jude C. Williams, M.H.

There was a time when every doctor was also an astrologer, for a
knowledge of astrology was considered essential for diagnosing and
curing an illness. *Healing Herbs and Health Foods of the Zodiac*
reclaims that ancient healing tradition in a combined reprinting of
two Ada Muir books: *Healing Herbs of the Zodiac* and *Health and the
Sun Signs: Cell Salts in Medicinal Astrology.*

The first part of this book covers the ills most often found in each
zodiacal sign, along with the herbs attributed to healing those ills.
For example, nosebleeds are associated with Aries, and cayenne
pepper is the historical herbal treatment. More than 70 herbs are
covered in all, with illustrations of each herb to aid in identification.

The second part of the book covers the special mineral or cell salt needs of each sign. Cell salts,
contained in fruits and vegetables, are necessary for the healthy activity of the human body.
For example, the cell salt of Libra is sodium phosphate, used to maintain the balance between
acids and alkalis. It's found in celery, spinach and figs.

In her introduction, Master Herbalist and author Jude C. Williams increases the practical
use of this book by outlining the basics of harvesting herbs and preparing tinctures, salves
and teas.

0-87542-575-5, 192 pgs., mass market, illus. $3.99

Prices subject to change without notice.